CASUALTY OF WAR

CASUALTY OF WAR

THE BUSH ADMINISTRATION'S
ASSAULT ON A FREE PRESS

DAVID DADGE

Prometheus Books

59 John Glenn Drive
Amherst, New York 14228-2197

Published 2004 by Prometheus Books

Inquiries should be addressed to
Prometheus Books
59 John Glenn Drive
Amherst, New York 14228–2197
VOICE: 716–691–0133, ext. 207
FAX: 716–564–2711
WWW.PROMETHEUSBOOKS.COM

08 07 06 05 04   5 4 3 2 1

Library of Congress Cataloging-in-Publication Data

Dadge, David.
    Casualty of war : the Bush administration's assault on a free press / David Dadge.
        p. cm.
    Includes bibliographical references and index.
    ISBN 1-59102-147-2
    1. Freedom of the press—United States. 2. War on Terrorism, 2001–
I. Title.

PN4745.D33 2004
323.44'5'0973—dc22

                                                                2003023766

Printed in Canada on acid-free paper

Casualty of War is dedicated to

Johann P. Fritz,

who has devoted his life to press freedom

and encouraged many others to do the same,

and to

Ellen

for all her help and kindly advice.

CONTENTS

ACKNOWLEDGMENTS

T he idea for *Casualty of War* came originally from an article written for the winter 2002 volume of the *Northwestern Journal of International Affairs*, and I am grateful to Editor-in-Chief Brian J. Link for suggesting that I write a piece on journalism after September 11. Now, with the book completed, I am indebted to a number of other people who have provided their help and assistance.

First and foremost, I should like to thank the people who consented to be interviewed: George Brock, Alan L. Heil Jr., Rohan Jayasekera, Ted Kaufman, Dr. Anthony Löwstedt, Toby Mendel, Joan Mower, Howard Rosenberg, Richard Sambrook, Karmal Samri, Danny Schechter, Joel Simon, Richard Tait, Kenneth Tomlinson, Myrna Whitworth, and others who wish to remain anonymous. All of them were tremendously giving of their time, despite their heavy work schedules.

My thanks also go to my colleagues at the International Press

Institute: Eva Grabmair Christiane Klint, Michael Kudlak, Diana Orlova, Martha Srokosz, and Barbara Trionfi. They are an inspiration and, as a team, have done much to make the International Press Institute the formidable global organization it is today.

At Prometheus Books, I would like to thank Vice President and Editor-in-Chief Steven L. Mitchell, who saw the merits of *Casualty of War* before many others, Senior Editor Mary A. Read, freelance editor Carol L. Thoma, typesetter Roz Gold, proofreader Michele Pelton-Fall, and indexer Laura Shelley. In their own way, each of them has done much to improve the final version of this book.

Outside of the workplace, I would like to thank my good friend David Kershaw, who aside from giving me his support and encouragement lent his critical intelligence to parts of the manuscript. Thanks also to Peter, Ralf, Isobel, Stephen, and Evita, all of whom, at one time or another, have been forced to listen to my views on the media and press freedom. That they did so without complaint is a true sign of our friendship. Special thanks also to Eryl Maedel, who was kind enough to give me her comments. My father, Roy, has been pivotal in forming my outlook on life, and I owe everything to the warmth, kindness, and bright intelligence of my mother, Doreen.

Finally, it goes without saying that the thoughts and opinions expressed in this book do not necessarily represent the views of the International Press Institute.

David Dadge

INTRODUCTION

For President George W. Bush, the realization that America had suffered its worst attack since Pearl Harbor came when his chief of staff, Andrew Card, walked over to him and whispered that a second plane had flown into the World Trade Center, this time into the South Tower. Already made aware of the first plane's flying into the North Tower, Bush, who had been listening to children read at the Emma E. Booker Elementary School in Sarasota, Florida, appeared to be shaken by the news. The effect would be the same for people all over the United States, and it would be reinforced by the repeated showing on television of the planes flying into the towers.

Even at a considerable distance in time from the events, the pictures of the planes flying into the towers, followed by the confusion on the streets of New York City and the subsequent collapse of both towers are horrifying. Indeed, it is difficult to convey any meaningful impression of the attacks—on so many levels, they are literally indescribable. And yet, it is still those television images, coupled with the images of Bush's initial reaction and his later speeches, which perhaps best define September 11, 2001. Although everyone in America had his or her own intense personal reaction to the terrorist attacks perpetrated by al-Qaeda, the communal response, the joint response that brought everyone together, was shaped and projected by the media.

The reporting of the television networks on September 11 was calm despite the confusion about the actual events. Before 9:00 A.M., reports came into the studios that a plane might have crashed into one of the World Trade Center towers. Minutes later, there were reports from eyewitnesses and reporters on the scene that a missile, possibly a plane, had exploded in the North Tower. While these reports were being relayed live on air, another plane flew into the South Tower. Shortly after 9:00 A.M., the television networks were confirming that there had been an attack on the World Trade Center. In the following hours, correspondents with the president would report on the movements of Air Force One from Florida to Nebraska via Louisiana; there would be reports on the attack on the Pentagon and the plane crash in Pennsylvania, as well as the news that airspace above the United States was being closed to prevent further attacks; and journalists and news anchors would report on the collapse of the Twin Towers. Slowly, as more information became available, the media began to make sense of the confusion, helping to dispel the fear of not knowing. It was a job they performed magnificently.

In a poll conducted after the attacks, the National Opinion Research Center (NORC) in Chicago examined the media and found that the role of television was pivotal during these early stages. According to the poll, 37 percent of Americans said they had first learned of the attack from television, while only 15 percent said they had been personally told of the attacks. The poll showed a marked contrast to one taken shortly after the assassination of President John F. Kennedy in 1963, which found that 24 percent of people had heard the news on television and 36 percent had been informed personally. Moreover, on the question of when they first heard of the attacks, some 70 percent of those polled said that they had heard within fifteen to thirty minutes of the first attack. The NORC research revealed just how quickly news of the attacks could be communicated by television.

Indeed, it is hard to avoid the conclusion that the original attacks in New York were perfect for the way in which television reports the news. The images of the planes, the clear weather, the disbelief of onlookers, the collapse of the towers all worked together to provide an overwhelming television event that eclipsed other similar occasions, such as the pictures of the space shuttle *Challenger* exploding in January 1986, the murder of Lee Harvey Oswald by Jack Ruby in November 1963, and the Zapruder film of the assassination of President John F. Kennedy. However, the images of the attacks told only one part of the story; there were other forms of media that would work to fill some of the gaps. In the days and weeks following the attacks, the print media would take over from the television networks: newspapers and magazines provided additional information, fleshing out the story and starting the long process of analyzing the attacks and their impact on the United States.

Significantly, if the film, photographs, and articles in the media helped to explain the attacks, there were also images that sought to calm and remove fear—images that would let frightened people know that their government was still in place, that the country's leaders were working to help the nation overcome this tragedy, and that a plan was being developed to retaliate against those who had carried out the attacks. These images included New York City Mayor Rudy Giuliani working tirelessly to regain a sense of normality in New York and President Bush standing at the Ground Zero site with a bull horn in his hand saying to the assembled crowd, "I can hear you. The rest of the world hears you, and the people who knocked these buildings down will hear all of us soon." Shown on television, these images characterized the United States' return from the brink of desperation and, in many ways, showed that the country was willing to fight back. The images were, therefore, essential to the recovery of the country after the devastation caused by the attacks.

The work of the television networks and the extensive reporting in the *New York Times*, the *Washington Post*, and many local newspapers revealed the true power of the media and its success at communicating information. It was a cipher for those difficult times, reflecting all the myriad fears, anxieties, and worries represented in

American society, but also willing to work hard to provide people with answers by questioning Bush administration officials; representatives from the State Department; members of the legislature; the Transportation Department; the FBI; the Department of Defense; and political pundits, military experts, psychologists, architects, civil engineers, safety workers, firefighters, policemen, Middle Eastern experts, experts on terrorism, and many more. In fact, almost anyone who could contribute to the ongoing story that was the September 11 attacks helped to sharpen the impressions of the events, signal the mood of the country, and define an appropriate emotional response.

Although the media were to be congratulated for carrying out this vital role, they were shortly to find out that, as well as reporting the story, they were about to become a part of the story. This subtle change, which took many journalists by surprise, occurred as a direct result of September 11 and could be seen in a *New York Times*/CBS News poll conducted shortly after the attacks. The poll discovered that 80 percent of Americans questioned were willing to trade personal freedoms for greater security. Based on these results, it was clear that Americans had suddenly developed a strong desire for security, a viewpoint supported by the discussions in the media at the time. While fighter planes patrolled the skies, newspaper articles discussed the usefulness of installing security cameras in public places—copying the British model, which had been instigated following a number of terrorist attacks—and the need for additional security at venues such as baseball and football games. The post–September 11 mood would be communicated to the Bush administration, causing them to act accordingly, confident in the knowledge that, although civil libertarians were worried by the decision to tighten security measures, they had the support of the majority of the American people. Another post–September 11 factor influencing the actions of the government was the belief that, for all intents and purposes, the United States was at war.

From the outset, the Bush administration used the language of war, which was reflected in President Bush's conversations and speeches at the time. On the day after the attack, Bush apparently told reporters that the attacks were acts of war, and the use of such language continued throughout September. Speaking to a joint session of Congress on September 20, 2001, President Bush said, "On September 11, the enemies of freedom committed an act of war against our country." The mood of the Bush administration was also reflected in the media, which used such phrases and captions as "America at War" or "America's War on Terror" in their reporting.

However, if the media were prepared to use the language of the Bush administration and the American public, they appeared to forget the expectation that during wartime they should forgo their traditional reporting duties. Instead of questioning and criticizing government decisions, the media would be required to provide enthusiastic support. But the role of cheerleader for the U.S. government did not sit well with some journalists. Caught between the pincers of a warlike environment and the demand for increased security, even at the cost of basic freedoms such as freedom of the press, the media were left with little room in which to maneuver. Rather than releasing some of the pressure by supporting the media's right to report independently, the Bush administration's officials criticized the media, creating in the view of some commentators a "censorious environment" reinforced by elements of the American public that called for expressions of patriotism.

As a consequence, there were attempts at censoring stories, and some journalists were removed from their positions while others were pilloried for expressing their views or upholding news values. Foreign broadcasters were criticized, pressure was applied on the television networks, a disinformation organization was created, and new laws that limited press freedom were swiftly passed through the legislature.

Casualty of War examines press freedom during the tumultuous period after the September 11 attacks and addresses two fundamental questions: Did the Bush administration attempt to pressure the media? and, What has been the wider impact on press freedom around the world of the war on terrorism?

Chapter 1

LOSING AMERICA'S VOICE

The Voice of America speaks. Today America has been at war for seventy-nine days. Daily at this time, we shall speak to you about America and the war—the news may be good or bad—we shall tell you the truth.

William Harlan Hale, first Voice of America broadcast in Europe,
February 24, 1942

Wei Jingsheng: "China's Conscience"

Thrown onto an airplane to the United States by officials from the People's Republic of China in mid-November 1997, Wei Jingsheng, one of the most outspoken critics of the Chinese government and its appalling human rights record, was allowed to leave the country as the result of successful negotiations between the Clinton administration and Chinese government officials. Wei's release was a personal victory for Clinton and his advisors, who had long sought to engage the Chinese government in economic discussion, while, at the same time, advocating democratic change in the country.

Wei's release marked the end of a bitter personal campaign against him by the Chinese government, which had sent him to prison for more than eighteen years, much of that time in China's notorious forced labor camps known as Laogai. In the late 1970s, the former journalist and editor of the magazine *Exploration* was believed to have earned the personal hatred of leader Deng Xiaoping when he demanded that Deng amend his "Four Modernizations"— agriculture, industry, science, and defense—to include a fifth modernization: democracy. Wei was arrested in 1979 and, in the first of many sham trials, sentenced to fifteen years in prison. He spent the first eight months on death row and the following five years in solitary confinement. Later, he was transferred to successive Laogai.

In 1993, Wei was paroled six months before the end of his sentence in a decision that many people believed was merely a cynical attempt to influence the International Olympic Committee while it was considering China as a possible host for the 2000 Olympic games. On his release, Wei bravely continued to call for democratic reform in the country.

Like all his previous hearings, Wei's prosecution was politically inspired. Indeed, his trial date had been announced only five days before the actual hearing. Although described by Chinese officials as an "open" hearing, in reality, the trial was open only to the close family of the accused, carefully selected journalists, and a small number of observers. All requests by European and U.S. diplomats to attend the trial were turned down. Moreover, the authorities refused the right of a legal team including two former U.S. Attorneys General to assist in Wei's defense. The trial started on the morning of December 13, 1995, and continued for five hours. During that time, Wei was given only one hour to put forward his defense. On several occasions, Wei was forced to stop his defense in midargument because of a debilitating illness. After the trial, the court sentenced Wei to fourteen years in prison.[1]

Now, however, Wei was flying to America after President Clinton had negotiated his release with Chinese President Jiang Zemin. True to form, Wei maintained that his release was not freedom but further exile. What Wei did not know, at the time of his flight to freedom, was that he was to encounter a debate over censorship in his newly adopted country every bit as vociferous as the debate in the country he had just left. Indeed, it seemed that Chinese officials were not the only ones who did not like Wei's criticizing China.

The trouble started almost immediately after Wei touched down in the United States. After a behind-closed-doors state dinner at the White House, at which Wei met President Clinton and various administration officials, the Chinese government complained bitterly that the United States was making political capital out of the journalist's release. Subsequently, Wei gave an interview in which he commented on his eighteen years in prison and the general human rights situation in China. The interview was due to be broadcast on both Worldnet and the Voice of America's Mandarin service, but State Department officials, National Security Council (NSC) officials, the director of the United States Information Agency (USIA), and an ambassador to China made frantic attempts to stop the VOA from broadcasting the interview.

News of the forthcoming broadcasts had found its way to James Sasser, U.S. ambassador to China, who contacted the NSC to express his concern that the interview would impede other negotiations with the Chinese government to free dissidents. He also told officials that an apparent condition of Wei's release had been a promise to the Chinese that the American government would not make political capital out of the case, a condition that Sasser believed had been broken by the interview with the VOA. Confirmation of the Chinese view was later given by foreign ministry spokesperson Tang Guoqiang, who said, "We are opposed to using Wei Jingsheng to engage in activities against the Chinese government."[2]

David Burke, founding chairman of the Broadcasting Board of Governors (BBG), told the *Wall Street Journal* that NSC officials contacted VOA director Evelyn Lieberman to "see if the interview could somehow not take place." Burke added that "[it was] disgraceful that anyone in government would circumvent the board of governors, which was designed to be a firewall [against] that kind of pressure."[3]

Presidential spokesperson Mike McCurry confirmed that National Security Advisor Sandy Berger had discussed the interview with Lieberman. McCurry said, "We would not make any effort to violate what is a very important principle—the editorial independence of the VOA. . . . At the same time, it is appropriate for the VOA to understand what the consequences of some of its broadcasts might be from our perspective."[4]

Officials from the Clinton administration also contacted the USIA director, Joseph Duffey, informing him of their dilemma. Duffey wrote to Kevin Klose, director of the International Broadcasting Bureau (IBB), which at that time oversaw the running of the VOA, stating that the interview could be "detrimental to the vital security interests of the U.S. government." The letter finished with the statement "I am now formally asking that the [Wei] program not be broadcast."[5]

Fortunately, Klose, with the support of the BBG, ignored the letter and went ahead with the broadcast of Wei's interview. Speaking afterwards, Duffey said, "After I learned it was going to be broadcast, I delayed the Worldnet telecast and I asked the VOA not to telecast it, but they did anyway."[6]

Commenting on the activities of the Clinton administration, Human Rights Watch (HRW) Asia's Washington director, Mike Jendrzejczyk, stated that he was shocked and added, "[HRW] can only assume from this that not offending Beijing is more important to the administration than exerting pressure on China to release more dissidents and improve its human rights record."[7]

The decision of the VOA to broadcast Wei's interview was a major victory for those who believed that the discussion of human rights should not be the sole preserve of ambassadors and administration officials talking to foreign governments behind closed doors. Holding out against those who had claimed that "vital interests" were at stake, the VOA showed that it was not merely the microphone of the federal government. Significantly, by refusing to bend to the government's will no matter what the pressure, the VOA sent a powerful signal that it could not be censored and was not prepared to allow the often narrow interests of the State Department and successive administrations to dominate its independent thinking.

As a forerunner to the argument over the airing of a report containing an interview with Taliban leader Mullah Omar in September

2001, the Wei case is extremely revealing. Not only are the two incidents similar in nature, but they involve similar arguments: (1) Does the VOA have the right to decide who speaks on its own airwaves? and (2) Should the VOA respect the State Department when it asserts that a vital interest is at stake?

Furthermore, the Wei incident highlighted the various institutions that were to play a significant role in the attempt to halt the airing of the Mullah Omar interview, and that have traditionally attempted to pressure the VOA: the State Department, the NSC, and, above both of these organizations, the Bush administration. The earlier State Department's attempt to smother the interview with Wei also shows the BBG protecting the VOA by operating as a firewall in the manner envisaged by Congress. If sense is to be made of the Omar case, the BBG's role needs to be fully appreciated, particularly because, in the six years between the two incidents, the role of the BBG had expanded dramatically.

KEEPING THE WOLF FROM THE DOOR: THE BBG, THE VOA CHARTER, AND LEGISLATIVE CHANGES IN THE 1990S

The International Broadcasting Act of 1994 consolidated all government-controlled broadcasting services not owned by the military under the IBB.[8] For the first time, the act created a board of governors, appointed by the president, composed of the director of the USIA and eight part-time members to be drawn equally from the Republican and Democratic parties. Viewed as a "firewall" between the VOA and outside interference, the BBG would "ensure independence, coherence, quality and journalistic integrity" in services such as the VOA.[9] Congress was also deeply concerned about interference, allowing the State Department, via the USIA director, to "provide information and guidance on foreign policy issues to the [BBG]" but otherwise ensuring the BBG's independence.[10] Congress was even more explicit when it said that the secretary of state is not to be "involved in the management or day-to-day decision making of the [USIA] or any of its operations or programs such as international broadcasting."[11]

Significantly, combining the International Broadcasting Act with the express statements from Congress made it possible to define a clear road map for the complaints made by the State Department about the activities of the VOA. In essence, the combination of the act and the Congressional statements invited the State Department to work through the director of the USIA with the BBG in its firewall capacity, examining the complaints at a considerable distance from the politicians.

The new legislative protection, which resembled a plan fleshed out by Assistant Secretary of State for Public Affairs William Benton after World War II, appeared to have as its sole concern the question of journalistic independence and the need to prevent possible government interference. Four years later, there would be further changes with the passage of the Foreign Affairs Reform and Restructuring Act of 1998, which focused on the BBG's role. The act was considered to be the single most important law affecting international broadcasters since 1953.

Under the 1998 act, the USIA was disbanded and all of its activities were relocated within the BBG. With the dissolution of the USIA, and with the role of the director of the USIA now defunct, the secretary of state or his designate took the director's place on the BBG.[12] Because of this act, the BBG's role became subtly different. In addition to its firewall role, it was now also in charge of the day-to-day running of the United States' international broadcasters.

In a Reorganization Plan and Report submitted to Congress by President Clinton on December 29, 1998, it was claimed under section IV, "International Broadcasting," that

> The BBG will become an independent federal entity. This provides a "firewall" between State and the broadcasters to ensure the integrity of journalism. The act thus ensures that the credibility and journalistic integrity of broadcasting will be preserved and enhanced. The act also provides "deniability" for State when foreign governments complain about specific broadcasts. The BBG will remain an important instrument of U.S. foreign policy by

telling America's story and otherwise serving broad American foreign policy objectives. The secretary of state will provide foreign
policy evidence to the BBG.[13]

For those employed at the VOA, the new legislation was viewed as a
positive step because it finally and irrevocably removed the country's
broadcasting outlets out from the control of the State Department.
Moreover, it handed control to a part-time body of individuals who
all worked outside of government and who were schooled in the
commercial media. With other jobs outside of their BBG role, all of
the board's members were largely insulated from pressure because
they did not depend on their federal jobs for a living. Perhaps more
important, they also understood the nature of press freedom. In the
words of the BBG's Communications Coordinator Joan Mower, "the
BBG was the only federal agency run by private citizens."[14]

In its dealings with the State Department, the BBG also felt that it
had a duty to protect the journalists at the VOA. BBG member Ted
Kaufman likened the relationship between the BBG, the VOA, and the
State Department to that between a publisher and the journalists of a
newspaper. In his opinion, just as it was the role of the publisher to
protect the journalists from the encroachments of advertisers, it was
also the duty of the BBG to protect the VOA from the State Department.[15] While perfectly prepared to listen to the State Department's
advice, the BBG made sure that it determined the final decisions, and,
as Kaufman said, on most broadcasting issues voting on the BBG was
not even close, with the board often expressing unanimity.

Buttressed by the BBG, the VOA's staff has also been protected by
the VOA Charter. Originally drafted in late 1958 and approved in
1960, the charter has become central to the working life of journalists
at the broadcasting organization. The idea for the VOA Charter originated with Director Henry Loomis and Program Manager Barry Zor-
thian, who commissioned a task force to define the VOA's mission. Set
out as a comprehensive statement of principles, the VOA Charter was
later endorsed by USIA Director George Allen. On July 12, 1976, President Gerald Ford signed the VOA Charter into federal law.

An examination of the VOA Charter reveals that it has attempted
to combine two competing roles, namely, news provider, on the one

hand, and presenter of "significant American thought" and "the policies of the United States" on the other. The news role is underlined by the use of traditional journalistic concepts such as "reliable and authoritative source of news" and "news will be accurate, objective, and comprehensive." These two roles represent the duality which is the VOA and are a consequence of the earlier debates over public diplomacy and the VOA's role.

On a day-to-day basis, the two missions of the broadcasting organization have been split between news and editorials (foreign policy statements). In effect, the two elements of the VOA's work operate much like a standard newspaper that contains both news and editorials. The VOA has been required by law to provide these editorial statements since 1984, and they are written by the Office of Policy, which produces and distributes the daily editorials to the various VOA language departments.

It has always been intended that the two missions should remain entirely separate, but there is a gray area that broadly relates to supporting factual news reporting with additional information in the form of interviews and reports. While this practice is common outside the VOA, it is often mired in controversy within the organization because some interviewees may express views contrary to American foreign policy. As a result, foreign policy makers and journalists have come to view each other with mutual suspicion—elements within the State Department are irritated that the VOA staff fail to follow the principle of reporting "the policies of the United States," while journalists are exasperated that State Department and NSC officials fail to understand the need to report objectively.

As previously mentioned, the intersection between news reporting and editorials articulating the policies of the United States is often the point at which journalists and certain members of the State Department have clashed. However, it is also the point at which there are genuine disagreements between different groups in the State Department which on no account should be seen as holding a single view on the work carried out by the VOA.

Although the State Department contains people who strongly believe that the VOA is part of the foreign policy apparatus, it also has career diplomats who believe that the independence and objectivity of the VOA provide a service to both the country and public diplomacy. These different threads have existed in the VOA since its inception, and they are part of a wider discussion on public diplomacy itself. To place the Mullah Omar interview within the context of this debate, it is important to briefly review the rise of public diplomacy and the creation of the VOA.

More Powerful Than All the Tyrants: Public Diplomacy and the VOA

When the State Department contacted the BBG on September 21, 2001, to prevent the airing of an interview with Taliban leader Mullah Omar, it was displaying an antagonism toward the Voice of America (VOA) that had long existed. The VOA's conflict with the U.S. State Department and Congress goes back beyond its formation in 1942 and is the product of a far older disagreement over public diplomacy and the dissemination of information.

In the early part of the twentieth century, American culture and politics were caught between the twin compulsions of isolationism and involvement in the outside world. With professional diplomacy in its infancy, little attempt was made to define a coherent view of America for the outside world, and the country's image abroad depended largely on private organizations. In the election of Woodrow Wilson in 1912, however, America found a president who believed that the country's democratic institutions could be exported to create peace and security. This view shaped Wilson's foreign policy and played a decisive role in America's decision to enter World War I.

As well as committing his country's military forces, Wilson recognized an attendant need to explain his actions and communicate them to the world. In April 1917, he created the Committee on Public Information (CPI), an organization designed "to teach the motives, purposes, and ideals of America so that friend, foe, and neutral alike might come to see us as a people without selfishness and in love with justice."[16]

As a body composed of professional diplomats, the State Department viewed the CPI's work as amateurish and lacking in obvious results, but this view hid a deeper worry that the organization was a direct threat to the State Department's own diplomatic activities. From the beginning, the department made every attempt to hinder the CPI's work. A further problem was a long-running argument over the benefits of public diplomacy. In the end, Wilson lost his battle with Congress and the CPI was closed down, even though it had shown the need for an organization to explain America's actions abroad and articulate its views on democracy. However, not until World War II was another attempt made to unify public diplomacy, this time by Franklin Roosevelt.

Elected in November 1932, Roosevelt laid the foundations for America's postwar public diplomacy programs. He created a network of government information programs ranging from extensive use of radio, including his own ground-breaking fireside chats, to courting editors to ensure the placement of ready-made articles for local newspapers. He also formulated specific public relations policies for agencies created under the New Deal.

When America entered the war in December 1941, therefore, the Roosevelt administration already had the makings of a strong public information network. The one overriding problem was the division between America's information programs at home and those abroad. To bring the organizations under a single roof, the Coordinator of Information (COI) was created in July 1941 with the dual role of reporting to the president on security issues and spreading propaganda abroad via the Foreign Information Service (FIS). The FIS was headed by Pulitzer Prize-winning playwright Robert Sherwood. Unfortunately, the dual role became too much of a burden for the COI, which was disbanded one year later.

Before the demise of the COI, however, on February 24, 1942, the FIS started broadcasting on short-wave radio in French, German, and Italian. This was later to become known as the VOA. In recognition of the problems attendant on America's entry into the war and fears over duplication by the organizations, the Roosevelt administration decided to separate the FIS and the VOA from the COI and placed them under the Office of War Information (OWI), formed in June 1942.

Speaking in that first European broadcast, journalist William Harlan Hale said, "The Voice of America speaks. Today America has been at war for seventy-nine days. Daily at this time, we shall speak to you about America and the war—the news may be good or bad— we shall tell you the truth." In its early days, the VOA used the British Broadcasting Corporation's transmitters to broadcast a series of fifteen-minute programs. Throughout 1942, the burgeoning organization signed a number of contracts for transmitters. By 1944, with its office in New York, the VOA had a staff of nearly three thousand and was broadcasting twenty-four hours a day in dozens of languages.

With the end of World War II, support for the OWI began to evaporate, but the director of the organization, Elmer Davies, lobbied the House Appropriations Committee for the creation of an international communication program that would give the world accurate information about America. Other influential voices were added in support of Davies and impetus was given by the report of a committee created by the State Department. Named after its chairman, Columbia University professor Arthur McMahon, the McMahon report investigated various information programs and concluded in its report that these activities were a necessary adjunct to foreign policy initiatives. The McMahon report also said that government organizations should impart full and fair knowledge of America without straying into the territory of the private media. In a statement that has profound implications for the early twenty-first century, McMahon concluded that the government could not be "indifferent to the ways in which our society is portrayed to other countries."[17]

On August 31, 1945, President Harry S. Truman terminated the OWI but transferred both its operations and those of the VOA to the Interim Information Service (IIS) under the auspices of the State Department. In speaking of his decision, Truman used the expression a "full and fair picture," a variant on the language used by McMahon. This phrase was to become the ethical principle for the VOA's reporting. The McMahon report itself was also to have an influence on later developments.

With the VOA's postwar future ensured, at least for the time being, a lively discussion took place regarding the principles that should guide the organization in its mission to tell the world about America. Inspired by the McMahon report and the words of Truman, the discussion led to the involvement of the Commission on Freedom of the Press (CFP), also known as the Hutchins Commission after its chairman, University of Chicago President Robert Hutchins. Formed in 1942, the commission included such notables as Reinhold Niebuhr, Harold Lasswell, Archibald MacLeish, and Arthur Schlesinger Sr.

Reacting to an article in the *Saturday Review of Literature* by Herbert Agar entitled "Must We Tell the World?" a CFP spokesman stated, "[T]he surest antidote to ignorance and deceit is the widest possible exchange of objectively realistic information—true information, not merely more information."[18] This view placed "truth" firmly at the center of the VOA's work and implied it was to provide information untainted by propaganda or political spin. The emphasis would be on allowing listeners to draw their own conclusions while being assured that they were receiving correct information. These early discussions were to inform the work and values of the VOA's journalists and would later become part of the VOA Charter.

Therefore, throughout the VOA's life, the State Department has played a fundamental role in shaping the news organization. In essence, the VOA journalists see themselves as the defenders of a heritage of objective reporting while the State Department, with its different frames of reference, views the VOA as a vehicle for projecting America's image abroad. The clash between these two opposing views can be seen in many of the VOA's dealings with government and in its charter.

How the State Department Sought to Quiet the VOA

In those first days and weeks after the September 11 attacks in New York and Washington, the Bush administration was quick to set out a clear and comprehensive military strategy, with its focus on both Afghanistan and the war on terrorism. However, the administration often appeared to have precious few ideas on a cohesive media strategy. Indeed, its chosen strategy often appeared to be overtly aggressive and unprepared, with little regard to the importance of free speech.

While officials from the Bush administration toured the countries of friends and neighbors to create a global alliance against terrorism, the world's media were involved in a struggle of their own—the search for newsworthy items and additional information to help their readers, listeners, and viewers comprehend what was happening. By taking part in this search, the VOA was no different from any other media organization; however, it was soon to discover that it was viewed differently by certain elements within the State Department.

On September 12, one day after the attacks in New York and Washington, the VOA interviewed an Egyptian terrorist known as Yassir al Serri. Although VOA staff were unaware at the time, the interview with al Serri was to have a direct bearing on the Mullah Omar news report. In the al Serri news report recorded in London, the VOA correspondent broadcast two interviews, one with a moderate Muslim cleric who warned that Western countries should not accuse Islamists or Arab groups without knowing the "full truth" of the situation, and one with al Serri who was identified only as "a leader of Egypt's largest Islamist group, the Gama'a Islamiya, which has worked to overthrow the Egyptian government." However, the correspondent failed to say that Gama'a Islamiya was a terrorist group that had killed fifty-eight foreign tourists and four Egyptians in a bloody attack in 1997.[19]

The report caused outrage in government circles. In the State Department, Richard L. Armitage, the deputy secretary of state, was particularly annoyed, and in Congress, North Carolina Senator Jesse Helms described the interview as giving equal time to Hitler.[20] The media also weighed in with a response, including *New York Times* correspondent William Safire, who wrote a critical opinion piece on the subject.

When discussing the al Serri incident with the media, members of the VOA staff said that the failure to properly identify the terrorist was a mistake but said that if the news organization was to remain credible, it needed to interview such people. Head of the VOA News Department Andre DeNesnera said the interview was part of the

VOA's "accurate, objective, and comprehensive reporting, providing our listeners with both sides of the story."[21] Commenting on the interview with al Serri, Myrna Whitworth, then acting director of the VOA, said that the overall news report could have been better balanced and al Serri better described, but she did not think it warranted the reaction the news report received.[22] Aside from the external criticism, the BBG was also deeply irritated by the al Serri news report.

Some of the anger from State Department officials, Senator Helms, the BBG, and the media would later be directly channeled into the debate over the Mullah Omar news report. For this reason, it is highly probable that the jaundiced view taken by the Bush administration over Omar originally stemmed from the al Serri interview. In an ironic twist, the BBG and the State Department would be discussing the al Serri news report on the day that Spozhmai Maiwandi, the head of the VOA's Pashto service, interviewed Mullah Omar.

The news that the Pashto service had made direct contact with the Taliban in Afghanistan was relayed at the 9:30 A.M. editorial meeting on September 21, 2001. At that meeting, normally attended by fifty or sixty people, the heads of the regional departments, the head of news, and the acting director of the VOA went through a rundown of the daily news reports. Reporters and the heads of news then discussed which events would be highlighted and described how they would be covered.

During the day's discussion, the newsroom and the South Asia and Central Division informed Whitworth that the VOA might be able to interview Taliban leader Mullah Omar. In fact, although Whitworth was unaware of this, the interview was being conducted by Maiwandi at the time of the daily editorial meeting. Responding to news of the interview, Whitworth discussed it with VOA News Department head DeNesnera and the South and Central Asia division. According to Whitworth, there was never any question that the interview would be broadcast live or broadcast without an accompanying report. "It was always discussed in the context of a background report," she said.[23] As a means of assessing the strength of the interview, Whitworth asked for a translation and a copy of the news report that would carry the interview. She also discussed the possibility of using President Bush's address to Congress in the same report.

As a result of the discussion, Maiwandi would hand over a translation of the interview to newsroom journalist Ed Warner, who would then draft a news report. The decision that the report would go through the newsroom was a new procedure instituted after September 11 and the al Serri interview to protect the Pashto and Dari services by giving all news reports an "additional editorial eye."[24] In effect, the news product containing the Mullah Omar interview would be reviewed twice, once inside the South and Central Asia Division and again by the newsroom.

At 11:00 A.M. on September 21, there was a conference call involving members of BBG, directors of the BBG staff, a State Department representative, and the acting director of the International Broadcasting Bureau. As the meeting drew to a close, the possibility of an interview with Mullah Omar was mentioned. A lengthy discussion followed about the appropriateness of the interview and whether it would confuse VOA audiences, coming as it did so shortly after the September 11 attacks. Whitworth told the callers that the interview had already been discussed with the South and Central Asia Division and the newsroom. The discussion with the "firewall" was complicated by the fact that a number of the board's members were in the process of leaving the country. Indeed, board member Ted Kaufman was already in Spain.

Though not rejecting outright the idea of an interview, the State Department representative was apparently concerned that the interview would not be conducted in an aggressive and objective manner. Afterward, the BBG apparently agreed to discuss the Omar interview among themselves, with the State Department representative invited to rejoin the discussion at 1:30 P.M. The BBG was then informed that the interview had already taken place. Subsequently, the BBG informed Whitworth that it wished to see a translation of the interview in order to carry out a proper assessment of its newsworthiness. Although Whitworth cannot confirm this, she thinks that the board members mistakenly believed that the interview was to be broadcast on its own, a belief easily disproved because Whitworth had already informed the BBG that Omar's comments would only be broadcast as part of a news report containing other interviews.

At around 3:00 P.M., a translation of the interview was faxed to the BBG and the State Department representative. In a discussion regarding the interview between the BBG and the State Department representative, participants expressed the view that the interview was too soft and that it would not enhance the credibility of the VOA. Later, Deputy Secretary of State Richard L. Armitage spoke to BBG member Tom Korologos and said that the VOA would be giving a platform to terrorists if it went ahead with the interview. After the conversation, the deputy secretary of state informed members of the State Department that the interview was not going to be broadcast on the VOA.

While these discussions were taking place, VOA staff in the newsroom were aware of the need to balance Omar's comments. As a consequence, it was decided that VOA staff would approach the former King of Afghanistan, Mohammad Zaher Shah, for his comments on the impending war against Afghanistan's Taliban government. Unfortunately, they could not obtain the desired interview, which led to a delay in the broadcast of the Mullah Omar news report. During this time, the story broke in the national media, which chose to lead with the State Department's opposition and the reactions of the VOA staff.

On September 23, 2001, a *Washington Post* article quoted an unnamed VOA staff member who said, "[When I heard,] I was stunned, absolutely stunned. . . . It goes against every principle of journalistic ethics." Another VOA staff member commented, "If this is an indication of the gag order they're going to impose on us, we can't do our jobs. . . . How can you talk about what we're fighting against if you don't give these people a voice?"[25]

With everyone keenly feeling the pressure, VOA News Director Andre DeNesnera e-mailed his staff, "The State Department's decision is a totally unacceptable assault on our editorial independence, a frontal attack on our credibility. As you know only too well, it takes a long time to build up credibility—and an instant to lose it." He continued, "I want to commend you for the sterling work all of you have done during these trying times—and I urge you not to fall under the spell of 'self-censorship.' If you do, 'they' have won."[26]

Using his daily briefing to the media, on September 24, 2001, State Department spokesperson Richard Boucher criticized the VOA. In response to a reporter's question, he said, "We didn't think it was right. We didn't think that the . . . Voice of America should be broadcasting the voice of the Taliban." Commenting on Omar's newsworthiness, Boucher said, "Unless he was going to accept the requirements of the United Nations, then there was no news or anything newsworthy in any interviews like that."[27]

Regarding Omar's message, Boucher argued, "Carrying the interview would be confusing to the millions of listeners to what is essentially a U.S. government broadcast, paid for by the U.S. government." Finally, on the decision not to air the interview, he said, "Whether it was the board of governors or the Voice of America that ultimately made this decision, it was the right decision, and we think good sense prevailed."[28] Boucher's statement showed that the State Department mistakenly believed that because the interview had not been aired before the weekend, the VOA had bowed to political pressure and was not planning to broadcast the interview. In fact, the VOA had halted the broadcast because it was still searching for additional context.

On September 25, 2001, the Mullah Omar news report was aired on the VOA. Having been dealt a fait accompli by the VOA, Boucher made the following comment at a press briefing on the following day: "We just don't think that broadcasting an interview with this man is in any way consistent with the [VOA's] charter, [and] considering the fact that U.S. taxpayers pay for this . . . we don't think that the head of the Taliban belongs on this radio station."[29]

A number of press freedom organizations also protested the State Department's attempted interference. Johann P. Fritz, director of the International Press Institute (IPI), said in a letter of support to the news director of the VOA:

> [B]y seeking to prevent the interview from being aired, the State Department has also damaged its own integrity. This is because arguments and viewpoints may only be truly evaluated when

exposed to opposing arguments. A failure to include such views will invariably lessen the impact of the State Department's own arguments and lead to a vacuum in which rumor, as opposed to fact, may become a determining factor. . . . [W]ith news organizations such as the VOA working on the key issues, it is to be hoped that the events currently unfolding will be reported without further damage to either the truth or the integrity of journalists.[30]

Secretary-General of the International Federation of Journalists (IFJ) Aidan White accused the American government of conducting "knee-jerk censorship," stating, "Governments must not use the current crisis as an excuse to compromise the credibility of journalism by trying to suppress opinions they don't like."[31]

Additional criticism came from the press itself. A *Washington Post* editorial stated that "the episode revealed an impulse to squelch facts that is never far beneath the surface in time of war or quasi-war, an impulse that is hardly less noxious when it retreats promptly under challenge."[32]

After the incident, a petition was circulated within the VOA calling for the organization to be allowed to carry out its job in accordance with its charter. Nearly two hundred staff members signed the petition, which proved an effective means of transmitting the staff's viewpoint to both management and the outside world. Despite considerable support from within the news organization, pressure from the outside forced the VOA to concede some ground. Influential politicians such as Senator Helms forced Whitworth to issue a statement that the VOA "will not give a platform to terrorists or extremist groups." The acting director later became one of the first casualties in the fallout from the Mullah Omar news report when Robert R. Reilly was appointed director of the VOA. Another casualty was Maiwandi. On October 26, 2001, the head of the VOA's Pashto service was informed that she was being given a "temporary promotion," when in reality the promotion amounted to her removal from active duty in the Pashto service. In a letter, VOA Human Resources said, "This action is not a reassignment from your current position. Your position of record remains Chief of the Pashto Service." Maiwandi, however, was to have no control over the day-to-day running of the service.[33]

Aside from her reassignment, Maiwandi has alleged that she was harassed. She claims, in particular, that she received "hate mail."[34] Responding to Maiwandi's reassignment, Executive Director of the Committee to Protect Journalists Ann Cooper said in a January 12, 2002, letter addressed to Reilly, "Maiwandi's reassignment . . . suggests that the VOA is sacrificing its hard-earned reputation as a reliable and independent news source to short-term political considerations. . . . Such a policy is a disservice to VOA's millions of listeners."

On October 2, 2001, President Bush announced that Reilly would take over as director of the VOA. Before his appointment, Reilly had worked for eleven years in the VOA Policy Office and was a host of its *On the Line* program. He was also responsible for reading VOA editorials to see that they conformed to State Department policy. Though not subject to Senate confirmation, the appointment needed the approval of the BBG, which was duly given at a later meeting between Reilly and the board.

Despite sponsoring the legislation that created the BBG, Senator Helms was a long-time critic of the VOA and had been angered by the Mullah Omar news report. According to a *Washington Post* article, Helms let it be known that he considered the organization to be a rogue agency that must be carefully watched. In an October letter to President Bush, he protested the possibility of a Middle East Radio Network being created under the umbrella of the VOA. Such a network, he feared, would promote "ideas contrary to American interests and values in the strained name of 'balance.'"[35]

The criticism led to the insertion of a clause in a pending congressional bill for the 2002 VOA appropriation stating that no interviews were to be undertaken "with any official from nations that sponsor terrorism." The clause stated Congress's expectation that the VOA "will not air interviews with any official from nations that sponsor terrorism, or otherwise afford such individuals opportunities to air inaccurate, propagandistic, or inflammatory messages."[36]

This clause forced Reilly to issue a memorandum on December 12, 2001, informing VOA staff members that they must heed "the letter and the spirit" of the provision. If the provision had been in force prior to the interview with Omar, it would have effectively censored the VOA. As a *Chicago Tribune* article pointed out, the provision could prohibit interviews with Syrian and Palestinian Authority officials because of their links with terrorism.[37]

With a new VOA director, a critical Congress, and an increasingly demoralized staff, the BBG's stance would be crucial. In previous instances of political pressure, the BBG had reacted quickly to provide protection for editorial decisions. Early signs were confusing, however, with those BBG members who gave interviews not entirely convincing in their support for the editorial independence of the VOA.

In the first such instance, it appeared that the BBG might have buckled under the pressure. BBG member Norman Pattiz said in an interview that the decision to air the Mullah Omar news report had been made by the VOA staff and not by the BBG. On the question of the BBG's role, he said, "We know what our mission is. We were set up by an act of Congress to ensure the independence of our news services, and we take it very seriously."[38]

Unfortunately, Pattiz's words seemed to show a misunderstanding of the BBG's role and the principle of journalistic independence. He appeared to give no direct support to the VOA journalists and their decision to release the Mullah Omar news report, and he gave no confirmation that the best people to make decisions about content are the journalists themselves. He, therefore, distanced the BBG from the actual decision by stating that the BBG had played no role. This comment must have further dented morale at the VOA.

On October 10, 2001, Marc B. Nathanson, then chairman of the BBG, supported by Tom Korologos another BBG member, gave evidence to the House Committee on International Relations. Nathanson said that U.S. international broadcasting had responded to the act of terrorism. He outlined the VOA's work and commented on the continuing debate over public diplomacy and the role of the VOA within that debate. Acknowledging that mistakes had been made, he alluded to the September 12, 2001, interview with al Serri: "The reporter who filed the story has been reassigned. The editors who handled the story have been admonished." With regard to the Mullah Omar news report, Nathanson played down its importance by stating that it involved mere minutes of broadcast time when compared with the thousands of hours broadcast since September 11: "In the end, we learned lessons about sure-footedness and the need for constant internal communication. We have issued extensive guidelines in an effort to follow the clear intent of legislation . . . ," and he concluded, "We will continue to tell the truth about terrorism and the United States' response to it."[39]

While Nathanson adequately discusses the work of the VOA, his testimony is more interesting for what it does not mention. The BBG member fails to state that it is the role of the News Department to set the news content of the VOA. As for his staff, while he says that, "overall, the vast majority of VOA reporting has been excellent," he also publicly admonishes a reporter and upbraids editors for their work—a management style not conducive to the promotion of good morale. Concerning the Mullah Omar news report, Nathanson says only that there were "passionate debates" on both sides.[40]

Elsewhere in his testimony, Nathanson states, "As BBG member Tom Korologos repeatedly reminds us, 'International Broadcasting is the most cost effective weapon in the foreign policy arsenal. Its low cost and high yield make it a great bargain. Our annual budget, of less than $500 million, is a fraction of a major weapons system.'"[41] These words compare editors and reporters to an unthinking piece of military hardware.

And what of the BBG's role as firewall? A December 14, 2001, memorandum from the BBG to all IBB employees stated, "We would like to reassure all of you that the board takes seriously its legislated role as a 'firewall' to protect the journalistic integrity of all our broadcasting services." Coming as it did two days after Reilly's memorandum saying that the VOA would have to follow the Congressional statement on terrorism, the e-mail to staff appeared to be too little, too late.

Irrespective of the pressure applied by politicians, media commentators were also quick to provide their own views on the al Serri and Mullah Omar news reports, leading to a debate in some sections of the media over whether the VOA had acted appropriately. One of the most critical articles came from journalist William Safire. In "Giving 'Equal Time' to Adolf Hitler," Safire says, "Even in peacetime, news credibility does not flow from splitting the moral difference between good and evil. In the climate of today's undeclared war, private media in democracies are free to join either or neither sides, but U.S. taxpayer-supported broadcasting is supposed to be on our side."[42]

Concerning the question of "splitting the moral difference," the VOA Charter says that a reporter's duty is to provide "accurate, objective, and comprehensive" news reporting. This statement does not imply reporting news from the middle ground as Safire comments but instead calls on journalists to report dispassionately, free of their own views and those of society. Significantly, the credibility of the VOA's news is entirely reliant on this duty. Safire's own views are based on notions of "support" and "patriotism" for a homegrown audience but fails to reflect what is needed to convince an audience in the Middle East that is already deeply suspicious of America and its values. Such an audience would expect contrary views to be censored on American broadcasting stations, particularly those connected to the government. By advocating this himself, Safire is merely reinforcing prejudices already deeply embedded among listeners in the Middle East.

On the question of the involvement of U.S. taxpayers, both Safire and Richard Boucher imply that they have a right to be involved in determining news policy. This view skews the relationship between those responsible for news, on the one hand, and the government and taxpayers, on the other. As IPI Director Fritz said in his October 2, 2001, letter of support to Andre DeNesnera, "The belief that editorial independence may be compromised because tax-payers provide funding is misleading. Editorial independence exists to protect objective and balanced reporting, irrespective of the narrow opinions of interest groups, whether these be government departments, publishers, or tax-payers."[43]

Elsewhere, the media pitted a former VOA director, Kenneth Tomlinson, against a former BBG governor, David Burke. Tomlinson, director of the VOA nearly twenty years ago, and the person who would eventually succeed Nathanson as chairman of the BBG, agreed with Safire that balance should not be the guiding principle of reporting. As a result, he found himself in disagreement with

Burke, the first chairman of the BBG, who said, "[The] VOA nearly validated the maxim that truth is the first casualty of war. It delayed four days in broadcasting the remarks of Mullah Omar. Why? Opposition from the State Department."[44] According to Tomlinson, the interview should have been surrounded with other voices ensuring that the listener was left in no doubt that Omar was an accomplice to some of the worst criminals in history.[45]

A speech by President Bush on February 25, 2002, set out his views on the VOA network. Speaking at the VOA's sixtieth birthday celebration, Bush said, "Tyranny cannot survive forever in an atmosphere of truth. The Voice of America is not neutral between America and America's enemies, between terrorism and those who defend themselves against terror, between freedom and between tyranny."[46] The speech did not mention how the "atmosphere of truth" was to be attained or how "truth" and partisanship were to coexist happily within the VOA.

In 2002, the VOA received support from an unexpected quarter. On April 16, it was given a Payne Award for Ethics in Journalism by the University of Oregon School of Journalism and Communication, and on June 27, VOA News Director DeNesnera received a "constructive dissent" award from the American Foreign Service Association, the union representing U.S. diplomats. The citation read, "His efforts to defend VOA's Charter and preserve the integrity of its news broadcasts demonstrate the qualities of intellectual courage and constructive dissent that exemplify this award."[47]

In another ironic twist, DeNesnera received the award at the State Department; however, Secretary of State Colin Powell, who was present at the start of the awards ceremony, was pointedly absent when the VOA received its award.

GRASPING THE HORNS OF A DILEMMA: SUPPORTING THE INDEPENDENCE OF THE VOA

Although the broadcast of the Mullah Omar news report was an important victory for press freedom and its supporters, it was not without its cost. The report became a clarion call for friends and enemies of the VOA alike, setting off a wide-ranging and intense discussion on public diplomacy. The debate revealed the intense pressure felt by many people during this period and showed just how far the events of September 11 were to inform decision-making processes and discussions on the subject of the media.

A number of strands within this debate reveal the thinking of various participants, all of whom were determined to shape the activities of the VOA. Participants ranged from the VOA staff and their supporters, who wished to validate their independence and reporting principles, to members of the administration and Congress, who saw in the incident a confirmation of their own worst fears—a "rogue agency" let loose within the halls of power.

The attempt to censor the Omar interview must be seen in the ongoing relationship between the State Department and the VOA, which has been plagued by such attempts. Clearly, there are people within the State Department who have little appreciation for the independent role played by VOA journalists. Moreover, these people fail to understand that rather than endangering the credibility of the VOA, interviews with terrorists like Omar can actually affirm and enhance credibility and objectivity.

For example, in 1999, the VOA conducted a telephone interview from its Washington office with Abdullah Ocalan, leader of the Kurdish Workers Party (PPK), causing a storm in diplomatic circles. On learning of the interview, Mark Parris, the U.S. ambassador to Turkey, wrote to then–Secretary of State Madeleine Albright and other U.S. officials in an attempt to prevent the interview from being broadcast. The letters argued that the broadcast would undermine U.S. foreign policy. Parris also sent a letter to the head of the VOA, in which he stated, "[By] assigning a platform to a terrorist by means of a broadcast against Turkey, the VOA will prove that America cannot distinguish between a terrorist leader and a legal human rights activist. Who will be the next 'political leader' interviewed on the VOA? Ebu Nidal or [Osama] bin Ladin? Will the VOA choose its guests from the foreign ministry list of terrorists from now on?"[48]

On this occasion, the VOA's position was supported by the State

Department and may have signaled another victory for the BBG. In a sign that the Clinton administration had learned from the Wei case, State Department spokesperson James P. Rubin said that the Ocalan broadcast demonstrated that "our media [are] free."

Interviews with Yasser Arafat, Somali warlord Mohammad Farah Aidid, President Jean-Bertrand Aristide of Haiti, and Fidel Castro have all spread alarm among elements of the diplomatic community who deem their views unsuitable for transmission over government airwaves. Such a position reflects the narrow view of State Department officials, who fear that the appearance of an Arafat or an Aristide on the VOA will undermine the foreign policy goals they are working toward.

This view, however, fails to answer the crucial question: How can America's policies be appreciated if listeners do not understand the opposing views or the context in which these policies are being shaped? It would appear that diplomats—and, by association, politicians—are often content with the sound of silence when it comes to opposing views and values. But these people fail to comprehend that, in the long term, they are actively undermining their own policies. The assessment of one's own arguments can come only when these views are placed side-by-side with opposing claims. To forge arguments in a vacuum is to invite cynicism, thus undermining one's own position.

Instead of discouraging interviews with Castro, for example, the State Department should welcome them. Such people have not only brought their own country's independent media to their knees but also criticized the American media for bias. As the Hutchins Commission, which was formed to examine freedom of the press, argued over sixty years ago, the appearance of a Castro on the VOA is an antidote to claims of bias. Furthermore, preventing the appearance of a Castro undermines the credibility of the VOA. If such interviews affirm the VOA's independence, then surely the State Department needs them to underpin its attempts to convince foreign listeners of the veracity of its policies. Politicians and diplomats, it would seem, spend undue amounts of time fearing the damage of words when silence is more destructive. There is no clearer example of this unwarranted fear than the State Department's attempts to prevent the VOA from airing the Mullah Omar news report.

Aside from being one element in the wider relationship between the VOA and the State Department, the attempted censorship of the Omar interview may reflect the relative inexperience of the Bush administration at that time. BBG member Ted Kaufman and BBG Chairman Kenneth Tomlinson concur on this point. Interestingly, Tomlinson has argued that the fact that the incident occurred when the BBG was in a period of transition had a direct bearing on the response of many of those involved.[49]

Kaufman has suggested that the incident might never have happened if Clinton had been president, not because of his liberal views but because the administration would have had the experience to deal with the situation. Tomlinson supports this view by stating that Secretary of State Powell told him on several occasions that the State Department would not try to censor the VOA, and, according to him, the fact that there have been no further problems is proof of Powell's statement.

For the BBG members, the failure to ask Omar tough questions and provide adequate balance were additional reasons for the BBG's apparent reluctance to entirely support the VOA. Kaufman said that his view of the situation was entirely directed by the need to provide appropriate balance to Omar's words but added that he was aware of individuals in the State Department who did not want to "give the microphone to the Taliban" at any cost.[50] On a similar note, Tomlinson said that "balance is not half-way between Washington and where the terrorists are, it is within the bounds of freedom and democracy."[51] According to these views, the BBG, while normally resistant to outside pressure, had not been fully persuaded that a substantive press freedom issue was involved in the Omar case.

Outside of the Broadcasting Board of Governors, there were those who believed that the Omar incident merely highlighted management and reporting problems in the Pashto service itself. These critics argued that the Omar interview was yet another example of a biased service, which was operating as the "Voice of the Taliban." This view was apparently supported by a report produced shortly before September 11 claiming a need for a "reaffirmation of balance" in the service's news reporting. However, Whitworth specifically rebutted these charges, stating in an interview that outside experts who examined translated texts of news reports delivered by the Pashto service found no such bias.[52] While acknowledging a possible need for additional management controls, the former acting director said that even before the September 11 attacks, the newsroom had decided that the Pashto and Dari services should hold joint editorial meetings and share interviews to create a more cohesive department. The existence of bias was also refuted by BBG Communications Coordinator Joan Mower, who said that the VOA had spent considerable amounts of money investigating bias in the Pashto service but had never found any. [53] Perhaps the real cause of the attempted censorship lay elsewhere, hidden in the relationships among the VOA, the BBG, and the State Department.

There can be no doubt that the events of September 11 sent shockwaves throughout both the Bush administration and the State Department. Tomlinson intuitively described the attack as having the same impact as Pearl Harbor, perhaps the best description of the overall impact of the tragedy on the United States. The attacks were staggering in their enormity and, at the same time, for the majority of people, absolutely incomprehensible. Afterward, the Bush administration and State Department would successfully shape a military response—the formation of the coalition of countries and the war on terrorism—but, given the freshness of the attacks, they remained excessively sensitive to news reports from either al-Qaeda or Taliban sources. Moreover, given the need for public diplomacy to justify the war on Afghanistan, the administration felt that a single, coherent message should be offered by all of the State Department's media outlets. Offering, as it did, an alternative view, the Omar news report cut across this pressing desire. Therefore, when its own broadcaster said that it had made contact with the leader of the Taliban, attempts were made to prevent the interview taking place. In the aftermath of the September 11 attacks, there appeared to be two camps within the State Department, both of which held equally firm views on the role of the VOA.

First, there were those who believed that freedom of speech is the cornerstone of democracy and that it was important that the VOA espouse this principle in regions of the world where it was almost unknown. This view was most often held by the many career diplomats who are convinced that it is possible to advance public diplomacy initiatives only if the VOA exists at arm's length from the State Department. For them, objectivity is an affirmation of credibility. But this view is countered by others in the service who believe that the VOA is essentially a part of the foreign policy apparatus of the United States and, as such, accountable to the State Department for its actions.

After the mistakes made in the al Serri case, the latter view gained ascendancy. And, for this reason, individuals within the State Department and the International Broadcasting Bureau, which houses the VOA, began closely examining VOA scripts for examples of bias or lack of balance. The Mullah Omar news report confirmed the worst suspicions of those who believed that the VOA was operating against the State Department's public diplomacy initiatives.

And what of the "firewall"—the BBG—which was supposed to stop outside interference in the everyday work of the VOA? When the September 11 attacks occurred, the BBG was going through a slow process of transition—with a new Republican president in the White House, the board was waiting for new appointments to change its composition. However, it still had a liberal democrat, Marc Nathanson, as chairman, while other board members were political holdovers from the time of President Clinton. In addition, both the VOA and the IBB had acting directors.

In the opinion of some commentators, this left the board in an untenable position. Significantly, Whitworth believed that in handling the Mullah Omar news report, "Nathanson tried to show that it [the BBG] was not a partisan board and that it was responsive at the most critical time in American history."[54] Therefore, according to Whitworth, in trying to show impartiality, the BBG failed to adequately protect the VOA.

The ramifications of this failure were widespread. It undermined the authority of the BBG, damaged morale at the VOA, and eventually forced the journalists to act on their own behalf when they released the news report without the support of the firewall members. As DeNesnera had said in his earlier memorandum, not to have done so would have meant that the censors had won.

Although it would appear that journalists and editors at the VOA held firm in the face of political pressure, the VOA and other institutions were wounded by the incident. Individuals also suffered, including acting director Whitworth, who was quickly removed after supporting her staff, and Maiwandi, who was reassigned after carrying out the original interview. And what of the damage done to the credibility of the State Department? What of the wider damage to the reputation of America's media abroad?

The State Department is impaled on the horns of a singular dilemma. It would very much like to dictate content, but it would also like to be believed. Unfortunately, its involvement in one undermines the other: control diminishes credibility. And yet, during times of crisis, such as the war in Afghanistan, the State Department will always revert to this involuntary desire to control information.

A further problem is the organization's seeming lack of understanding of journalists. The State Department must accept the fact that journalists do not check their ethical obligations at the entrance to the VOA's offices. For journalists, words such as "objectivity" and "balance" have real and meaningful implications. They exist to encourage credibility, to ensure that listeners believe what they are hearing. For this reason, the VOA Charter expressly mentions "objectivity." This notion cannot be wiped away with poorly defined calls to represent American policy abroad. Instead, the State Department needs to understand such principles and incorporate them into its thinking and behavior, creating a much-needed change in the relationship between politicians and journalists. If the State Department cannot do this, then it might as well employ information offices to communicate the news as opposed to reporting on it, but, doing so would mean once again being caught in the conundrum that is public diplomacy. Employing information officers rather than journalists would undermine the credibility of the broadcaster. Losing credibility risks losing the message. Losing the message means sacrificing the opportunity to change opinion in regions where America is most resented. This, in turn, could mean the loss of America's voice at a time of great need.

The important debate over the loss of credibility and the undermining of America's voice echoes the words of famed journalist Edward R. Murrow, who said, "We must be believable. To be believable, we must be credible. To be credible, we must be truthful." If this is not to be undermined, the State Department must do more to develop a better working relationship with the VOA. The belief that the VOA is merely part of the U.S. foreign policy apparatus should not be allowed to triumph over the VOA's ability to report independently and free of outside interference.

Although unsuccessful, the Bush administration's attempt to prevent the Omar broadcast should be seen as its first attempt to control the free flow of information. The administration's next move would be against the Qatar-based television broadcaster Al-Jazeera.

NOTES

1. House Republican Committee Policy Perspective, "The Trial of Wei Jingsheng," December 12, 1995.

2. Reuters News Service, "China Says Don't Use Dissident to Oppose Beijing," December 18, 1997.

3. Amy Williams, student editor, "White House Tried to Stop VOA Broadcast of Dissident Wei Jingsheng into China," http://www.bulldog.news.net (accessed December 1, 2003).

4. "White House Defends Contacting VOA on Wei Story," *Washington Post*, December 18, 1997.

5. Center for Security Policy, "Kow-Towing to China: Clinton's 'Engagement' Policy Means Joining Beijing in Stifling Human Rights in America," December 18, 1997, http://www.centerforsecuritypolicy.org (accessed December 1, 2003).

6. Simon Beck, "Storm over Block on Wei TV Broadcast: White House Red-Faced after Censorship Admission," *South China Morning Post*, December 19, 1997.

7. Ibid.

8. Public Law 103-236, Foreign Relations Authorization Act, Financial Year 1994–95.

9. Statement on International Broadcasting Programs, June 15, 1993, *Published Papers of William J. Clinton*, vol. 1, pp. 857–58.

10. 22 U.S.C. ß6205.

11. S. Rep. No. 103-107, at 49 (1994).

12. Reorganization Plan and Report, December 30, 1998. Pursuant to Section 1601 of the Foreign Affairs Reform and Restructuring Act of 1998, as contained in Public Law 105-277, Omnibus Consolidated and Emergency Supplemental Appropriations Act, 1999.

13. Ibid.

14. Joan Mower, telephone interview, February 28, 2003.

15. Ted Kaufman, telephone interview, March 6, 2003.

16. George Creel, *How We Advertised America* (New York: Harper & Brothers, 1920), p. 237.

17. George Mackenzie, "A Brief VOA History," *VOA News*, http://www.voa.gov (accessed December 22, 2003).

18. L. White and R. D. Leigh, *Peoples Speaking to Peoples: A Report on International Mass Communication from the Commission on Freedom of the Press* (Chicago: University of Chicago Press, 1946).

19. William Safire, "Giving 'Equal Time' to Adolf Hitler," *Seattle Post Intelligencer*, September 21, 2001.

20. Ibid.

21. Ibid.

22. Myrna Whitworth, telephone interview, March 14, 2003.

23. Ibid.

24. Ibid.

25. Ellen Nakashima, "Broadcast with Afghan Leader Halted, State Department Pressures Voice of America Not to Air Voice of Taliban," *Washington Post*, September 23, 2001.

26. VOA internal memo, VOA News Director Andre DeNesnera to news staff, September 24, 2001.

27. U.S. Department of State, daily press briefing, Richard Boucher, spokesperson, September 24, 2001.

28. Ibid.

29. U.S. Department of State, daily press briefing, Richard Boucher, spokesperson, September 26, 2001.

30. Johann P. Fritz, director, International Press Institute, letter to Colin Powell, secretary of state, October 8, 2001.

31. Aidan White, quoted in International Federation of Journalists' press release, September 28, 2001.

32. Editorial, "Resisting the Censor's Impulse," *Washington Post*, September 26, 2001.

33. Frank Smyth, "The Price of Propaganda," March 21, 2002, Tom Paine.commonsense, http://www.tompaine.com (accessed August 28, 2003).

34. Spozhmai Maiwandi, quoted in ibid.

35. Senator Jesse Helms (R-NC), letter to Pres. George W. Bush, October 4, 2001.

36. James Warren, "VOA Chief Restricts Airing of Interviews," *Chicago Tribune*, December 14, 2001.

37. Ibid.

38. Cable News Network, "VOA Asked Not to Air Taliban Leader Interview," September 25, 2001, http://www.cnn.com/US (accessed December 1, 2003).

39. Marc B. Nathanson, testimony before the House Committee on International Relations, http://www.house.gov/international_relations (August 28, 2003).

40. Ibid.

41. Ibid.

42. Safire, "Giving 'Equal Time' to Adolf Hitler."

43. Johann P. Fritz, letter to Andre DeNesnera, October 2, 2001.

44. David Burke, editorial, "A Truthful Voice," *Washington Post*, October 10, 2001.

45. Kenneth Y. Tomlinson, "VOA Led Astray?" *Washington Times*, October 14, 2001.

46. George Bush, quoted in "President Salutes VOA's Sixty-Year Commitment to Freedom," PR Newswire, February 25, 2002.

47. Agence France-Presse, "VOA Official Who Defied U.S. State Department over Taliban Interview to Be Honored," June 26, 2002.

48. Turkish Press Review, "U.S. Ambassador Against Ocalan Interview on VOA," June 1, 1999, http://www.hri.org (accessed December 1, 2003).

49. Ted Kaufman, Broadcasting Board of Governors, telephone interview, March 6, 2003; Kenneth Tomlinson, chairman, Broadcasting Board of Governors, telephone interview, March 7, 2003.

50. Kaufman telephone interview.

51. Ibid.

52. Whitworth telephone interview.

53. Mower telephone interview.

54. Whitworth telephone interview.

Chapter 2

AL-JAZEERA
A Platform of Controversy

You mean to tell me that all this trouble comes from this matchbox?
—President of Egypt Hosni Mubarak on
visiting the Al-Jazeera offices, 2001

A FLOWER IN THE DESERT?

In May 2001, independent journalist Nizar Nayyouf was released after spending ten years in a Syrian prison. Originally imprisoned on January 10, 1992, for disseminating false information and for being the secretary-general of a proscribed organization, Nayyouf routinely faced torture at the hands of his guards. The Syrian journalist was beaten and subjected to the "German chair," a torture method that contorts the spine, leaving him partially paralyzed below the waist.[1]

On his release, Nayyouf flew to Paris for medical treatment.

Syrian security officers then turned on his family, still living in Syria, when they publicly refused to criticize the journalist. Since 2001, Nayyouf's family has suffered violence, continuous harassment, and threats of exile. Family members have been attacked in the streets, threatened with dismissal from work, and forbidden from attending university. Closed off from the outside world, the family members have lived in almost permanent fear from a vindictive regime that shows no remorse for its activities.[2]

While this incident represents one of the worst excesses, the impulse to suppress the independent media exists in many of the countries in the Middle East. In the past few years, however, new leaders have assumed power in Jordan, Morocco, and Syria. While these changes initially offered the possibility of a new liberalizing process, those hopes were dashed when, despite claims to the contrary, the business of suppression continued as usual. The harassment of journalists, repressive legislation protecting both leaders and religion, and limits on the free flow of information are used by these countries to stifle debate and obstruct calls for democratic change.

Other countries have also failed to make a break with the past. In Bahrain, Kuwait, and the United Arab Emirates, the situation has improved slightly but a credibility gap exists between what the governments allow to be printed and what the Arab public wishes to read.[3] Elsewhere, there are countries where press freedom is virtually nonexistent. Expression of independent thought was crushed long ago in Iraq and Libya, and journalists who have sought to practice their profession have often been imprisoned or forced into exile.

The primary problem for journalists throughout the Middle East is the attitude of the ruling families, parties, or religious groups. Accustomed to governing without criticism, these groups have failed to adjust to the request of their populations for more information, more debate, and more freedoms—requests motivated by increased exposure to outside media, the Internet, and globalization. Frightened, or in some cases appalled, by this clamoring for information from their citizens, governments have employed a number of invidious tactics to subdue the media, thereby playing down the calls for increased democratization.

With an underlying ambivalence toward a free press, coupled with state apparatuses that are attuned to snuffing out dissent, Arab journalists face arbitrary arrest, interrogation, and imprisonment. All of these are traditional weapons in the hands of some rulers, and they have been applied liberally. Not surprisingly, the Middle East and North Africa are "the second biggest prisons" for journalists, with twenty-eight journalists held behind bars on January 1, 2002.[4] Nearly half of those imprisoned were in Iran, where a sudden blossoming of the media under a moderate government has since been crushed by conservatives exerting their authority. According to press freedom organization Reporters Sans Frontières (Reporters Without Borders [RSF]), there were also seventy arrests and sanctions applied against a further fifty media outlets.[5]

Repressive laws are also used against the media. With no elected legislatures in many of the countries, the passage of new laws is often at the discretion of a leader or a small coterie of advisors. Press codes are created with little or no discussion among the media, and mandatory licenses for both journalists and media outlets can be revoked for the slightest breach.

On October 9, 2001, several new restrictive laws were enacted against the media in Jordan. Adopted as part of new antiterrorist legislation, the measures allowed for the permanent closure of newspapers for defamation. At the same time, prison sentences for insulting the royal couple and the crown prince were updated.

Freedom of information is also virtually unknown in many Arab countries, and governments continue to act secretly and without accountability. Egypt is representative of these countries; on March 10, 2001, there were reports that the country was seeking to pass a law that made it an offense, punishable by five years imprisonment, to photograph or publish government documents. Furthermore, the movement of journalists in the region is often restricted, with certain countries applying a prohibition on travel outside the capital; elsewhere, official "minders" are provided.

According to a report by the Committee to Protect Journalists (CPJ), there are an estimated four million Internet users in the Middle East.[6] The Internet has led to a flood of information, previously unobtainable, into the region, forcing countries to come to terms with the technology. Although some Middle Eastern countries have clamped down on the Internet, others have attempted to accommodate it. The United Arab Emirates is an example of the latter attitude; the country has sought to make itself the Internet center of the Middle East. Overall, to a greater or lesser extent, Internet content is still controlled by Arab governments, but the censor's grip is loosening.

According to Dr. Anthony Löwstedt, an IPI press freedom analyst, the region has its fair share of undemocratic cultures where there is little equality and human rights are undervalued. Löwstedt makes the point that governments react negatively to criticism, and politicians are thin-skinned and often vengeful. Significantly, many Middle Eastern governments refuse to accept the media's traditional role of balancing and checking political institutions. Speaking of democracy in the region, Löwstedt said, "[These] are undemocratic countries ruled by unelected governments. This makes it difficult for the media to challenge [them] in the same way they would in a democracy."[7] Because of these problems, the Middle East continues to suppress the independent media, and it is deeply resistant to change. One country, however, appears to be swimming against the current—namely, Qatar. It has introduced changes to its media environment and, as a result, has had a profound effect on other countries in the region. Located on a peninsula bordering the Persian Gulf and Saudi Arabia, Qatar is slightly smaller than the American state of Connecticut and has a population of approximately 750,000. On September 3, 1971, the country formally declared its independence, and a palace coup in February of the following year saw Emir Ahmed exiled and Deputy Ruler and Prime Minister Sheikh Khalifa bin Hamad al-Thani take his place. Sheikh Khalifa provided much-needed leadership and a degree of stability and prosperity previously unknown in the country.

Once a center for the pearl market in the Middle East, the country is now almost completely dependent on oil production. Oil was discovered in 1939 by the Petroleum Development Qatar Company, and the country's North Dome Field is the third largest liquefied gas reserve in the world. In total, almost 85 percent of the country's revenue is derived from oil, and attempts to diversify into other fields have met with varying degrees of success. There is, however, a growing acknowledgment among Qatar's leaders that the country needs to break free of its reliance on oil, thus tax incentives have been offered to encourage internal investment.

On June 27, 1995, Sheikh Khalifa was dethroned by his son, Sheikh Hamad bin Khalifa al-Thani. The coup was the culmination of several weeks of in-fighting during which Sheikh Khalifa had tried to regain many of the powers transferred to his son. Many experts believe that Sheikh Hamad's hand was forced by corruption in his father's administration. Hours after assuming control, the new emir gave a television address in which he said, "I am not happy with what has happened, but it had to be done and I had to do it." In the days that followed, a number of countries formally recognized the change in leadership, including the United Kingdom and Saudi Arabia.

Almost immediately after the bloodless coup, Sheikh Hamad set Qatar on a course of pro-Western modernization, while at the same time mending fences with his far larger neighbor Saudi Arabia. The shift in policy was motivated by a desire to improve ties with Western countries, particularly the United States. Sheikh Hamad also indicated a desire to follow in the footsteps of Kuwait, perhaps the most liberal country in the Gulf region.

Since starting the drive toward greater democracy in Qatar, Sheikh Hamad has held municipal elections with the full participation of women; controversially allowed Israel to maintain a commercial office in the capital, Doha; and called for the rehabilitation of Iraq after the Gulf War, thereby asserting a degree of independence from Saudi Arabia. In 1999, he started on perhaps his greatest challenge—a constitution for the country. To achieve this goal, Sheikh Hamad formed a thirty-two-member committee to draft a constitution and announced that it would be in place within three years. Such changes represent the seeds of a growing democracy in the country, although it should be remembered that parliamentary elections have yet to be held and political parties are still prohibited.[8]

Within the media sector, Sheikh Hamad has instituted a number of improvements. A report by IPI in 2001 said "Qatar is . . . one of the most liberal powers in the Arab world in relation to press freedom and expression."[9] The report noted that the media are becoming increasingly confident and that satellite dishes and the Internet are more prevalent. Confidence within the media was further increased when, in 1999, Sheikh Hamad abolished the Ministry of Information and its Censorship Department, which had tightly controlled the media during the reign of Sheikh Hamad's father.

Speaking to the Qatari newspaper *Al-Watan*, the emir said that he believed Qatar's future lies "in establishing the building blocks for a democratic state, especially a free, balanced, and fair media." Moreover, he stated that he respected the media and would not attempt to control them.[10] These and other views have won the emir a number of plaudits from Western commentators, who see the country as one of the few bright lights in the Gulf region.

However, there is also a darker side to the media in Qatar, a division in the country's attitude between the foreign and the domestic news fronts. Sheikh Hamad is a fervent supporter of the media's right to report foreign news, but he has not been so supportive on the domestic front. According to an unnamed journalist who spoke in March 2001, the media are still intimidated and self-censorship is widespread. He told Reuters, "[A]s a reporter, you still assume that certain things are taboo. Seventy percent of the problem is actually the journalists' own inhibition."[11]

Problems over the portrayal of women still exist. In 1998, a newspaper editor, Malcolm Ward of the *Peninsula*, was fired on instructions from the government after he published a fashion picture showing a woman's breast. The photograph was declared to be in violation of the Press Law and its publication a religiously unacceptable act.[12] In the same year, a member of the civil service was arrested for criticizing Sheikh Hamad's policies. As these examples indicate, there is often a gap between appearance and reality in Qatar. While it is true to say that the Ministry of Information has been abolished, media censorship is now conducted by the Ministry of Religious Endowments.[13] Censorship has merely been shifted from one agency to another.

But for every step backward, there have been many steps forward, and while the country does not meet international standards on every issue, it is far ahead of many other countries in the region. Without doubt, the crowning achievement of Sheikh Hamad's open media policy is the Qatari-based satellite network Al-Jazeera ("The Peninsula"). Funded by Sheikh Hamad but with an independent editorial policy, the network has grown into one of the most widely known television channels in the world, much to the consternation of Qatar's Middle Eastern neighbors and a number of other countries as well.

Ironically, Al-Jazeera and its editorial independence arose from an act of censorship. In June 1994, a joint venture was set up between World Service Television (later known as BBC World Wide Television) and the Rome-based Orbit Communications Corporation (OCC), a subsidiary of the Saudi Arabian company Mawarid.[14] The project created an Arabic-language channel, funded by Saudi Arabia and transmitted across the Middle East and North Africa. Named the BBC Arabic Television Channel, its aim was to re-create the success of the BBC World Service Radio's Arabic Service.

Unfortunately, there were problems over editorial independence. At the beginning of the venture, the OCC had promised that the BBC would be given the right to develop its own news and reporting, but these assurances vanished once the station started broadcasting. During its brief life, there were several heated meetings between the BBC and OCC officials at which the BBC was accused of failing to appreciate "Saudi sensibilities"—code for any reporting disliked by the Saudi Arabian ruling family.[15]

Disagreement about censorship allegedly culminated in an argument over a special documentary on Saudi executions. On April 20, 1996, the BBC Arab Television Channel was closed down by the OCC. Seizing their opportunity, the founders of Al-Jazeera recruited the BBC editorial staff and, in doing so, inherited the BBC's fierce independence and distinctive reporting style. After hiring the staff, the department was moved from London to Doha, where the Qatari government offered the news organization a sizeable subsidy. In November 1996, Al-Jazeera reportedly received $140 million from

Sheikh Hamad to help the station in its first five years, with a view to the television station's becoming financially independent after this period. Since then, Sheikh Hamad has been paying approximately $100 million a year to Al-Jazeera. With a viewership of almost thirty-five million, Al-Jazeera now employs almost 350 journalists and 50 foreign correspondents in over thirty-one countries.[16]

From the start of its twenty-four-hour-a-day broadcasting life in 1999, Al-Jazeera has been determined to provide daily news, documentaries, and talk shows with content never before seen in the Middle East. The channel examines many of the most topical issues for Arabs in the region, from the Israeli-Palestinian conflict and the war in Afghanistan, to human rights issues in Saudi Arabia and the Algerian civil war.

All of these programs seek to challenge the status quo, offering information and debate not presented by other regional broadcasters. In 1996, Al-Jazeera was the first Arab station to maintain a policy of interviewing Israeli commentators and politicians, and in May 2000, the Israeli television channel Matav signed a contract to carry Al-Jazeera as part of a bundle of different channels. One program that typifies this independent stance is *The Opposite Direction*, which is similar in style to CNN's *Crossfire*. Taking guests who emphatically disagree with one another, the weekly two-hour program uses phone-ins and faxes from viewers to increase dramatic tension and promote debate. The program has produced notable successes and gained a reputation for raucous argument that often offends viewers. Nonetheless, *The Opposite Direction* attracts important guests, including Jordan's deputy prime minister, as well as intellectuals, academics, and a number of ambassadors from various countries.

Even before September 11, Al-Jazeera had a steadily growing reputation for reporting news in the Middle East that had brought it to the attention of other media organizations such as Britain's Sky News and America's CNN. Its reputation was further enhanced by Al-Jazeera's reporting of the destruction of Buddhist statues by the Taliban in March 2001. Al-Jazeera carried exclusive footage of the Taliban blowing up the statues, which had been carved into a sandstone cliff face in the second century and measured fifty-three meters and thirty-eight meters, respectively. For many viewers around the world, this footage was their first exposure to the ultraconservative religious views of the Afghan rulers.[17]

The success of Al-Jazeera has made it a target among Qatar's Middle Eastern neighbors. Since its formation, the Qatari government has faced constant pressure, which both it and Al-Jazeera have always resisted, to tone down or soften the satellite station's reporting.

"THE VIEW AND THE OTHER POINT OF VIEW"

Al-Jazeera Washington Bureau Chief Hafez Al-Mirazi once commented in an interview, "Al-Jazeera has a margin of freedom that no other Arab channel enjoys. Our motto is 'the view and the other point of view.'"[18] Because they have provided the "other point of view," countries as varied as Iraq and India have angrily denounced the network. Indeed, since Al-Jazeera first started broadcasting, bureaus have been closed, journalists expelled, and ambassadors withdrawn from Qatar, and Sheikh Hamad has been berated at the Gulf Cooperation Council (GCC). It is doubtful that any other media organization in the world has faced such pressure.

In their anger, many countries have targeted not Al-Jazeera, but Qatar. With their views on Al-Jazeera often clouded by the restrictions applied to their own media, the rulers of these countries believe that appeals to the Qatari government will resolve the dispute. But Sheikh Hamad has made it clear from the outset that, although Al-Jazeera is publicly funded and its chairman is his relative, its editorial independence is guaranteed and beyond his power to influence. Arab media have also been critical. In December 1998, the Arab States Broadcasting Union (ASBU) refused to admit Al-Jazeera because it refused to act in solidarity with traditional Arab views and media.

Al-Jazeera has been a thorn in Jordan's side on many occasions. In 1998, the Jordanian Press and Publications Department (PPD) cancelled the accreditation rights of journalists working at Al-Jazeera and closed the Jordanian bureau. According to Lyad Qattan, director general of the PPD, the decision was made owing to "deliberate insults against the Jordanian people and political system" in a program criticizing the 1994 Wadi Araba agreement which strengthened relations between Jordan and Israel. The Wadi Araba agreement was also at the heart of the disagreement in 2002 when Jordanian officials rebuked the Qatari government for an Al-Jazeera program that criticized the Jordanian royal family. On August 6, 2002, *Opposite Direction* participants berated King Abdullah II and his late father, King Hussein, for signing the 1994 peace accord with Israel. During the program, the guests attacked Jordan's policies toward the Palestinian National Authority (PNA) and Iraq, implying that father and son were "agents" of Mossad and the CIA. Within twenty-four hours, Mohammed Adwan, the Jordanian information minister, had closed the Al-Jazeera bureau in his country, revoking its license and banning its journalists from practicing their profession in Jordan.

Defending the decision, Adwan said that the program had been a "defamation" against the country and an "undermining [of] Jordan's national policies. . . ." Indeed, it had "surpassed all kinds of decency in its programs by attacking the nation's leaders and its nobilities."[19] The Jordanian Senate likewise accused Al-Jazeera of playing a "destructive role" and of attempting to "sow the seeds of sedition among the Arabs." Newspapers in the kingdom also attacked the Qatari network.

In an editorial, the Jordanian newspaper *Al-Ra'y* said that Al-Jazeera was attempting to split the Arab ranks over such issues as Palestine and Iraq. Under the headline "Al-Jazeera Satellite Channel: Suspicious Role and Poisoned Messages," the newspaper printed several articles, one of which accused the station of close ties with Israel: "it is necessary to adopt a clear stance on this satellite channel and the political cover which provides it with support to serve suspicious goals." Another article accused Al-Jazeera of hypocrisy because of its perpetual failure to focus on Qatar. In a decision that increased tension, Jordan recalled its Qatari ambassador for talks on how to deal with the incident.[20]

A protest letter from the Committee to Protect Journalists to the prime minister of Jordan dated August 8, 2002, stated that the decision violated "basic standards of press freedom that are the hallmark of open societies" and noted that King Abdullah II had said on a number of occasions, "'The sky is the limit' for press freedom in Jordan."[21] Robert Menard, general-secretary of RSF, also said that the actions of the Jordanian government were "unacceptable for a country that seeks to be seen internationally as respecting freedom of expression."[22]

Another country that has been deeply irritated by Al-Jazeera is Saudi Arabia. Qatar and Saudi Arabia share a common border, and disagreements between the two countries have been frequent. In late July 2002, a series of articles appeared in *Al-Watan* and other Saudi newspapers attacking the Qatari foreign minister and, by implication, Al-Jazeera for having its own Middle East policy. It is unlikely that these criticisms were published without the express permission of the Saudi Arabian government. The Saudi government has intermittently made calls for the station to be boycotted.

An *Al-Watan* editorial published on July 28, 2002, under the headline "Al-Jazeera's Channel and Gangrene" stated, "This malicious gang that made up what is called 'Al-Jazeera' is working intensively with all means and ways to destabilize GCC [Gulf Corporation Council] countries, by producing artificial, self-styled, and malicious programs." Quoting the Qatari foreign minister, who said that the network often caused a headache, the article continued, "In an attempt on our part to cure this gangrene and the chronic headache caused by this channel to our Qatari brothers, we suggest a remedy similar to the one used to cure gangrene, which is amputation or severance prior to the spreading of the disease to other organs of the body."[23]

In a situation that replicated Jordan's behavior, the government of Bahrain said on May 11, 2002, that it would no longer allow Al-Jazeera to report from its territory. Consequently, reporters from the network were unable to cover municipal elections. Bahrain officials accused Al-Jazeera of using its programming to "harm Bahrain." It also said Al-Jazeera had "links with Israel." Kuwait carried out a similar act in 1999 when it closed Al-Jazeera's bureau and revoked journalists' work permits for broadcasting a program on women's rights titled "*Sharia* and Life," which criticized Sheikh Jaber al-Ahmed al-Sabah, the emir of Kuwait. A Bahraini official later declared that the closure was the result of the sheer "audacity" on the part of the satellite station.[24]

The temporary closure of Al-Jazeera's office in the city of Ramallah on the West Bank of the Jordan River by the PNA revealed official sensitivity over the broadcaster's portrayal of Yasser Arafat. After showing a trailer on March 19, 2001, covering the war in Lebanon, PNA officials informed Al-Jazeera that it had two hours to remove the trailer from its broadcasting scheduling because it portrayed Arafat in an unflattering light. The station chose to ignore the objections, and three days later security forces prevented Al-Jazeera staff from entering the bureau.

Although happy to cover the speeches of Saddam Hussein, Al-Jazeera has not always had a friendly relationship with the dictator. In July 2002, Iraq prevented Diyar al-Omari, an Al-Jazeera journalist, from working for ten days because of his dispatches. In protest, the station closed down its Iraqi bureau for the length of the ban. It later reopened.

Countries outside the Middle East have also protested the work of Al-Jazeera. North African countries such as Algeria and Morocco have vehemently attacked the station. On January 27, 1999, the Algerian government allegedly went so far as to cut off the supply of electricity in the capital, Algiers, to prevent the airing of a program on its long-standing and bloody civil war. Morocco has withdrawn its ambassador from Qatar because of alleged Al-Jazeera criticisms of the country, only to return him several months later.

In the summer of 2002, the Indian government complained that Al-Jazeera's coverage of rioters attacking a mosque, a close-up of the Koran being burned, and scenes in which a mother claimed that her son had been named a militant by members of the armed forces were all profoundly detrimental to the image of India. In total, twenty stories were listed by the Indian government. Officials blamed the reporting of Al-Jazeera's Indian correspondent, Nasir M. Shadid. Interestingly, after this incident, India's immigration department repeatedly delayed Shadid's re-accreditation.[25]

Set against this background, U.S. State Department efforts in October 2001 to persuade Sheikh Hamad to use his influence to tone down Al-Jazeera's reporting may be seen as another in a long series of failed attempts. From an outsider's perspective, the decision to intervene looked like a badly handled and rather clumsy attempt by one of the freest nations in the world to censor a media outlet in another country. The overwhelming reaction was confusion. Why had the State Department decided to try this? And why had it not foreseen that it would be rebuffed?

The attempt to influence Al-Jazeera's reporting served only to reinforce the impression that the Bush administration had no overarching strategy for the media; instead, it appeared to react to situations as and when they occurred. Such reactions reinforced the view that Powell's discussion with the emir of Qatar was an attempt to control the free flow of information, something that should have been appreciated by American officials as nearly impossible at the outset of the war in Afghanistan. The circumstances surrounding the meeting between Sheikh Hamad and State Department officials help to clarify the Bush administration's actions in this instance.

BATTLING FOR HEARTS AND MINDS

Before September 11, Al-Jazeera was virtually unknown outside the Middle East; however, the war in Afghanistan brought the network to the attention of the world. As has been said elsewhere, the rise of Al-Jazeera parallels that of CNN during the Gulf War, with both stations delivering important exclusives.

During America's preparations for war in Afghanistan, there were expectations from media analysts that CNN would repeat its successes in the first Gulf War, but the sight of CNN airing footage clearly marked with the Al-Jazeera logo alerted many media commentators to the fact that, in this war, Western broadcasters were not the only ones vying for news.[26] If the overall effect of this exposure was to win Al-Jazeera new viewers, its activities also created apprehension among the Bush administration.

By September 19, 2001, Al-Jazeera was the only news station operating in the Taliban-occupied part of Afghanistan. On October 7, 2001, the broadcaster was able to air footage of America's first strike on Afghanistan; it also provided reactions to the attack from the civilians and members of the ruling Taliban. The other news organizations, with their journalists far away in the territory held by the anti-Taliban Northern Alliance, were forced to sit on the sidelines while the story of the initial attacks unfolded. On the same night, Al-Jazeera broadcast another exclusive—a speech from terrorist Osama bin Laden.

While this speech was the first by bin Laden after September 11, it was not the first shown by Al-Jazeera. In January 2001, the network broadcast footage of bin Laden's attendance at his son's wedding, and on September 20, 2001, it rebroadcast a bin Laden speech delivered in 1998 and originally shown in 1999. The network also quoted from a faxed message that allegedly came from bin Laden.

A number of these videos contained anti-American sentiments such as "We want our land to be freed of the Americans . . ."; "these events have split the world into two camps, the camp of the believers and the camp of the infidels"; and "To America and its peoples . . . I say . . . that America and those who live in it will not be able to dream of security before we live it on the ground in Palestine, and before all the infidel armies leave the land of the Prophet."

In addition to airing statements from al-Qaeda and bin Laden, Al-Jazeera showed the torching of the vacant American embassy in Kabul on September 26, 2001, by angry demonstrators protesting the plans to attack Afghanistan. Three days later, on September 29, Al-Jazeera reported that three soldiers from America's special forces had been captured—a claim denied by Taliban and American officials alike.

Heavily involved in military planning and seeking support for the war in Afghanistan, the Bush administration became alarmed by the portrayal of anti-American expression on Al-Jazeera. On September 20, 2001, in an address to Congress, President Bush said, "Americans are asking, 'Why do they hate us?'" Although his speech was an important rallying call to both America and its allies to fight global terrorism, it also reflected a growing awareness within the administration that hatred and resentment of American policy existed in large pockets around the world, particularly in the Middle East.

Furthermore, there were American fears that the spread of this hatred might undermine the alliance among key countries in the region that was being painstakingly put together to combat terrorism in Afghanistan. There were also security concerns in the Bush administration—albeit contentious ones—that the unedited videos from bin Laden might be used to pass on coded messages; a possibility exacerbated by the fact that Western broadcasters were airing Al-Jazeera footage. For these reasons, the Bush administration became increasingly sensitive to such news. Moreover, as the Voice of America case proved, American officials were unwilling to view the pronouncements of a bin Laden or a Mullah Omar as news. A combination of these different elements led the Bush administration to attempt to censor Al-Jazeera, beginning on October 3, 2001, with the visit of Sheikh Hamad to the State Department in Washington. According to news reports, Secretary of State Colin Powell asked Sheikh Hamad to use his influence to "tone down" the reporting of the Qatari network. At the same meeting, Sheikh Hamad was told that the news channel was unbalanced and anti-American and airing vitriolic and irresponsible statements. A U.S. official later told CNN that the two men had entered into "a frank exchange" and "there should have been no mistake of where we were coming from."[27] The discussion came one day after the American embassy in Doha had formally complained that the network tended to "interview analysts who argued that it was the U.S.'s foreign policy which brought about the September 11 plane attacks."[21] Alluding to the rebroadcast 1998 interview with bin Laden, embassy officials argued that it was too flattering to the terrorist.[28]

In response, Sheikh Hamad confirmed that the conversation with Powell had taken place and said, "We heard this from the U.S. administration, and also from the previous administration. . . . Naturally we take these things as a kind of advice." He argued that Al-Jazeera was not under his control and he was unable to influence its editorial policy: "Parliamentary life requires you have a free and credible media and that is what we are trying to do. . . . Al-Jazeera is one of the most widely watched [television stations] in the Arab world because of its editorial independence and its willingness to provide a platform of controversy."[29]

Within Al-Jazeera there was also anger at the attempt to influence editorial policy. On October 4, Muhamad Jasim al-Ali, managing director of the network, countered the criticism: "We have been accused of being the voice of Iraq because of our coverage, and now that we are the only people with access in Afghanistan, we are accused of being pro-Afghani. . . . We give equal coverage to both sides and that is our role. We present both sides." Al-Jazeera journalists also denied that they were given strict guidelines from the Editorial Department on how to report the war in Afghanistan.[30]

As with the earlier VOA case, the State Department's actions were immediately condemned by press freedom and media organizations. Johann P. Fritz, director of the International Press Institute, said in a letter to Powell, "In the opinion of IPI, the attempt to curtail the news reporting of an independent television station, based in another country, is an infringement of editorial independence and has serious consequences for press freedom." Countering the view that Al-Jazeera was unbalanced, Fritz continued, "Editorial independence protects news reporting and this includes the freedom to portray often uncomfortable or controversial viewpoints."[31]

Outraged that a country perceived as one of the strongest advocates of press freedom should attempt to censor the media of another country, the Arab media were particularly critical. In Iran, the reformist daily *Nowruz* said, "This censorship is meant to secure U.S. interests but in fact threatens world interests," and the *Daily Star* of Beirut commented, "The United States has said and done some fairly ridiculous things [in the Middle East but] . . . the latest shenanigan sets new standards for juvenility and hypocrisy."[32] Elsewhere in the Middle East, the prevailing view was one of double standards. Many critics pointed out that the question of balance could not be determined by viewing Al-Jazeera in isolation. Only by examining a cross section of the media, they argued, could support of the American-led war on Afghanistan be balanced by the views aired on Al-Jazeera. Other commentators offered a counterargument to the State Department's view, namely, that the media in America were "kindling feelings of revenge."

In America, the response of some media was to castigate Al-Jazeera, often using vitriolic and inflammatory language of their own. National Public Radio stated that the network should "come with a health warning," while the influential journalist and news anchor Dan Rather pondered on television whether there was "any indication that Osama bin Laden has helped finance this operation." Perhaps the most influential statement came from the *New York Times* on October 10, 2001. Al-Jazeera, the newspaper said, "often slants its news with a vicious anti-Israel and anti-American bias" and broadcasts "deeply irresponsible reporting [that] reinforces the region's anti-American views."[33] Additional criticism of Al-Jazeera came from the British media, which described the network as "bin Laden television."[34]

One of the most caustic attacks on Al-Jazeera—similar in vein to William Safire's attack on the VOA—came from commentator Zev Chafets, who wrote in the *New York Daily News* that the station was "one of the most potent weapons in the Islamic access arsenal." Chafets claimed that Al-Jazeera was attempting to present the bombing campaign in Afghanistan as "unjustified slaughter" and, as a result of this bias, was sapping the will of the American people to win the war. After stating that Powell's interference was "fair," he said that the Bush administration could not expect assistance from Arab countries whose governments feared their own people. Chafets concluded by inviting the American military to shut the network down.[35]

Al-Jazeera was also censured by the U.S. State Department on October 7, 2001, when it chose to air a prerecorded al-Qaeda video. In a phrase calculated to spread alarm, bin Laden's aide Suleiman Abu Ghaith said, "The storm of airplanes will not be calmed, if it is God's will." According to Colin Powell, the video used inflammatory language that would increase tension in the region. Later in the month, Defense Secretary Donald Rumsfeld also weighed in against the network by claiming that it failed to make value judgments about images it aired. In an interview on October 28, 2001, Rumsfeld was asked whether the images of Afghan children injured by allied bombing were fake. While accepting their veracity, he said that the continual playing of these images amounted to propaganda for the Taliban. Tensions between the Bush administration and Al-Jazeera were heightened further when, on November 3, the network aired another video of bin Laden speaking to the world. Then, more than one week later, the American air force bombed Al-Jazeera's offices in Kabul, leading to widespread claims that the bureau had been deliberately targeted to halt footage showing damage caused by American bombing sorties.

Dropped on the night of November 13, the bomb destroyed Al-Jazeera's Kabul office and damaged the nearby BBC bureau. The blast almost killed BBC reporter William Reeve, who was on air at the time the bomb exploded and was forced to hide under his chair as a result of the explosion. Reacting to the blast, Ibrahim Hilal, editor-in-chief of Al-Jazeera, said that he believed the bureau had been targeted by the American air force. Speaking to reporters, Hilal said that Al-Jazeera's office had been on a Pentagon bombing list from the start of the air campaign but claimed that military planners would not bomb it while Al-Jazeera was the only media outlet in Kabul. However, the arrival of a BBC bureau, staffed by journalists William Reeve and Rageh Omar, allegedly made it a target. In support of his views, Hilal claimed that the military must have been aware of the bureau's existence because he had given the American government details of its location. He also said that Americans were regularly intercepting communications between Al-Jazeera's head office and the office in Kabul, a fact apparently proven by the Bush administration's awareness of a video featuring bin Laden prior to its airing.[36]

Claims that Al-Jazeera had been a target were quickly dismissed by the Pentagon. At a press briefing held on November 14, Rear Admiral Craig Quigley stated that a weapon had apparently gone astray and that the American military were doing everything to "only target military targets." Speaking from America's military command center for the Afghan campaign, Colonel Brian Hoey told a November 16, 2001, conference on journalism in Barcelona: "The U.S. military does not and will not target media. We would not, as a policy, target news media organizations—it would not even begin to make sense." The colonel also said that the military had not been given the position of the Al-Jazeera office.[37]

Claims of a mistake by the military were followed up by a brief letter from Victoria Clarke, assistant secretary of defense, stating that the building was a known al-Qaeda facility in central Kabul and there were no indications that this or any nearby facility was used by Al-Jazeera. Interestingly, the letter appeared to ignore the fact that the Kabul bureau was housed in a residential area and, with satellites clearly visible on the roof, was recognizable as a media outlet. Furthermore, residents of the area, including members of the diplomatic community, were aware of the station's existence.[38]

Despite appearances to the contrary, it is unlikely that the American air force deliberately targeted the Al-Jazeera offices. Although the station was a source of concern for the Bush administration—which was obviously embarrassed by the photographs of the victims of the bombing campaign—it is doubtful that it would have risked the lives of civilians to silence the television network. Casualties would have undermined the administration's attempts to explain and justify its actions in Afghanistan, and the incident would have incensed those supportive of the administration. Furthermore, aware of the international outrage caused by the bombing of the Usce Business Center in Belgrade in April 1999, which killed seventeen people, the Bush administration would have been unwilling to risk the same worldwide condemnation. The attack in Serbia caused great damage to the credibility of NATO, endangering Western support for curbing Slobodon Milosovic. A repeat performance might have had similar results.

SHOOTING THE MESSENGER
AND LOSING THE MESSAGE

"We are getting hammered in the Arab world. . . . Many feel that Al-Jazeera is trying to run the divide and fuel the flames of fundamentalism," a State Department official told CNN.[39] Significantly, the statement provides an insight into the mind-set of the Bush administration shortly after the September 11 attacks. With the war on Afghanistan in its infancy, their essential concerns focused on the image of America, particularly in the Middle East, and on fears that Al-Jazeera might be encouraging support for al-Qaeda.

Already by mid-October, the television network was showing footage of damage to civilian homes and appalling injuries to civilians, particularly children. Moreover, the message of bin Laden and the al-Qaeda terrorist group was being reported as news and broadcast to nearly thirty-five million viewers in the region. At the time, it seemed that the more American military spokespersons tried to impress with the accuracy of their munitions, the more Al-Jazeera attempted to explode this myth by showing the results of the bombing. In the war of military spin versus the visceral images of war, there was likely to be only one winner in a Middle East region already skeptical about the reasons for the attack.

How was the challenge of Al-Jazeera to be met? Unfortunately, rather than countering the negative image, the Bush administration made the decision to, first, soften Al-Jazeera's reporting by prevailing upon a "friend" and, second, applying pressure through the comments of individuals such as Powell and Rumsfeld in the hope that managers and editors at the station would stop repeating the images of war and start censoring the comments of bin Laden. The fact that the attempt failed did not lessen its impact.

In October 2001, a U.S. official made the following comment: "This is a battle for public opinion. We're doing everything we can to win this battle." If this were true, then the very public image of this battle—played out in the newspapers and on the television sets of the world—was censorship and pressure. As America's ally, Britain was faced with the same problem but reacted completely differently. British Prime Minister Tony Blair made the decision to counter the negative images using the same medium—Al-Jazeera. It would not be the last time that there were substantial differences in approach between the two countries.

Already known for his reading of the Koran in order to gain a greater understanding of the Middle East, Blair, along with his director of communications, Alasdair Campbell, chose to communicate the views of the allies and justify the attack on Afghanistan. Together, the two laid out a communications strategy designed to allay the fears of Muslims and firmly blame bin Laden and al-Qaeda for the September 11 attacks. To achieve this goal, Blair visited the region, wrote articles for newspapers, and, on October 9, 2001, appeared on Al-Jazeera. Discussing the September 11 attacks, Blair said, "There were hundreds of Muslims killed. There were women and children killed. And I felt this was an act of injustice. . . ." His interview reinforced the idea that the allies were attacking terrorism and not Muslims. Enroute to Oman during his trip to the Middle East, Blair said that it was becoming increasingly clear to him that there was a need to improve communications in the region.[40]

By appearing on television, Blair revealed a deep understanding of the medium, an understanding that had so far eluded the Bush administration. If Al-Jazeera voiced anti-American feeling, it could be negated by those who sought to justify the war in Afghanistan. The clue for Bush administration officials was in the station's motto, "The view and the other point of view." For too long the administration had allowed "the view" to exist in isolation; Blair and Campbell provided the "other point of view." It was a strategy in profound contrast to the attempts by Powell and Rumsfeld to silence the station.

Blair's appearance on Al-Jazeera led to a shift in the Bush administration's approach to the network. Powell was the first top American official to be interviewed on Al-Jazeera, and on October 15, 2001, Condoleezza Rice, the United States National Security Advisor, appeared. On the following day, Rumsfeld also made an appearance. These interviews allowed American officials to explain their policies directly to the people of the Middle East. But the damage had already been done.

At stake in this incident were thirty-five million Arab viewers, who, while horrified by September 11 and sympathetic to the need to capture the perpetrators, were deeply skeptical about the attack on Afghanistan. The strategy developed by Blair and Campbell recognized a need to reach out to these people and an understanding that this captive audience, if treated properly, could be persuaded of the correctness of the allies' behavior. Failure ran the risk of embedding or reinforcing the resentment of America for years to come. Why, then, did the Bush administration jeopardize this core constituency by seeking to censor a medium valued by many Arab people? And, perhaps more pertinent, why were officials oblivious to the potential damage cause by the intervention?

In his October letter to Powell, IPI Director Fritz worried that the U.S. State Department was trying to create a two-tiered approach to news reporting by allowing news reports in the United States but preventing similar news stories from being aired in the Middle East: "By doing so, the U.S. State Department is seeking to sanitize reporting and is denying the right of individuals the right to receive information."[41] In effect, the State Department was saying that freedom of the media would continue in the United States but had to be suppressed, as it always had been, in the Middle East. The result was a startling double standard.

Taking Russia as an example of how successive American governments have viewed freedom of the press, it is possible to see just how far this double standard extends. Regarding the Russian government's pressure on their own television network owners, consider the following statements from American officials: "Russia's international standing will be severely damaged, we believe, if the government lets stand actions that are intended to intimidate the media," "We certainly see the future of the independent media . . . as a major test of democracy in Russia," "Freedom of speech and pluralism in the media are essential elements of a democratic system. . . . These gains are put in jeopardy so long as the Russian government use[s] political pressures and intimidation to limit people's access. . . ."[42]

Obviously, these statements support the independent media. Why, then, the lack of support for Al-Jazeera? For the media to be independent, they must be allowed to express thoughts and opinions that are often uncomfortable or difficult to accept. But in the case of Al-Jazeera, the U.S. government wished to apply its own shifting meaning of "independence" and decide when and where a media organization might exercise free thought.

Another side of the same coin was the way the U.S. government viewed Al-Jazeera before September 11. In his letter to Powell, Fritz seizes on this. The letter quotes from the 2000 edition of the U.S. State Department's Human Rights Report, which says that Al-Jazeera "operates freely." This statement, Fritz argues, places "the U.S. State Department . . . in the curious position of seeking to restrain the very same organization which it rightly commends. . . ." Fritz adds that "by attempting to censor Al-Jazeera, the U.S. government is identifying itself with countries that have abysmal human rights records."[43]

Concerning the State Department's charges that Al-Jazeera broadcasts anti-American and inflammatory remarks, it is difficult to winnow out the network's real relationship with the Middle East. Indeed, there appear to be two prevailing views. In an *Asian Wall Street Journal* article, Amir Taheri asserts that the station's programming favors radical Islamists. He makes the point that of thirty-five frequently invited guests, thirty were linked to radical Islamist organizations.[44] Alternatively, Nadim Shehadi, director of the Center of Lebanese Studies at Oxford University, says, "I don't think Al-Jazeera has an anti-American agenda. It simply provides a forum for public opinion—and most people in the region happen to be anti-American."

Nor are inflammatory remarks the sole preserve of the journalists from Al-Jazeera. Speaking on his program, *The O'Reilly Factor*, after the September 11 attacks, Bill O'Reilly said, "The U.S. should bomb the Afghan infrastructure to rubble—the airport, the power plants, their water facilities, the roads. . . . The Afghans are responsible for the Taliban. We should not target civilians, but if they don't rise up against this criminal government, they starve, period."[45] If the American military had followed O'Reilly's advice and bombed power plants and water facilities, they would have breached the Geneva Convention.[46] In an even more inflammatory *New York Post* article titled "Simply Kill the Bastards," journalist Steve Dunleavy discussed those "cities or countries" that shield terrorists. "Bomb them into basketball courts," he advised.[47]

While these statements do not reflect the mainstream media's reaction, the authors were not subjected to pressure or censorship by the Bush administration, nor should they have been. They represented an understandable, though extreme, expression of shock and outrage at the attacks. However, such articles are as inflammatory as Al-Jazeera's broadcasts. As before, a double standard is in play, with the State Department making all the rules.

The attempt to soften Al-Jazeera's reporting failed, and deeply damaged America's image abroad. As with the VOA case, the U.S. government's credibility was at stake, together with its reputation for upholding freedom of the press. When examining the attempt to soften Al-Jazeera'a reporting, members of the Bush administration should reflect on the newspaper columns, opinion pieces, and television reports that appeared after this incident and ask themselves whether, in the Middle East, they softened or hardened opinions. It is extremely doubtful that they managed the former.

In the lead-up to the war in Afghanistan, the Bush administration sought credibility in the Middle East. After its attempt to censor Al-Jazeera, it could only struggle to be believed. A clear example of this struggle can be seen in the case of the mistaken bombing of Al-Jazeera. If there had been no attempted censorship, would the belief that America deliberately bombed Al-Jazeera have been so easily accepted? The attempted censorship fed the existing cynicism in the region, making the public diplomacy struggle much more difficult than it had been.

Denied in its attempts to interfere with the reporting of the VOA and Al-Jazeera, the Bush administration's next struggle over censorship would be with a much more malleable opponent—the news divisions of America's major television and cable networks.

NOTES

1. Michael Kudlak, *Fifty World Press Freedom Heroes* (Vienna: International Press Institute, 2000), p. 40.

2. Johann P. Fritz, letter to Jacques Chirac, October 7, 2002, http://www.freemedia.at (accessed December 3, 2003).

3. "We . . . know that what we are allowed to publish is not what the readers want." Abdel Rahman al-Rashed, editor in chief of *Al-Sharq al-Awsat*, quoted in Joel Campagna, *Attacks on the Press: Overview: The Middle East and North Africa* (New York: Committee to Protect Journalists, 2001), p. 468.

4. Introduction to Reporters Sans Frontières, *North Africa and the Middle East,* Annual Report 2002 (N.p.: Reporters Sans Frontières, 2002). Some reports consider North Africa and the Middle East as a single region.

5. Ibid.

6. Campagna, *Attacks on the Press.*

7. Anthony Löwstedt, interview, November 27, 2002.

8. In November 2003, Sheik Hamad stated that the country will soon create a constitutional court to allow for the issuance and implementation of the constitution. Press Digest, London-based Arab newspapers, Reuters News, November 19, 2003.

9. Anthony Löwstedt, Qatar Report, *IPI World Press Freedom Review, 2000* (Vienna: International Press Institute, 2000), p. 249.

10. Sheikh Hamad bin Khalifa al-Thani, quoted in "Emir Says Qatar on the Road to Democracy," BBC Monitoring Service: Middle East (*Al-Watan* Web site), February 14, 2001, http://www.factiva.com (accessed December 1, 2003).

11. Löwstedt, Qatar Report, p. 249.

12. Peter Goff, editor, "Qatar Country Report," *IPI World Press Freedom Review* 1998, http://www.freemedia.at (accessed August 28, 2003).

13. U.S. Department of State, *Qatar Country Report on Human Rights Practices for 1997* (Washington, DC: GPO, 1997).

14. Ian Richardson, "Sand in Auntie's Face," *Independent* (London), April 28, 1997.

15. Mohammed El-Nawawy and Adel Iskandar, *Al-Jazeera: How the Free Arab News Network Scooped the World and Changed the Middle East* (Boulder, CO: Westview Press, 2001), p. 31.

16. Ibid.

17. Sayed Salahuddin, "Taliban Say Took Twenty Days to Destroy Giant Buddhas," Reuters News Service, India, March 26, 2001.

18. Hafez Al-Mirazi, quoted in Nawawy and Iskandar, *How the Free Arab News Network Scooped the World,* p. 34.

19. Mohammed Adwan, quoted in "Jordan Vents Anger over Al-Jazeera Programme," *Khaleej Times, Middle East,* August 9, 2002, www.khaleejtimes.co.ge (accessed December 1, 2003).

20. Xinhua News Agency, "Jordan Calls Back Ambassador over Closure of Qatari TV Office," August 10, 2002.

21. Ann Cooper, letter to His Excellency Ali Abu al-Ragheb, Committee to Protect Journalists, August 8, 2002.

22. British Broadcasting Corporation, "Jordan Carpets Qatar over TV," August 8, 2002, http://www.bbc.co.uk (accessed December 1, 2003).

23. Editorial, "Al-Jazeera's Channel and Gangrene," *Al-Watan*, July 28, 2002.

24. Ann Cooper, letter to Youssed Muhammad al-Samait, Committee to Protect Journalists, June 22, 1999.

25. International News Service, Southeast Asia Edition, "India Asks Al-Jazeera Correspondent to Leave," July 7, 2002, http://www.southasia.insnews.org (December 1, 2003).

26. At the start of the war in Afghanistan, CNN and Al-Jazeera signed an exclusivity contract regarding news feed.

27. CNN, "Bin Laden and Partner Appear in Unity Video," October 4, 2001, http://www.cnn.com/world (accessed December 1, 2003).

28. Kim Ghattas, "Ruffled Feathers Nothing New for Al-Jazeera TV," IPS Newsfeed, October 8, 2001.

29. Sheikh Hamad bin Khalifa al-Thani, quoted in Ghattas, "Ruffled Feathers."

30. Ibid.

31. Johann P. Fritz, letter to Colin Powell, October 8, 2001.

32. BBC Worldwide Monitoring, "Middle East Press Criticize U.S. Pressure on Al-Jazeera," October 11, 2001, http://www.factiva.com (accessed December 1, 2003).

33. "Censorship in Pashto and Arabic," *New York Times*, October 10, 2001.

34. Chris Hughs, "War on Terror—Fighting Back—Bin Laden Television," *Mirror* (London), October 10, 2001.

35. Zev Chafets, "Al-Jazeera Unmasked: An Arab Propaganda Machine in the Guise of Real Journalism," *New York Daily News*, October 14, 2001.

36. Matt Wells, "Al-Jazeera Accuses U.S. of Bombing Its Kabul Office: TV Channel Targeting of Building Denied by Pentagon," *Guardian* (London), 17 November 2001; and Matt Wells, "Media: How Smart Was This Bomb? Did the U.S. Mean to Hit the Kabul Offices of Al-Jazeera TV?" Guardian (London), November 19, 2001.

37. Matt Wells, "Al-Jazeera Accuses U.S. of Bombing Its Kabul Office, TV Channel Targeting of Building Denied by Pentagon," *Guardian* (London), November 17, 2001.

38. Ann Cooper, letter to Donald Rumsfeld, January 31, 2001.

39. Human Rights Watch, "U.S. Presses for Censorship of Jazeera TV," October 15, 2001, http://www.hrw.org (accessed December 22, 2003).

40. Tony Blair, quoted in "Prime Minister Tony Blair's Interview with Al-Jazeera," October 9, 2001, www.globalpolicy.org (accessed December 1, 2003).

41. Fritz, letter to Powell.

42. Steven Boucher, State Department briefing, June 16, 2000, www.usinfo.state.gov; Philip Recker, State Department briefing, November 12, 2000, www.usinfo.state.gov; Boucher, State Department briefing, April 18, 2001, www.usinfo.state.gov.

43. Fritz, letter to Powell.

44. Amir Taheri, "Boob Tube: Unveiling Al-Jazeera," *Asian Wall Street Journal*, December 11, 2001.

45. Bill O'Reilly, *The O'Reilly Factor*, Fox TV, September 17, 2001; Russell Mokhiber and Robert Weissman, "Kill, Kill, Kill," *Counterpunch*, November 15, 2001, http://www.counterpunch.org (accessed December 1, 2003).

46. Protocol, Additional to the Geneva Conventions, 1977, Article 54(2). "It is prohibited to attack [or] destroy . . . objects indispensable to the survival of the civilian population, such as . . . drinking water installations and supplies and irrigation works."

47. Steve Dunleavy, "Simply Kill the Bastards," *New York Post*, September 13, 2001.

Chapter 3

EXECUTIVES' PRIVILEGE

Only the suppressed word is dangerous.

Karl Ludwig Börne, journalist

TALKING TO THE ENEMY

Reminiscing with Larry King about his experiences in the 1991 Gulf War, CNN journalist Peter Arnett commented, "I was in Baghdad for the people who look at CNN." Implicit in his statement was the belief that television reporters serve their viewers and not their country. The distinction has not always been fully appreciated by politicians.

One of the few reporters to remain in Baghdad at the start of the American air campaign, Arnett provided CNN with regular updates on the attack. Taken by his Iraqi minders to view bombed-out housing, ruined factories, and injured Iraqi civilians, Arnett built up an image of the war that contrasted with the pristine and antiseptic imagery portrayed in video clips and by military briefings. As a result, the allies were prevented from presenting the air war as merely a series of surgical strikes, guided by laser and undertaken with pin-point accuracy. It was a message not everyone wished to hear.

From the outset, Arnett faced extensive criticism. Critics pointed to the constraints applied by the Iraqis who arranged all his visits and accompanied him everywhere. Moreover, he was forced to write down everything he wished to say on air, so that revisions could be made by censors. Arnett was given no choice regarding the changes. Columnist Jim Wooten* wrote that, although CNN was laudable in its attempts to bring news from behind Iraqi lines, the tightly con-trolled coverage was the legitimate target of allied jamming. Tele-vision critic Walter Goodman later called Wooten's view an invita-tion to a "censorship party."[1] The Accuracy in Media group appar-ently went further then mere criticism of Arnett and CNN, sending thousands of postcards to CNN imploring executives to dismiss Arnett; others accused him of betraying the troops.

Pentagon disapproval was heaped on Arnett after he reported the story of a "baby milk plant" destroyed in one of the bombing raids. Accompanied by 1990 footage of the plant in operation, Arnett's report stated that the factory, valued at $150 million, pro-duced huge quantities of powdered milk and was the sole provider for the country's infants. Almost immediately afterward, a spokes-person for the Pentagon claimed that the plant was a legitimate mil-itary target. Later, CNN said that the veracity of Arnett's report was in doubt. Adding to the pressure on Arnett, White House spokes-person Marlin Fitzwater said the plant was a site for the production of chemical weapons. He also claimed that the president had been angered by Arnett's report.[2] Official irritation at Arnett's reporting continued after his controversial interview with President Saddam Hussein. Viewing it as an exclusive that was too good to turn down, Arnett went through elaborate security checks, including being dis-infected, before interviewing Hussein. When Hussein asked whether he had a long list of questions, Arnett simply replied that

---

*Columnist for the *Atlanta Journal*, not the ABC correspondent.

he had questions to which the world wanted answers. CNN was heavily criticized for allowing Hussein to appear on international television and for enabling him to put "a message across that could be detrimental."[3]

Arnett's experiences highlight a fear held by governments in general—that public support for war can be eroded by pictures of innocent civilians injured in fighting. As the debate over the Hussein interview reveals, this fear was exacerbated by a belief in military and political circles that the enemy's appearance on television would incite or inflame tension. Underpinning these views was the belief that, in times of war, the country should unite to confront its foes. While this notion is attractive, the ethical obligations of journalists to report fairly and independently prevent them from doing so.

Faced with journalists willing to talk to the enemy, successive administrations have found other means to circumscribe the activities of the media. In the first Gulf War, the media drowned in a pooling system that prevented them from reporting without severe restrictions.[4] However, the government could do little, apart from increasing the number of their own briefings and official denials, to prevent the reporting of Arnett and his colleagues in Baghdad.

Facing a similar challenge after September 11, the Bush administration chose a novel method of exhausting the oxygen of publicity previously given to the speeches of bin Laden and his fellow al-Qaeda terrorists. Indeed, the Bush administration provided an object lesson in how to heighten fears over security and propaganda in the minds of media executives without the need to justify its assertions.

WATCHING YOU BROADCASTING HIM

If the media were in doubt as to the Bush administration's mood in the days and weeks after September 11, the September 26, 2001, press briefing by Bush spokesperson Ari Fleischer was to be a rude awakening. In stark contrast to a period of calm reflection by policy makers on how the United States intended to react to the September 11 attacks, this dictatorial statement alerted the media to a sea change in political affairs. It heralded a time when to be out of step with the government was to be out of step with the American people.

When asked about the president's reactions to the televised comments of comedian Bill Maher, who had commented on the war in Afghanistan on his show, *Politically Incorrect,* Fleischer said, "it's a terrible thing to say . . . they're reminders to all Americans that they need to watch what they say, watch what they do. This is not a time for remarks like that; there never is. . . ." (See chapter 4.) Crystallizing the Bush administration's attitude toward criticism, Fleischer's statement was deeply damaging to the concept of free speech after September 11 because it refused to accept that dissent was part of the ongoing dialogue about the September 11 attacks. In subsequent weeks, the Bush administration would be further angered by the activities of the major news networks and cable channels.

Taking their lead from Al-Jazeera, ABC News, CBS News, CNN, Fox News Channel, and NBC/MSNBC aired, in its entirety, a taped message from Osama bin Laden on October 7, 2001. Mixing religious phraseology with imagery taken from the Israeli-Palestinian war and the allied bombing raids of Iraq, the terrorist stated that God had struck against America and destroyed its largest buildings. He added that the "winds of change were blowing against the infidels who occupy the land of the Prophet Mohammed. May peace and God's blessings be with him." Two days later, on October 9, 2001, the same networks aired a taped statement by al-Qaeda spokesperson Suleiman Abu Geith. Originally delivered to Al-Jazeera staff in Kabul, the tape showed Abu Geith calling upon all Muslims to wage a jihad against America: "You must fight if you are able-bodied; there is no excuse. The time is now. This is the word of God." In a chilling statement, Abu Geith said that the "land would burn with fire under their feet, God willing" if the Americans and British failed to leave Afghanistan.

Confronted with al-Qaeda's messages beamed directly into the homes of millions of Americans and with its own faltering public diplomacy activities, the Bush administration elected to discuss the broadcasts with the television and cable networks. This decision also recognized bin Laden's success at delivering his message to the outside world. On the morning of October 10, 2001, Condoleezza Rice held a conference call with leading media executives from ABC News, CBS News, CNN, Fox News Channel, and NBC News. During the twenty-minute conference call, Rice requested that the news networks remove all "inflammatory language" from future broadcasts of bin Laden. Rice also expressed her concern, highlighted by security agencies, that the messages might contain codes instructing al-Qaeda members to carry out further attacks on the United States and its allies. At all times, the national security advisor stressed, the media executives should keep in mind national security when exercising their independent news judgment. Finally, Rice expressed the fear that bin Laden's messages would incite Muslims in moderate countries such as Malaysia and the Philippines. After delivering her message, Rice left the media executives to discuss the issue among themselves by telephone.[5]

Reflecting on Rice's words, the media executives agreed that they would televise only abbreviated versions of any future tape issued by al-Qaeda. Each broadcast would be accompanied by short reports containing "appropriate text," and there would be no excessive repetition of the messages. It was the first time in modern memory that the news networks had consulted each other on policy.[6]

Afterward, each news network gave its own reaction to the meeting. Implying that media executives were in a special position to determine when it was in the public's interest to be denied information, the president of CBS News, Andrew Heyward, said, "This is a new situation, a new war, and a new kind of enemy. Given the historic events we're enmeshed in, it's appropriate to explore new ways of fulfilling our responsibilities to the public." Walter Isaacson, chairman of CNN, commented, "It was very useful to hear their [the Bush administration's] information and their thinking." Regarding Rice's statement, he said, "We're not going to step on the landmines she was talking about." Speaking of bin Laden, the president of NBC, Neal Shapiro, said, "[Rice's] biggest point was that here was a charismatic speaker who could arouse anti-American sentiment getting twenty minutes of air time to spew hatred and urge followers to kill Americans." Owner of the Fox News network, Rupert Murdoch, went still further, saying that his news organization would do "whatever is our patriotic duty."[7]

However, the *New York Times* reported some skepticism among media executives, quoting one media executive as saying, "What sense would it make to keep the tapes off the air if the message could be found transcribed in newspapers or on the Web? They'd get the message anyway."[8] That this comment was anonymous speaks volumes about the atmosphere at the time, revealing a media executive who did not wish to appear out of step with his colleagues.

Where the Bush administration had probably expected criticism, it curiously found support. One of America's most beloved newsmen, Dan Rather of CBS, appeared to back the decision, saying, "By nature and experience, I'm always wary when the government seeks to have a hand in editorial decisions. But this is an extraordinary time. In the context of this time, the conversation as I understand it seems reasonable on both sides."[9]

A press briefing by Ari Fleischer later on October 10, 2001, after the Rice conference call, throws additional light on the government's thinking. Fleischer said that the president was pleased with the decision of the news networks and reiterated that the messages of bin Laden could be used to communicate to his followers around the world: "Dr. Rice asked the networks to exercise judgment about how these prerecorded, pretaped messages will air. She stressed that she was making a request, and that editorial decisions can only be made by the media." Allaying fears that the government would attempt to centralize the editing of the bin Laden messages, Fleischer confirmed that it was up to the networks to exercise judgment on how to handle the tapes. Speaking of the coded messages, he admitted, "There's no hard indications [*sic*]. . . . It's a specific level of concern."[10]

The joint agreement of the media executives was to have a considerable impact upon the editorial policies of the news organizations. Moreover, it was to provide further evidence that, after September 11, the media executives would have a greater say in the activities and content of news. Normal editorial procedures appeared to be abandoned in favor of bringing the news into line with pro-government thinking on the war on Afghanistan. Under the guise of worries over bias, media executives in some news organizations introduced new guidelines that created a hazy line over which news was not to be taken. This was particularly true in the world's most famous twenty-four-hour news organization—CNN.

Toward the end of October, CNN's head of standards and practices, Rick Davies, sent a memorandum to his staff saying:

> As we get enterprising reports from our correspondents or Al-Jazeera, we must continue to make sure that we do not inadvertently seem to be reporting uncritically from the perspective or vantage of the Taliban. . . . Also, given the enormity of the toll on human lives in the U.S., we must remain careful not to focus excessively on the casualties and hardships in Afghanistan that will be a part of this war, or to forget that it is the Taliban leadership that is responsible for the situation Afghanistan is now in.[11]

Concerning newscasters, Davies said they would be required to end each report with a prepared statement along the lines of "We must keep in mind, after seeing reports like this, that the Taliban regime in Afghanistan continues to harbor terrorists who have praised the September 11 attacks that killed close to 5,000 innocent people in the U.S." Alternatively, the news anchors could say, "The Pentagon has repeatedly stressed that it is trying to minimize civilian casualties in Afghanistan, even as the Taliban regime continues to harbor terrorists who are connected to the September 11 attacks that claimed thousands of innocent lives in the U.S."[12] Where relevant, newscasters were to say, "The Pentagon has said that the Taliban continues to harbor the terrorists and the Taliban forces are reported to be hiding in populated areas and using civilians as human shields." The memorandum concluded with "Even though it may start sounding rote, it is important that we make this point each time."[13]

Speaking about the memorandum to the *Washington Post*, Chairman Walter Isaacson of CNN said, "I want to make sure we are not used as a propaganda platform. We're entering a period in which there's a lot more reporting and video from Taliban-controlled Afghanistan. You want to make sure people understand that when they see civilians suffering there, it's in the context of a terrorist attack that caused enormous suffering in the United States."[14]

The new guidelines drew different responses from other news organizations. NBC News Vice President Bill Wheatley said, "I'd give the American people more credit."[15] In contrast, Fox News Vice President John Moody argued that "Americans need to remember what started this. . . . I think people need a certain amount of context or they obsess on the last fifteen minutes of history. A lot of Americans did die."[16] In sharp contrast to Wheatley, the executive producer of the *CBS Evening News*, Jim Murphy, said, "I wouldn't order anybody to do anything like that. Our reporters are smart enough to know it always has to be put in context."[17]

It is difficult not see the CNN directive as one of the most abject statements ever handed to the news staff of a television organization. Not only does the statement reduce news to a prepared formula, but it sacrifices nuance and objectivity for a simplicity of outlook that is deeply insulting to the intelligence of both newscasters and viewers. Furthermore, the fact that the guidelines were not directed at CNN's international service indicated the creation of a two-tiered system providing news tailored to the viewer's location. Rather like the twin tracks of a railway, international viewers were to be sped away and given news undiluted by so-called context and assisted by the comments of independent and objective journalists, while, on the other track, CNN anchors would provide the American domestic audience with constant reminders of why war was being fought and where the responsibility for civilian casualties lay. As a consequence, the statement heralded a new period for news in America. Previously, television programming had been based on viewer preferences; now news reports could be packaged in much the same way.

Perhaps the best retort to this type of qualified news came from a spokesperson for the British Broadcasting Company (BBC). Responding to questions about the CNN memorandum, she said, "Correspondents may or may not decide to put in this sort of detail in their reports—to put things in context."[18] Her view was shared by the BBC's director of news, Richard Sambrook, who said he thought the editorial policy was a "mistake."[19]

Encouraged by its first real success in the struggle to control the flow of information, the Bush administration sought to use the same arguments against the print media to prevent the publication of complete transcripts of bin Laden's speeches. Although the question of the print media had first arisen in Fleischer's press conference, in which he had refused to rule out the possibility of approaching them, the administration was to discover that American print media executives were not as receptive as their colleagues in television.

On October 11, 2001, the executive editor of the *New York Times*, Howell Raines, took a morning phone call from Fleischer, who made a request identical to that made by Rice on the previous day. Raines responded that it was the newspaper's practice to keep its readers fully informed of the news. Although he stated that he was prepared to listen to the administration on security matters when there was a specific danger, he said that the newspaper would use its own judgment.[20]

While it appears that Raines was the only executive approached directly, other newspapers reacted to the idea in a similar fashion. The executive editor of the *Washington Post*, Leonard Downie Jr., was quoted by *Newsday* as saying that he would not regard a request by the administration as inherently improper, but he would need evidence of a specific threat: "If there was a real possibility of them [al-Qaeda] sending a message to Washington-based terrorists, we would want to hear about it and consider it." Interestingly, Downie stated that he did not view the approaches as a constitutional issue but saw them as the result of conflict over the free flow of information. When asked to provide his opinion on the Bush administration's approach to Raines, the editor of *Newsday*, Anthony Marro, said he would deal with each case individually but reiterated Raines's point that the goal of a news organization is to provide its readers with information.[21]

Significantly, there were mixed initial responses from news organizations around the world to the decision of the American news organizations. In Britain, Independent Television News (ITN) said it would review all items on their individual merits, while the BBC said that it had received no requests regarding the bin Laden and al-

Qaeda material. In the Netherlands, NOS Television said that it was not showing the video tapes in their entirety, but it remained unconvinced that they could be used as a medium to send coded messages. Organizations in France and Italy, however, decided to err on the side of caution. France's TF1 announced that it would stop the live broadcasts because of the possibility of codes, while the Italian TG4 network said that it would no longer air bin Laden material.

British Prime Minister Tony Blair had originally taken the view that the news broadcasters should make their own decisions. Indeed, he was quoted as saying, "We will leave it up to them."[22] Shortly thereafter, he underwent a volte-face that led to his communications director, Alasdair Campbell, meeting with senior media executives. The reaction of the British television networks to the prime minister's change of heart makes an interesting comparison with the actions of their American counterparts.

Rather than holding a conference call, the British government elected to fax a letter to the three main news television networks— the BBC, ITN, and Sky News—asking for a meeting. A spokesperson for Blair said that the participants would discuss media issues and the war in Afghanistan. His spokesperson also stated that bin Laden and the Taliban "have a built-in-advantage in that they put out pictures which are carried out around the world in full. I think that there is a real danger they could be sending out messages to terrorist members of their network." Using the example of the allegation, later proved false, that a women's hospital had been bombed, the spokesperson also asked the media to be "more skeptical" when dealing with Taliban claims. Downplaying any potential confrontation, he said that the British government was not at war with the media, it was merely raising issues that were not part of the "normal government-broadcaster relationship."[23]

Speaking of the Taliban's claims, the prime minister's communications director Alasdair Campbell accepted the right of journalists to enter Afghanistan as the guests of the religious group, but added, "If you are in a conflict situation where access to information and pictures is controlled by a regime which harbors terrorists, clearly you are going to have to be pretty skeptical about what they are being shown because there is an in-built advantage at the very least for the Taliban propaganda machine being able to pump out whatever it chooses."[24]

On October 15, the BBC's News Director Richard Sambrook, ITN Editor-in-Chief Richard Tait, and Sky News head Nick Pollard met with Campbell. At the forty-five-minute meeting, Campbell stated his view that the media organizations had reported responsibly and allayed fears that the government wished to sensor footage. He outlined the government's views on the tapes and the Taliban claims regarding the bombing campaign, expressing the government's irritation at the media's habit of seeking extreme Islamic voices for interviews. Finally, he said that he and Blair were pleased that an open channel existed between the government and the media.[25]

Afterward, reflecting on the meeting, both Tait and Sambrook described it as friendly, constructive, and nonconfrontational. In an interview, Sambrook said that his recollection was that although the government said it recognized that the broadcasters had a perfect right to broadcast, there was nevertheless a danger that the messages might be coded. Responding to this assertion, Sambrook asked Campbell on several occasions whether the government was unhappy with the way in which the broadcasters handled the bin Laden messages, to which Campbell replied that it was not.[26]

During the conversation with Campbell, Tait said that the bin Laden tapes were in the public domain and that they were clearly newsworthy by virtue of the fact that the al-Qaeda terrorist stood accused of committing the biggest terrorist atrocity of all time. For this reason, Tait said that ITN would continue to report on the tapes but that it would do so responsibly, making clear any doubts over the dates of recording or the tapes' provenance. Tait summed up this view by saying that he understood the nature of the government's concern but thought that the broadcasters were behaving responsibly.[27]

In a clear rebuttal of government interference, the three news organizations issued a unique joint statement after the meeting that said, "The best people to judge what to broadcast are the broadcasters themselves." Moreover, the statement said, "We will continue to exercise care in our handling of all material. As responsible broadcasters, we are mindful of national and international security issues and the impact [that] reports can have in different communities and cultures. . . . We also believe that the provision of independent and impartial news is a fundamental part of a free society and the democratic process. . . . But we will retain the right to exercise our own independent, impartial editorial judgment."[28]

A government spokesperson later commented that the meeting had not been a forum for complaint but a genuine attempt to make the broadcasters aware of possible difficulties. The media executives were also keen to dispel talk of prior restraint: "There had been talk of censorship. That hasn't happened and it is not likely to," explained Sambrook.[29]

While the British media managed to firmly rebuff the government while upholding editorial independence, the government was able to air its views and could claim that the media were at least aware of the potential pitfalls. Unlike the Bush administration, Blair's government did not seek to take the argument to the country's print media, perhaps because doing so would have led to a rejection similar to that of the *New York Times* in the United States. With the media determined to hold on to their impartiality, the government was left to resolve the question of what to do about al-Qaeda and Taliban propaganda. Such fears led Campbell to make an unscheduled two-day visit to Washington, D.C., at the end of October.

While in Washington, Campbell met with Karen Hughes, an advisor to the president. The two communication specialists discussed the development of a joint communications and media strategy for the war against terrorism. Commenting on the meeting, a spokesperson for the prime minister noted the need to ensure that messages reached across different time zones, particularly because the war against the terrorists was likely to be a protracted one. The meeting was also an acknowledgement that al-Qaeda had a sophisticated propaganda machine that needed to be combated both at home and abroad.

During their meeting, Campbell and Hughes agreed on the creation of a joint information body—the Coalition Information

Center (CIC)—with offices in Islamabad, London, and Washington. The organization was to be responsible for a range of public diplomacy tasks, including acting as a clearing house or "war room" for information, coordinating interviews with allied officials, and the provision of roving ambassadors. According to a CIC staff member, the aim would be to "beat down misconceptions about our motives . . . [to make] the case that this is not a battle of Christianity vs. Islam or West vs. East."[30] The existence of the CIC proved that there was an alternative to telephone conference calls with media executives and the resulting bad publicity.

Bearing in mind the reaction of the leading U.S. media executives, the Bush administration's approach to the cable and news networks was a complete success. Condoleezza Rice's carefully expressed allusions to propaganda and security fears touched a nerve with leading media executives and, given the climate at the time, acted as a subtle reminder of the dangers faced by all Americans.

On November 3, 2001, Al-Jazeera broadcast a new bin Laden video. However, the five American networks and cable channels aired only fragmentary clips, with a number of them refusing to show a moving image; instead, brief remarks were relayed over a frozen still-shot taken from the video. Unlike the previous tape, the major newspapers failed to carry a transcript. The cautionary warnings had, therefore, exceeded all expectations. But was the government right in its worries over security? And, if it had other motives, why were the electronic media so quick to fall into line without any evidence supporting the government's broad claims?

SELF-CENSORSHIP: A COLLEGIAL EXPERIENCE

In October, Executive Director of the Project for Excellence in Journalism Tom Rosenstiel was quoted in the *Washington Post* as saying, "We need to know who Osama is, what he [is] like. . . . We need to learn about the enemy. . . . The American democratic system is predicated on the idea [that because] of our diversity of viewpoints, we're more likely to find the truth."[31] Rosenstiel's words issued a challenge to both government and media alike. By emphasizing truth and plurality, Rosenstiel was stating that the views of bin Laden and al-Qaeda, however distasteful, deserved to be heard. Implicit in his statement was the view that by broadcasting the terrorist's words, America was not only affirming its rich tradition of free expression but also exposing the divide between its own democratic practices and the values expressed by bin Laden and his followers. Furthermore, while the inclination to shun or turn away from bin Laden's attempts to incite hatred might be understandable, his words deserved to be confronted and comprehended. Only by placing arguments alongside the views of bin Laden rather than isolating them, or by calm and patient explanation, could people around the world fully appreciate the war on terrorism.

To paraphrase the words of the Commission on Freedom of the Press, the true antidote to ignorance and deceit is more information. Why then did the Bush administration, with the acquiescence of the major news networks and cable channels, seek to provide less?[32]

In the October 10 telephone conference, Rice had expressed the following concerns: first, that coded messages might be relayed to other members of bin Laden's terrorist organization, and second, that his words might inflame Muslim populations around the world. Later, there was some confusion over which of these concerns was more important. In his press conference, Fleischer said that the codes were the primary concern, but this statement was contradicted by the media executives, who said that the threat of incitement was Rice's main worry.[33] Despite the confusion, many media organizations led with the question of the codes, and, with its implicit threat to security, this concern was to have the greater impact on the public consciousness. But while it gained general acceptance, the perceived threat did not stand close scrutiny.

From the outset, questions were raised concerning the effectiveness of bin Laden's communication through video tapes. An anonymous media executive disputed the administration's view immediately after the conference call, and others also questioned it. In an editorial supporting the media's position, the *Times* of London said it doubted the feasibility of sending messages via the Western media, while the online weekly magazine *Electronic Media* said that, in this age of technology, bin Laden had other more direct means of contacting operatives.[34] A commentator on CNN also downplayed the possibility by claiming that bin Laden's communications methods were too sophisticated. Appearing in a CNN chat room, the host of CNN's *Reliable Sources*, Howard Kurtz, said, "If there is any credible evidence about bin Laden sending messages, it hasn't been shared with the media or the public. I'm certain he has other ways to communicate with his followers, but that doesn't mean the Western media should make it easier for him." ABC news correspondent Bob Zelnick, appearing on a Public Broadcasting Service (PBS) television program, said, "I don't think there was anything, any proof that he was sending signals." Their views reflected a growing cynicism over the question of codes. Elsewhere, supporters of the code theory could express themselves only in the vaguest of terms.

As previously mentioned, Fleischer believed that al-Qaeda, with little access to conventional forms of communication, was seeking to pass on messages through the media, but he conceded that there was no hard evidence for this view. An anonymous administration official stated that the precaution was based on a "hunch" and "commonsense," adding that although CIA analysts had discovered nothing unusual, bin Laden's language was replete with fuzzy images suggestive of possible coded messages.[35]

Two of the severest difficulties for bin Laden, if he was indeed trying to send coded messages, concerned broadcast length and translation. He could have no guarantee that Western media would broadcast the messages in their entirety, thus the tapes would probably be edited, making it impossible to guarantee the delivery of coded messages. An additional complication was the translation from Arabic into English. If bin Laden could not ensure that certain parts of his speech would appear on television, he was equally unable to guarantee that certain English phrases would be used by the translator.

Adding his own view on the subject of possible coded messages in the bin Laden tapes, BBC news director Richard Sambrook said that all of the U.K. broadcasters had taken random extracts from the bin Laden tapes and had, by and large, voiced over them. Consequently, he considered coded messages to be an extremely random way of communicating because the terrorists would never know which forty-second segment of their twenty-minute tape would be broadcast.[36]

In an article in the *National Post*, Sarah Schmidt interviewed linguistic experts who stated that the CNN broadcast of the bin Laden speech on October 7, 2001, had been "butchered" by the translators. The article quoted Bernard Haykel, an associate professor of Islamic studies at New York University, who explained that "the translations were very poor; bin Laden was using very sophisticated and theological language, but the translators were neither linguists nor theological scholars."[37] This analysis threw further doubt on the ability of bin Laden to deliver coded messages to terrorists.

Supporters of the theory pointed out that a precedent did exist for the use of codes. In World War II, the Allies placed coded messages in the radio broadcasts of the BBC. However, they, unlike al-Qaeda, had complete control of the medium. Therefore, what the London *Guardian* newspaper described as a "spine chilling theory" could, in all probability, be discounted.

The question of propaganda and incitement to hatred still remained. In revealing that Rice had spent much of her time during the conference call discussing this issue, the news executives were acknowledging the government's true reasons for limiting bin Laden's exposure on television, namely, the desire to stem the flow of information from al-Qaeda and its supporters to the outside world. This need had been precipitated by the initial failure of the public diplomacy effort in the Middle East. Blair had admitted as much during interviews, and this failure was also accepted among political circles in Washington. One American official went so far as to say that the ball had been dropped in the early days of the war.

As a result of the failure to win the public diplomacy battle, the televised comments of bin Laden were finding fertile ground in the Muslim world. Profoundly disturbed by the effect this acceptance could have on the alliance, particularly in Pakistan, the Bush administration felt that a strategy was needed to counteract the al-Qaeda propaganda. An aspect of this strategy involved negating the impact of the media. This view can be supported by examining the way the administration dealt with the media after September 11. A continuous theme running through the Mullah Omar incident at the VOA, the attempt to "tone down" Al-Jazeera, and Rice's conversation with the news networks was the Bush administration's desire to control information. In the case of the VOA, the administration had said that Omar was not "newsworthy," that Al-Jazeera was broadcasting "vitriolic and irresponsible statements"; and that the news networks were airing "inflammatory language." All of these charges were used to justify subsequent attempts to restrain the media. However, if the question of incitement in a foreign country is stripped away, what remains is an administration deeply unhappy that the "other side" was receiving air time through the world's media. The words of a government official speaking in October are especially revealing: "This is a battle for public opinion. We're doing everything we can to win it."[38] As hinted at by the official, information is a key component in the overall strategy to win a war. It is the natural instinct of governments to try to silence the enemy's voice and opinions, thereby controlling the images of war. This philosophy is predicated on the belief that, with the enemy's voice muted, it is easier to influence opinion at home and abroad. Without other sources of news to balance the official interpretation of events, the media are also weakened and more likely to accept government "truths." For this reason, it was helpful to the Bush administration that Secretary of State Colin Powell and Vice President Dick Cheney had been involved in the first Gulf War and were well versed in this type of "battle."

During the 1991 Gulf War, as defense secretary and chairman of the joint chiefs of staff, respectively, Cheney and Powell had presided over one of the most poorly reported conflicts involving the United States in the latter half of the twentieth century. Aided in this achievement by Pentagon spokesperson Peter Williams, Cheney and Powell ensured that the lesson learned from Vietnam was practiced in the Gulf: keep the war short and control the news media. The U.S. media were chained down in a restrictive "pooling system," which at the outset had been warmly welcomed but later was used to prevent journalists from getting to the front line. For this reason, little or no footage exists of the military engagements, and the government's and military's interpretation of the war cannot be refuted.[39]

Many years later during the war in Afghanistan, news anchor Peter Jennings and ABC's chief national security correspondent John McWethy had the following conversation on ABC's *World News Tonight* in early October.

> Jennings: "We've been [at war] three days now, [and] we've had three photographs of bomb damage. . . ."

> McWethy: "It appears, Peter, that the Pentagon does not want to share the details of what is going on. [The government] keeps saying that it is a different kind of war, and so far it has been a war with very little information."[40]

To the detriment of the media everywhere, certain government officials hoped it would long remain so.

Concerned by the success of al-Qaeda's propaganda and increasingly worried that it was losing the information battle, the government had every incentive to censor the media. Why, though, did the news networks accede to such requests? In the words of Press Secretary Ari Fleischer, the conference with Rice had been a "collegial conversation,"[41] which might imply either that both parties were vested with equal power or that it was conducted with all the friendliness and chumminess of a conversation taking place in a college dining hall. Whether "collegial" or not, the words of the media executives, expressed immediately after the conversation, offer proof of the persuasiveness of Rice's arguments.

Speaking on Al-Jazeera, Rice provided her own view of the conversation. "My discussions with the network executives were very fruitful, and I think they [the executives] have been very responsible, because they understood that having a fifteen-minute or twenty-minute tape that was pre-taped, prerecorded sat there and did nothing but incite hatred . . . was a matter of propaganda, and it was inciting attacks against Americans."[42]

In response, the media executives called this "a new type of war"

(Heyward) and stated that "[we'll do] whatever is our patriotic duty" (Fox's Murdoch), "We're not going to step on the landmines [Rice] was talking about" (Isaacson). Spokespersons for their respective news organizations went even further, saying such things as "in deciding what to air, CNN will consider guidance from appropriate authorities," "[CBS is committed to] responsible journalism that informs the public without jeopardizing American lives," and "a free press must . . . bear responsibility not to be used by those who want to destroy America and endanger the lives of its citizens" (Fox News). Only ABC and NBC acknowledged the role of editors and journalists in making these decisions.

Based on these comments, the editor's voice seems to have been almost completely excluded from the dialogue with the U.S. government. Professional objectivity, independence of the media, editorial control, and journalistic judgment were ignored or overridden by the majority of media executives in their haste to accept the government's arguments. With the exception of one network executive, who undermined his own comments by remaining anonymous, the incitement and coded message arguments were accepted across the board, with no attempt to support the journalists in the news networks. As with the VOA, journalists in these media outlets must have been infuriated by the apparent willingness of the media executives to accept the government's view that they were not responsible enough to decide what to broadcast, particularly when the actions of the U.S. media executives were compared with those of their British counterparts whose joint statement said, "The best people to judge what to broadcast are the broadcasters themselves." In contrast to his American counterparts, former British Independent Television News Editor-in-Chief Richard Tait said that he was "able to go back to the [ITN] newsroom and say that they could use the Osama bin Laden material if editorially appropriate [and] as they thought . . . necessary [in order] to cover the story properly." The difference on the other side of the Atlantic was palpable.[43]

After siding with the government against their own editors, the U.S. media executives showed a willingness to dismiss another major tenet of journalism—its skepticism toward the claims of government.

This skepticism is best expressed by Sambrook of the BBC: "This idea that the tapes may contain hidden messages is very hard to prove or disprove. . . . I think it's up to the government to show this is a serious issue rather than merely raising the possibility [that it is]."[44]

Fundamental to the work of journalists is their duty to corroborate facts. Famously, in the Watergate case, the executive editor of the *Washington Post*, Ben Bradlee, told *Washington Post* journalists Bob Woodward and Carl Bernstein that they had to find at least two sources to corroborate each statement. This example stresses the importance that journalists and editors place on getting their facts straight. But such an attitude appears to have been ignored or disregarded in the case of the Rice conference call.

If a source had walked into the offices of any one of the network executives and said, "I have a story that I want you to air. However, in offering this story to you, I will provide no evidence as to its veracity, no corroboration, no 'hard indications.' Instead, I will give you only 'hunches' and 'commonsense' and speculation," in all probability, the story would never have been aired. And yet, this scenario almost parallels what occurred when the network executives took the call from Rice. Essentially, the government was saying, "We have no proof, but your broadcasting is endangering national security." Following such a line of argument, a modern-day version of the Pentagon Papers* would never have been published. This is an indication of how far removed today's media are from their counterparts of the 1970s.

Briefed by the capable Rice, the media executives accepted her arguments with nary a complaint and then proceeded to strip away decades of healthy skepticism toward government while ignoring or excluding the editorial judgment of their own editors and, in some cases, rewriting the values of the news organizations they headed. It is no wonder, then, that Rice described the meeting as "fruitful."

Another possible factor in explaining the behavior of the American media executives is the tangled relationship between the major television networks and government. While there is no evidence that

---

*The secret study of decision making about the Vietnam War leaked to the *New York Times* and resulting in a federal court battle between the government and the press.

the Bush administration ever offered inducements to the networks in return for their acquiescence, the interconnection may have preyed upon the minds of those running the television networks, encouraging them to place greater faith in the words of Rice than they might otherwise have done. Certainly, in the period immediately before and after September 11, plans were being discussed by the Federal Communications Commission (FCC) that may well have had a coercive effect. These plans reveal how a conflict of interest can arise between the television news networks themselves and the ethical duties and obligations of the journalists who work for them.

Before September 11, a major concern of the television networks was the question of diversity in the American media market. With an awareness of the need to generate increased profits, a number of networks were seeking to expand by purchasing other media organizations but were prevented from doing so by the United States' restrictive broadcasting rules. On April 19, 2001, the body responsible for the regulation of the television networks, the FCC, voted three to one in favor of removing the rule preventing one television company from owning another.[45]

At the same meeting, the Republican-dominated commission, chaired by Bush appointee Michael Powell, the son of Secretary of State Colin Powell, discussed the possible amendment of the "cross ownership rule," which prevents a local newspaper from owning a local television station.[46] The media networks also wanted the FCC to review the rule that prevented a television network from owning stations with a combined reach of more than 35 percent of all American homes.

By August of 2001, Michael Powell was seeking to overhaul all of the rules, proclaiming that it was important to determine whether they "served their intended purpose." According to *USA Today*, the rule changes would make it theoretically possible for one chief executive officer to run AOL Time Warner, which owns CNN, and purchase "NBC, Clear Channel Radio, and the *New York Times*."[28] On the question of the timetable for the review, *USA Today* said that some rules might be settled by summer while others would be examined in 2002.[47]

At the time of the Rice conference call in October 2001, the organization Fairness and Accuracy In Reporting (FAIR) reported that the FCC, now with its full complement of five commission members, had unanimously voted for a review of the rules. This ruling suited Rupert Murdoch (the owner of the Fox TV Network), who had recently acquired station owner Chris-Craft and was in potential violation of FCC rules owing to his other media purchases in the New York area. According to USA Today, the global media company Viacom was in the same position because of its ownership of CBS.[48] Furthermore, General Electric, the owner of NBC, was one of the biggest contractors with the Pentagon, with contracts worth $1.7 billion in 1999.[49] The profit that could be derived from such mergers provided a powerful incentive to agree with government.

It is entirely possible that the government exploited this relationship. Danny Schechter, executive editor, journalist, and writer for mediachannel.org, said in an interview that the FCC's decision to review the ownership rules was one of the "hidden stories" of September 11: "the administration was lobbying hard for changes in the regulatory environment when [the attacks] happened; when there is so much money at stake, so many interests involved, no one wants to antagonize the government unnecessarily."[50] If so, this was government exploitation of the environment in which the television networks operated and not a direct manipulation of the networks themselves. The words of Morris Ernst of the American Civil Liberties Union (ACLU) are also significant in relation to the government's influence over broadcasting. Speaking in the 1930s, Ernst said, "So long as the department [the FCC] can determine which individuals shall be endowed with larynxes, it does not need additional power to determine what shall be said." This discussion of profit and FCC rules reflects a higher, corporatized world, above and beyond the news room where strategy and market positions have replaced the everyday considerations of "objectivity" and "balance." Moreover, the profit-over-ethics mentality may explain why journalists were largely excluded from the discussion of the bin Laden tapes and why many of the networks failed to defend their own editorial policies.

An interesting denouement to the story of the bin Laden tapes occurred in mid-December when the White House released a tape that had been discovered in an al-Qaeda safe house. The tape showed bin Laden in a jocular mood apparently boasting of his role in the September 11 attack and claiming that he had underestimated the damage and loss of life that would be inflicted by the airplanes. Commenting on the tapes, Bush said, "This is bin Laden unedited[,] . . . a man who is so devious and so cold-hearted that he laughs about the suicide bombers that lost their lives."[51]

Realizing the propaganda value of the tape, the Bush administration encouraged the networks to use it, which they did. The Voice of America translated parts of the tape into dozens of languages and placed them in news reports alongside interviews with key Bush advisors. A version for the Middle Eastern media was also prepared with subtitles and a transcript in Arabic. "People who speak Arabic can watch it in the original language with the subtitles and the sound in Arabic," said State Department spokesperson Richard Boucher.[52] The incident showed that not all bin Laden tapes were to be restricted viewing.

NOTES

1. Walter Goodman, "What We Saw, What We Learned," *Columbia Journalism Review* 30 (May/June 1991).

2. After the war, French contractors and technicians from New Zealand who built the plant confirmed that it had been used for the sole purpose of making powdered milk. Mark Crispin Miller, "A Lesson in U.S. Propaganda," January 3, 2003, http://www.alternet.org (accessed December 1, 2003).

3. Peter Arnett, Third Annual John S. Knight Lecture, Stanford University, April 8, 1991.

4. John R. MacArthur, *Second Front: Censorship and Propaganda in the Gulf War* (Berkeley: University of California Press, 1993), pp. 146–98.

5. "The Public's Need to Know," Century Foundation Homeland Security Project, http://www.homelandsec.org (accessed December 1, 2003).

6. Bill Carter and Felicity Beringer, "At U.S. Request, Networks Agree to Edit Future bin Laden Tapes," *New York Times*, October 11, 2001.

7. Ibid.

8. Ibid.

9. Dan Rather, quoted in ibid.

10. "Transcript of October 10 White House Briefing by Ari Fleischer," *U.S. Newswire*, October 10, 2001.

11. Matt Wells, "CNN to Carry Reminders of U.S. Attack," *Guardian* (London), November 1, 2001.

12. Howard Kurtz, "CNN Chief Orders 'Balance' in War News, Reporters Are Told to Remind Viewers Why U.S. Is Bombing," *Washington Post*, October 31, 2001.

13. Ibid.

14. Ibid.

15. Ibid.

16. Ibid.

17. Ibid.

18. Wells, "CNN to Carry Reminders of U.S. Attack."

19. Richard Sambrook, telephone interview, December 9, 2002.

20. Bill Carter, "White House Seeks to Limit Transcripts," *New York Times*, October 12, 2001.

21. Ken Fireman, "U.S. Asks of Newspapers: No Unedited bin Laden Comments," *Newsday*, October 12, 2001.

22. Giles Elgood, "UK: Broadcasters Will Screen bin Laden Video," Reuters News Service, October 11, 2001.

23. Paul Waugh, "Air Strikes on Afghanistan—Downing Street—Broadcasters Summoned for 'Propaganda Talks,' " *Independent* (London), October 15, 2001.

24. Adam Sherwin and David Charter, "TV News Chiefs Resist Any Interference by No. 10—War on Terror—Propaganda," *Times* (London), October 16, 2001.

25. Ibid.

26. Richard Sambrook, telephone interview, December 9, 2002.

27. Richard Tait, telephone interview, January 10, 2003.

28. "Joint Statement: BBC News, ITN, Sky News," October 15, 2001, http://www.bbc.co.uk (accessed December 1, 2001).

29. Sherwin and Charter, "TV News Chiefs Resist Any Interference by No. 10."

30. Judy Keen, "Information 'War Room' Deploys Its Own Troops," *USA Today*, December 12, 2001.

31. Tom Rosenstiel, quoted in Paul Farhi, "The Networks, Giving Aid

to the Enemy? Unedited bin Laden Video Sparks Debate," *Washington Post*, October 12, 2001.

32. Commission on Freedom of the Press, *Peoples Speaking to Peoples* (Chicago: Chicago University Press, 1946), p. 1.

33. Ari Fleischer and Condoleezza Rice, quoted in "Transcript of October 10 White House Briefing by Ari Fleischer."

34. Electronic Media, "Video bin Laden: Let the Editors Do the Editing," *Times* (London), October 22, 2001.

35. "Media Asked to Downplay bin Laden," Tulsaworld.com, http://www.tulsaworld.com (October 11, 2001).

36. Sambrook telephone interview.

37. Sarah Schmidt, "Speech Translation Inaccurate, Experts Say," *National Post* (Ontario), October 9, 2001.

38. T. Christian Miller, "U.S. Strikes Back," *Los Angeles Times*, October 12, 2001.

39. MacArthur, *Second Front*, pp. 3–36.

40. Farhi, "Giving Aid to the Enemy?"

41. Ari Fleischer, quoted in "White House Briefing Speaker: Ari Fleischer," Federal Document Clearing House, October 10, 2001, http://www.factiva.com (accessed December 3, 2001).

42. White House EmediaMillWorks, "Interview of National Security Advisor Condoleezza Rice by Al-Jazeera TV," October 16, 2001, http://www.factiva.com (accessed December 3, 2001).

43. Tait telephone interview.

44. Jay Rayner, "The Battle for Afghanistan: Propaganda and Media," *Observer Newspaper*, October 14, 2001.

45. Kalpana Srinivasan, "FCC Relaxes Network Ownership Rules," Associated Press, April 19, 2001.

46. According to a Fairness and Accuracy in Reporting (FAIR) Action Alert dated April 20, 2002, the FCC was disposed to provide waivers to this rule. For instance, Rupert Murdoch's News Corporation owns a New York television station and the *New York Post*.

47. David Lieberman, "Media's Big Fish Watch FCC Review Ownership Cap," *USA Today*, July 9, 2001.

48. Ibid.

49. Natasha Haubold, "Where Does the Pentagon's Money Go?" *Federal Computer Week*, February 17, 2001.

50. Danny Schecter, interview, December 12, 2002.

51. George Bush, quoted in Elizabeth Becker, "A Nation Challenged:

Public Relations; U.S. Spreads Word of bin Laden Tape," *New York Times*, December 15, 2001.

52. Richard Boucher, quoted in Elizabeth Becker, "A Nation Challenged: Public Relations; U.S. Spreads Word of bin Laden Tape," *New York Times*, December 15, 2001.

Chapter 4

"IN CIPRO WE TRUST"

*When a whole nation is roaring Patriotism at the top of its voice, I am
fain to explore the cleanness of its hands and purity of its heart.*
—Ralph Waldo Emerson

ALL BEWAIL THE CHIEF:
THE "OUTING" OF THE CRITICAL AMERICAN

When ABC's Peter Jennings finally left the studio on September 12, he had been on air for seventeen hours
straight. Exhausted, the network's news anchor had covered the
tragedy of the terrorist attack from shortly after 9:00 A.M. eastern
daylight time (EDT) until 2:00 A.M. the next day. During that time,
Jennings reported on the crashes of Flights 77 and 93, the horror of
the attacks on the World Trade Center towers, and the reactions of
the government to the catastrophe. All of this reporting was con-

ducted in a fog of confusion, but throughout, Jennings remained calm and authoritative as he sought to explain what had happened. Using its substantial resources, ABC produced some "steadfast" and "comprehensive" reporting of that fateful day.[1] None of this, however, prevented Jennings from being lambasted for his alleged criticisms of President Bush.

In the days following the attack, ABC received more than 10,000 e-mail messages and telephone calls from enraged viewers who claimed that Jennings had slighted the president. The complaints were soon echoed in the media. According to his critics, shortly after noon on September 11, when speaking of the president's failure to return to Washington, Jennings had said that some presidents handled crises better than others. The statement was subsequently relayed to talk radio host Rush Limbaugh, who denounced Jennings, calling him a "fine son of Canada" (the journalist was born in Toronto). Limbaugh also said that the comment was evidence of "foolish, whining, babyish, unrealistic selfishness on the part of liberals."[2] The problem with these accusations is that they were based on a misunderstanding of what Jennings had actually said.

Speaking on Jennings's behalf, ABC's Executive Vice President Paul Friedman said that the accusations were depressing for both ABC and Jennings. He added that the journalist felt he had done a good job on the day in question and was being quoted out of context. ABC also provided details of his comments. According to a transcript, Jennings said, "None of us should be surprised that the security services take the president's safety seriously, but there was a psychological aspect because the country looks to the president on occasions like this to be reassuring to the nation. Some presidents do it well, some presidents don't."[3] After learning of the context in which the statement was made, Limbaugh retracted his accusations.

Jennings was vindicated, but his story provides ample evidence of the country's mood immediately after the attack. Brought together by a national tragedy unknown since the Japanese attack on Pearl Harbor, the American public experienced "an intense feeling of community" in the days and weeks that followed.[4] This emotion was to shape the way America reacted to this horrific act of terrorism.

It is worth remembering that, at the time, both the public and the administration were completely in the dark as to who the perpetrators were and the reasons for their attack. Indeed, such was the scale of confusion that, for the first two hours, the television networks, like the military and the Bush administration, were unclear on what exactly was happening. Afterward a shared sense of grief, anger, and incomprehension permeated the air and the people turned to their leaders for support and guidance. The realization of America's vulnerability produced an emotional covenant that would be intuitively recognized across the country. In return for leadership and security, the public traded unstinting and uncritical support during a difficult initial period when both the Bush administration and the American people were adjusting to the new threat.

Unfortunately for the media, a number of journalists failed to recognize this unspoken pact between the American people and their government. In the new post–September 11 world, a journalist could find him- or herself stranded in the no-man's land between the public's desire for strong government and the journalist's traditional duty to provide analysis and opinion. In the aftermath of the attacks, the normally wide band of freedom of expression became narrower and more restrictive, with the main focus on explaining the "who" and the "how." Any attempt to delve deeper, to provide the "why" or an analysis or critique of how America's leaders were performing, was rejected by much of the public as unpatriotic.

Journalists who were used to exposing politicians for their questionable activities now found themselves under intense scrutiny. The pressure on an "offending" journalist could be considerable, as the Jennings incident shows. Recognizing the change in the public mood, a number of administration officials sought to extract political capital from the situation. Comments by presidential spokesperson Ari Fleischer that the media should be careful and by Attorney General John Ashcroft that criticism of the administration "only aids terrorists" and "gives ammunition to America's enemies" exacerbated the situation. Talking on the *O'Reilly Factor*, a military officer argued that people who do not support the government are treasonous.[5] Whether they intended to do so or not, these members of the Bush administration inflamed the public and curtailed freedom of expression through these comments.

As a consequence, the media were pushed further and further away from their traditional role as the watchdog for American society. Criticized by the government and the public alike, the media found themselves confined to the role of furnishing information on the attackers and the victims. Greater scrutiny was discouraged. The media, particularly the print media, performed this newly imposed role admirably. But, in acceding to the public's implicit demands, the watchdogs were acknowledging that their claws had been clipped.

If further proof were needed, the fate of journalists and commentators who failed to heed this subtle coercion served as a timely reminder to others to remain silent. On television, the first victim of this new climate of intolerance was the host of ABC's *Politically Incorrect*, Bill Maher, a reputed polemicist who discussed topical issues with a panel of celebrities. When the show came back on air after the attacks, Maher announced, "[F]eelings are going to get hurt, so that actual people won't." Commenting on whether the terrorists who had flown the airplanes into the World Trade Center towers had been cowards, Maher said on his September 17, 2001, show, "We have been the cowards lobbing cruise missiles from 2,000 miles away. That's cowardly." When a guest agreed, the host said, "Staying in the airplane when it hits the building . . . say what you want about it, [it's] not cowardly. . . ."[6] The remarks were widely taken as an attack on the American military. The situation was further inflamed by another talk show host, Dan Patrick, who told his Houston listeners to contact the sponsors of Maher's show, FedEx Corp. and Sears, Roebuck and Company, to register their anger.

The impact on Maher's show was immediate. On the same day that the controversial episode was aired, FedEx Corp announced that it was withdrawing its regular thirty-second advertising spot. Two days later, on September 19, 2001, Sears, Roebuck followed suit by announcing the cancellation of its advertising on *Politically Incorrect* after receiving complaints from customers. A spokeswoman for the company, Lee Antonio, said, "Bill and his guests have every right to voice their freedom of speech and we applaud that. However, we have the right to air our broadcast advertising where we feel it's appropriate to reach out to our customers."[7]

In an attempt to salvage the situation, ABC issued a press release saying that, although the network remained sensitive to the tragedy and would help viewers cope with it, a forum for the expression of the "nation's diverse opinions" was needed. Maher also defended his comments, saying that they were meant for "politicians who, fearing public reaction, have not allowed our military to do the job they are obviously ready, willing, and able to do, and who now will, I'm certain, as they always have, get it done."[8] Maher's statement showed a failure to fully understand the situation in which he found himself. It was not his specific criticism of the military that was the cause of the problem, it was the act of criticism itself that was taboo. Therefore, the hemorrhaging of affiliates and advertisers from the show continued.

Angered by Maher's comments, the ABC affiliate WJLA-TV in Washington, D.C., decided to drop the show, refusing to air *Politically Incorrect* on September 20, 2001. On the following day, WJLA's president Chris Pike said that the ban would continue on a day-to-day basis. In an e-mail to viewers who complained about the comments made on Maher's show, Pike said, "We at WJLA were also offended by the insensitive remarks. . . . [A]t this time of great sorrow in our nation, and our community specifically, we have tried to maintain the highest level of sensitivity in our local news coverage, on-air promotion, and advertising. Although we strongly defend the right of free speech, Mr. Maher's ill-timed comments demonstrated a lack of feeling for the victims of this tragedy."[9] Siding with Pike, ABC stations in Des Moines, Sioux City, St. Louis, and five other Sinclair Broadcasting group stations also dropped the show.

Adding to the pressure on Maher, on September 26, 2001, Fleischer said, "[I]t's a terrible thing to say. . . . [Maher's comments are] reminders to all Americans that they need to watch what they say, watch what they do. This is not a time for remarks like that; there never is. . . ."[10] Fleischer's remarks led columnist Maureen Dowd to comment in the *New York Times* that "Mr. Fleischer acts offended—and vindictive—when someone has the nerve to challenge the

White House while our country is a target. But, especially when we are a target, we should not suppress the very thing that makes our foul enemies crazed with twisted envy. . . ."[11] Even with Dowd's support, Maher was forced into a further round of apologies, but even these efforts failed to stem the criticism.

On May 14, 2002, the Associated Press announced that *Politically Incorrect* had been cancelled. The last show was recorded on June 27, 2002, and aired the following day. ABC chairman Lloyd Braun said that Maher's comments had nothing to do with the decision to replace his program with a new one starring comedian Jimmy Kimmel. "We made a decision to go with straight entertainment programming in late night," Braun said. "That's just a scheduling opportunity that we felt over the long term had more potential."[12]

Reacting to ABC's decision, Maher stated that his show had been "politically annihilated." Others agreed with him. On June 22, 2002, the Los Angeles Press Club gave its President's Award to *Politically Incorrect*. The prize was presented to Maher by the *Los Angeles Times* columnist and club president Patt Morrison at the Press Club's annual awards.

As with the case of Peter Jennings, there appeared to be a genuine misunderstanding about the nature of the comment. However, unlike the ABC anchor, Maher's real crime was to offer criticism at a time when much of the viewing public believed it to be inappropriate. Two print journalists, Dan Guthrie and Tom Gutting, also discovered that comments about President Bush were also unacceptable, although unlike Maher they did not have the initial support of their employers. Perhaps the most alarming aspect of these journalists' cases was how quickly their respective publishers rushed to join the side of their critics.

Dan Guthrie was probably the first print journalist to suffer the consequences of believing that nothing had changed after September 11. A columnist and copy editor for the *Daily Courier* in Grants Pass, Oregon, Guthrie wrote in a column on September 15, 2001, that President Bush had "skedaddled" after the terrorist attack. He added, "Most of his aides and Cabinet members split for secret locations, too." Speaking of the airline passengers who struggled with the hijackers, Guthrie said, "They put it all on the line. Against their courage the picture of Bush hiding in a Nebraska hole becomes an embarrassment." Reacting to the criticism of the president, dozens of people protested, and Guthrie even received a death threat. The publisher of the *Daily Courier*, Dennis Mack, was outraged by the column and dismissed Guthrie immediately. Later, Mack was quoted as saying that Guthrie had turned the article into a personal attack on Bush and had failed in the task of writing about the "president being on the frontline." Mack then made Editor-in-Chief Dennis Roler apologize to the readers. Writing in the newspaper, Roler said that criticism of the president and his cabinet should be responsible and that calling President Bush a coward during the present crisis was neither responsible nor appropriate.[13]

Tom Gutting had similar problems at the *Texas City Sun*. In a column published on September 22, 2001, Gutting was critical of Bush's actions on the day of the attacks. Gutting accused the president of "flying around the country like a scared child seeking refuge in his mother's bed after having a nightmare." Gutting finished the column by comparing the president unfavorably with New York City Mayor Rudy Giuliani, who was "highly visible, not hiding underground in Nebraska." Gutting's comments caused numerous protests. Like Dennis Mack, the *Sun*'s publisher, Les Daughtry reacted quickly to the protests by writing an apology for Gutting's column on the front page of the next day's edition. "I offer an apology for this newspaper's grave error in judgment in allowing such a disruptive piece as Tom Gutting's 'Bush Has Failed to Lead U.S.' to make it to print," he wrote.[14] The publisher ended his statement with the words "May God bless President George W. Bush and other leaders. And God bless America." According to Gutting, the next day, Daughtry called Gutting into his office and informed the journalist that he could no longer work with him, promptly terminating his employment contract.[15]

The dismissal led to a spirited debate in some parts of the American media. Gutting himself appeared on ABC's *Nightline* and, during the program, admitted that he might have been wrong about the president. However, he pointed out that debate was fundamental to a democracy. In an online article titled "Censoring Dissenting Voices Is a Danger to Us All," Gutting argued that to justify beliefs we must expose them to arguments. In his view, such exposure strengthens the principles of the argument.[16] Others, though, disagreed. Writing in the *South Bend Tribune*, Bill Moore, a journalist who had mentored Gutting, called the story ill-timed.

Both Guthrie and Gutting were victims of local newspaper owners, but TV-critic-turned-columnist Howard Rosenberg faced intense pressure at the prestigious *Los Angeles Times*, although his publisher remained loyal to him. The incident was to show that nobody was immune from the censorious mood of the public. A line had been drawn and those caught on the wrong side were subject to vitriol, including, in the case of Rosenberg, racist jibes.

In a column published on September 14, Rosenberg stated that Bush "lacked size in front of the camera when he should have been commanding and filling the screen with his presence." The response was immediate, with over a thousand e-mail messages and telephone calls protesting his column and his ostensible lack of patriotism. A number of readers told Rosenberg to leave the country and "live with the Arabs." Several other e-mail messages addressed him as a "Jew." In the words of Rosenberg, "My patriotism wasn't just questioned, it was assaulted, and many e-mailers equated my column with terrorism. . . ."[17]

Twelve days later, Rosenberg sought to defend the column by admitting that his timing had been wrong but he did not regret the language he had used. In a well-written defense of freedom of expression, Rosenberg questioned the prevailing view of "My country right or wrong." He went on to make a connection with My Lai and other excesses, arguing that if journalists in Vietnam had followed this view, that massacre would never have been discovered. Commenting on the hate mail, Rosenberg said that he was surprised at the number of these responses. While accepting that he is an opinionated writer, he said that "it was as if I had called for the assassination of George Bush. It was frightening that there were so many Americans who felt that way." On the question of his journalistic judgment, Rosenberg said, "[W]hether I was right or wrong was not the issue, the point was . . . that as an American and as a journalist I had a First Amendment right to express my opinion. Call me dumb, call me stupid, but that is the way it goes."[18]

In addition to the public, a number of radio talk-show hosts exercised their power over the mainstream media. Having been denied the opportunity of successfully buttonholing Peter Jennings as an anti-patriot, Rush Limbaugh had a second opportunity to embarrass the ABC network. This time, he managed to force the president of ABC News, David Westin, to make a very public apology.

Speaking at a Columbia University journalism forum on October 23, 2001, Westin was asked whether the Pentagon and the World Trade Center towers were legitimate military targets. Denying that the World Trade Center towers were a suitable target, he stated that he did not have an opinion on the Pentagon. In a defense of journalism, Westin said that his job was to say "what is" and not "what ought to be." He finished his answer by saying, "As a journalist I feel strongly [that] that's something that I should not be taking a position on. . . ." Westin's failure to condemn the attack on the Pentagon drew swift responses from Limbaugh and others, such as Internet gossip columnist Matt Drudge. Managing to hold out for over a week, Westin finally buckled on October 31, 2001, when he issued a statement saying, "I was wrong. . . . Under any interpretation, the attack on the Pentagon was criminal and entirely without justification." The statement also said, "I apologize for any harm that my misstatement might have caused."[19]

Westin had attempted to defend the basic tenets of journalism, namely, objectivity and independence of thought, yet instead he found his words treated as an attempt to justify the terrorist attack on the Pentagon. As Howard Kurtz said in the *Washington Post*, Westin's words could be interpreted as "taking a pass on mass murder."[20] Whether this assessment is accurate or not, in this new environment, the Westins of the media were given few opportunities to explain themselves.

For this reason, there was a growing awareness among journalists and commentators that silence at this juncture was preferable to being outed for a lack of patriotism. Few wanted to lose their jobs or be forced into an embarrassing—and very public—retraction. Arguments, it seemed, could not be won against the combined might of public opinion, statements by Bush administration officials, and comments by conservative talk-show hosts—all of them reinforcing each other's position in a cycle of accuse and re-accuse.

In the days after September 11, the American flag and, in particular, tiepins in the shape of the flag became extremely popular as a sign of unity. A number of commentators wore these pins on networks such as CNN and Fox News Channel, and NBC prominently displayed flag graphics to reinforce the patriotic message. Tim Russert of NBC's *Meet the Press* wore a red, white, and blue ribbon on September 16, 2001. But the use of the patriotic emblems by television anchors led to a debate on whether they were overtly political and sent the wrong message to the viewers. Pat Dolan, the news director of News 12 in the New York City area, ordered a flag ban in a memorandum issued to his staff. His brother James Dolan, president of the station, disliked the decision but told interviewers that he would not overrule Pat. As a consequence of the ban, "A number of clients are talking about running their ads somewhere else," said an official from the station.[21]

Pat Dolan's memorandum led to biting criticism from Fox News Network anchor Brit Hume, who said, "This is not the flag of the Bush administration or the Democratic party, this is the flag of the country itself." When other news networks were asked for comments, NBC stated that it had no policy, but CBS spokesperson Sandra Genelius said, "As a rule, our people do not wear their hearts or their politics on their sleeves."[22]

While the larger networks discussed the merits of wearing a tiepin free from political pressure, the training station KOMU TV in Columbia, Missouri, which is affiliated with the University of Missouri School of Journalism, had considerable difficulties when it followed the lead of News 12. On September 17, 2001, News Director Stacy Woelfel sent an e-mail message to news staff informing them that the newsroom was not the place for personal statements in support of any cause, no matter how deserving. "This includes," he said, "the little red, white, and blue ribbons that a lot of people are sporting these days. Our job is to deliver the news as free from outside influences as possible." The message was passed anonymously to Missouri legislator Republican Matt Bartle, who protested Woelfel's decision. Rejecting the idea of objectivity, Bartle said, "This is a matter of simple decency and respect for our fellow human beings." In a statement that must have shaken the University of Missouri School of Journalism, he said, "I am going to be evaluating far more carefully state funding that goes to the School of Journalism. If this is what you are teaching the next generation of journalists, I question whether the taxpayers of this state will support it." Another state legislator, Republican Chuck Purgason, also criticized the decision, as did Republican legislator Carl Beardon, who noted ominously that he sat on the House Budget Committee.[23]

When asked for his opinion, the dean of the School of Journalism, Dean Mills, commented that the school tried hard to outline ethical guidelines for the students, but that the decision over the tiepins was one that only Woelfel could legitimately make. Supporting Woelfel, the School of Journalism issued a statement that said, "We . . . strongly support the right of faculty editors to make editorial decisions in our newsrooms." Perhaps more attuned to the political realities, Chancellor Richard Wallace chose not to support Woelfel's decision. "[The University of Missouri] deeply regrets that the policy has caused offense to KOMU viewers and other citizens," a statement from the chancellor's office commented. "This action . . . did not in any way reflect the policy of the university."[24] Initially withdrawn, the $500,000 state finance bill for the School of Journalism was reinstated in 2002.[25]

The incident proved that state legislators were quite capable of applying their own distinct brand of pressure on the media. The chancellor of the university appeared to recognize this fact and tried to appease the politicians, but the journalists rallied and held their ground. As had happened before, the political reaction was based on a misunderstanding about the role of journalists. Woelfel's decision was based on the belief, taught in most journalism schools, that journalists should be above society in order to report independently, that they should be the objective communicators of news, free of all constraints whether political, social, or emotional. With little appreciation of the ethics of journalism, politicians mistook Woelfel's stance as a rejection of America and its values. In Senator Bartle's eyes, the emblems were a question of "simple decency"; for Woelfel, it was a case of removing symbols that might make viewers identify the journalist with the news being read. These opposing views were difficult to reconcile.

There is no doubt that with dismissals by publishers, the withdrawal of sponsorship, the refusal of affiliated television stations to carry controversial programs, the clarion calls of radio talk show hosts, the public's ire, and the questions of legislators, critical Americans, including journalists, were very much an endangered species after September 11. Those brave enough to step forward were punished for their refusal to accept that American society was no longer tolerant of dissent and criticism. The attitude of many people was that dissent should be punished.

A clear example of this type of thinking can be seen in the case of Peter Werbe's syndicated radio show, which was dropped by Santa Cruz's KSCO-KOMY-AM. Werbe was an outspoken critic of the bombing in Afghanistan and the killing of innocent civilians. On October 6, 2001, the station's co-owner Michael Zwerling voiced his criticism of the show. Even Zwerling's mother, Kay Zwerling, condemned the show's political content: "Partisanship is out—we are all Americans now," she said. Such a statement, which implied that the attacks made everyone American, went to the heart of the problem. But, as Teresa Barton argued in the *South Bend Tribune*, the equation was wrong: Dissent did not equal treason, and unity did not equal patriotism.[26] Many people, though, felt differently.

Writing in the *New Statesman*, Scott Lukas summed up the view of many journalists when he said that if in November 2001 he had written a story on why the attacks happened, people would have written to his newspaper saying, "Fire the guy."[27] However, Lukas's article failed to suggest when the time for writing such a story would be right. And this was the essential problem with the "wait and see" argument: As the words of Fleischer implied, there never is a good time for dissent. Indeed, according to the "dissent equals treason" perspective, there is only a bad time.

Throughout September, October, and November of 2001, journalists were continually reminded of the need to be cautious. On September 25, 2001, an editorial in the *Investor's Business Daily* argued that "America is not a disgrace, no matter what [the dissenters] splutter." The article finished ominously: "When America returns to peace, it would do well to remember those who embarrassed themselves during war."[28] Commenting on Bill Maher, James V. Plummer of the *Times Union* wrote, "I think there is an apology owed to the people of the United States from this man or the station that allows him to almost commit an act of treason."[29]

With the prevalence of such sentiments, it was impossible not to appreciate that lapsing into silence was the best way of avoiding trouble. Even journalists who courageously supported their colleagues felt the need to distance themselves from what had actually been said. Talking of the comments by Maher, Kathleen Parker of the *Milwaukee Journal Sentinel* wrote, "[The comments] may have been in poor taste, poorly timed or ignorant but. . . ." Bill Moore distanced himself from Gutting when he said, "I also didn't agree with what he recently wrote in the *Texas City Sun.* . . ."[30] Such statements acknowledged the public's intense need for a patriotic response from the media.

Aside from this covert pressure, distortion played a considerable role in the attacks on journalists. In the cases of Jennings, Maher, Westin, and Woelfel, what was actually said came a poor second to its perceived meaning, which was often defined by those with their own agendas. As a consequence, journalists found themselves accused of criticizing the president (Jennings), or the military (Maher), implying that the murder of civilians was justified (Westin), or failing to be patriotic (Woelfel). These distortions were yet another means of stifling dissent. Executive Editor of *mediachannel.org* Danny Schechter described the entire process as a "calculated misinterpretation of information as a way to try to enforce a conformity of view."[31] In the uproar over the apparent message, few people were interested in taking the time to understand what was being said. For this reason, the messengers themselves were rendered powerless as the distortions took on a life of their own.

What of government pressure? In probably the best assessment of the government's behavior during this period, the editor of the online magazine *Salon*, David Talbot, suggested that the government had created a censorial atmosphere in which a herd mentality existed, bent on punishing dissenters.[32] Fleischer's statement that Americans should "watch what they say, watch what they do" set the tone for the way the media were to be treated, particularly when taken together with Ashcroft's comment that criticism aided the enemy. These statements by members of the Bush administration were exhortations for journalists to censor themselves, as Fleischer made clear when he reinforced his message by saying that there is never a good time to voice dissent. Given the strength of the passions at the time, both Ashcroft and Fleischer should have used their positions to call for tolerance and calm. Their failure to do so exacted a high price from the media.

On the subject of the pervading atmosphere at the time, Web editor and journalist at the Index on Censorship organization Rohan Jayasekera believed that the government's actions were simple attempts at bluster designed to avoid giving the media proper information. According to Jayasekera, deliberately limiting information is a "weapon of war that you need to control in the same way that you need to control every other tactical, strategic objective. . . . Their only weapon is this sense of moral outrage that anybody would question their government and their military during the time of war."[33] On the question of the environment that journalists were working in, Schechter argued, "I agree there was a censorious environment, but I would go further; I believe there was a self-censorious environment."[34]

Additional proof of the powerful forces acting on the media came in May 2002. Speaking at the News World Asia conference, Rena Golden, the executive vice president and manager of CNN International, said, "Anyone who claims the U.S. media didn't censor itself is kidding you. It wasn't a matter of government pressure but a reluctance to criticize anything in a war that was obviously supported by the vast majority of the people. . . . And this isn't just a CNN issue—every journalist in this room who was in any way involved in 9-11 is partly responsible."[35] While Golden understated the part played by the government, her statement was a tacit admission of the pressure to conform that would have found support among many journalists.

Confronted by the enormity of the September 11 tragedy, many journalists felt compelled by the prevailing environment to reject their traditional role of questioning the government while others succumbed to the desire to offer their patriotic support. The effects of such patriotism on the media were to be damaging.

JOURNALISM AND THE SUBTLE UNDERTOW OF PATRIOTISM

After September 11, the American flag could be seen across the United States: On cars and buses, on tiepins attached to women's dresses and the lapels of men's suits, hung from windows in residential areas, displayed in shop windows, and tied to bridges and underpasses. The message of the flag was that the American people had come together during a critical period in their country's history and were ready and willing to support their government in the "war against terrorism." Spurred on by this behavior, the media adopted many of the symbols in a display of solidarity.

As previously mentioned, in certain newsrooms, flags figured prominently on banner headlines and on tickertapes displayed at the bottom of screens. Some journalists also began to wear their own individual symbols of support. The language used by media outlets was also patriotic; TV screens used headlines such as "America under Siege" or "America Strikes Back." These headlines reinforced the strong feelings of unity, togetherness, and community among the population.

A second event occurring on the heels of the attacks in New York, Washington, and the downing of the airliner in Pennsylvania also created in the media a sense of unity with the public—namely, the anthrax attack on media outlets. Coming after September 11, the posting of letters laced with anthrax to media outlets and politicians heightened tension and fear among Americans. "Death by Mail . . ."

(*Time*), "Anthrax anxiety" (*Newsweek*), and "High Anxiety" (*US News and World Report*) were only some of the frightening headlines that appeared at the time.

The attacks started on September 18 when letters containing granular anthrax were sent to the *New York Post* and to the NBC studios in New York. Four days after the initial attack, on September 22, 2001, an editorial page assistant discovered blisters on her fingers and was later found to have the cutaneous form of anthrax. Just over one week later, Bob Stevens, a photo editor at the *Sun* in Boca Raton, Florida, started to feel ill. He was hospitalized but died on October 5 from inhaling anthrax. The panic among media outlets increased when a letter containing anthrax was also sent to the *National Enquirer*, while hoax letters were also sent to the *New York Times*, a science reporter, the *St. Petersburg Times*, CBS News, and Fox News.[36]

At the beginning of October, Erin O'Connor, assistant to NBC anchor Tom Brokaw, was prescribed the antibiotic Cipro after suffering from the cutaneous form of anthrax. Speaking on October 15, Brokaw finished his broadcast by holding a medicine bottle up to the camera and, with all the drama of a Hollywood actor delivering a line, said, "In Cipro we trust. . . ." Tinged with melodrama as it was, the phrase indicated that the media and the public were united in the face of anthrax.

Brokaw's comment epitomizes the media's behavior after September 11. His comment pierced the veil of objectivity normally surrounding journalists, and although it enabled the public to identify with the media, it also alerted viewers to the fact that, from now on, the news was to be treated subjectively. It was "them" against "us."

Driven by the events of September 11 and the anthrax attacks, Fox News was emblematic of this new stance. The channel's tone was set early on by its owner, Rupert Murdoch, who said that he would do his patriotic duty. Indeed, the declared position of the channel was "be accurate, be fair, be American"[37]—it struck a chord with many people and, as a result, the channel increased its percentage of viewers. NBC anchor and Washington bureau chief Tim Russert also felt the need to declare his patriotism. "Yes, I'm a journalist," he said. "But first, I'm an American. Our country is at war with the terrorists, and as an American, I support that effort wholeheartedly."[38]

However, Russert failed to answer the important question of how, given his views, he could retain his skepticism and objectivity. Essentially, was a journalist who declared his support for the war effort capable of asking the right questions of administration officials? Could such a journalist hold government to account? Questions such as these led to a debate among the media, with a split between those who thought the media should remain impartial and those who felt that the media should articulate the national mood.

This discussion was closely followed by media groups, with some conservative groups congratulating members of the media for setting aside their objectivity in order to devote themselves to patriotic sentiment. Based on the comments of some journalists at the time, this perspective appeared to be victorious. What was the reasoning behind this result? Although it is difficult to reach a definitive decision on why the media, particularly the television networks, decided to jettison their journalistic objectivity, many writers have suggested that network executives were pressed to do so by economic factors, by advertisers, and by parent corporations. Such a view treats patriotism as merely another preference displayed by audiences. Seen through this prism, the television networks merely bundled news into the form most desirable to the American audience at the time. The result was a designer news founded on brand America.

But, this fails to explain why the journalists themselves echoed the views of the media networks. The journalists were not compelled to wear patriotic tiepins, nor were they forced to appear on television chat shows on which they espoused their support of president and country. Perhaps the real reason was a deep-seated need to be seen as members of the community and to reflect its views and perspectives. During this period, journalists became popular again. A poll conducted by the Pew Research Center in November 2001 showed that, after September 11, 69 percent of Americans believed that journalists "stand up for America." Before the attacks, only 43 percent had supported this statement. While this need for acceptance was a human response to the crisis, it failed to appreciate the harm that such patriotic comments could do to the image of American journalism.

Appearing on the *Late Show with David Letterman* on September 17, CBS anchor and editor Dan Rather made the following statement, "George Bush is the president. He makes the decisions. As just one American, wherever he wants me to line up, just tell me where." Rather later apologized to Letterman for his display of emotion. The chat show host responded to Rather's emotion by taking the anchor's hand and saying, "You're a professional, but good Christ, you're a human being." Coming as they did from possibly America's most prominent journalist, Rather's words appeared to endorse the notion of the "patriotic but objective journalist"; they were not the only such comments from journalists.

Elsewhere, the Sinclair Broadcast Group (SBG), which later refused to air *Politically Incorrect*, started airing its own ninety-second editorials shortly after September 11. On November 4, 2001, the SBG issued an editorial criticizing the national coverage of the war on terrorism, in particular, those media outlets airing footage from Qatari-based Al-Jazeera. The vice president of SBG challenged viewers to participate in the new editorial process by starting a dialogue with the television stations over the news they carried.

On September 18, a Fox News anchor interviewing the German ambassador to America said that America looked forward to working with Germany in the task of wiping out the terrorists who carried out the attacks. Such a statement typified the reporting style of the Fox News Channel, which from the outset had shown an extraordinary willingness to abandon journalistic objectivity in its scramble for the patriotic high ground.

In December, the chairman of the Fox News Channel, Roger Ailes, said that terrorism is evil and that America does not engage in it. Talking to the *New York Times*, Fox News anchor Brit Hume said, "The fact that some [Afghani] people are dying, is that really news? And is it to be treated in a semi-straight-faced way? I think not." Perhaps the most flagrant example of the rampant patriotism shown at Fox News was the behavior of Geraldo Rivera, who joined the news organization to report on the war in Afghanistan. "I'm feeling more patriotic than at any time in my life. Itching for justice—or maybe just revenge," the talk-show-host-turned-war-correspondent said.

Rivera promised that on finding bin Laden, "I'll kick his head in, then bring it home and bronze it." Rivera also admitted that he was carrying a gun for self-protection and stated that he would not hesitate to shoot a terrorist. In perhaps his most ridiculous outburst, Rivera said in November that he had a New York fire department hat that he wanted to place on the head of bin Laden. "I want to put [the hat] on—on the body of his—you know, the head of his corpse." Explaining his reaction, he said, "It's deeply personal, on the one hand. On the other, it is my professional calling."[39] Based on Rivera's statements, it was difficult to separate the would-be executioner from the would-be war correspondent.

As Deputy Director of the Committee to Protect Journalists Joel Simon said in an interview, Rivera's activities in Afghanistan "blurred the boundaries" between being a journalist and a possible combatant. "One of the things that has kept journalists safe is the perception that they are neutral observers who will listen to all sides and report honestly what people tell them."[40] The comments of Ailes, Hume, Rather, and Rivera showed little appreciation of the possibility that by aligning themselves so readily with the American government, they were endangering the independence of the media as a whole. By expressing their support for the government's actions, by wearing emotive symbols, by revealing their desire for revenge or hoping for the chance to kill bin Laden, journalists were undercutting and undermining the objectivity that journalists so badly needed to report in safety from the conflict zone.

Reporting the war in Afghanistan was an extremely dangerous job. According to IPI Death Watch, a total of 109 journalists were killed between the start of 2001 and the end of 2002.[41] Many of those killed were journalists operating in a conflict zone. On the battlefield, journalists needed to be viewed as neutral if they were not to face attack from one side or the other. However, the patriotic comments of colleagues at home chipped away at this perception, making an already dangerous job even more dangerous. At a time when journalists are increasingly being seen as "legitimate targets" for soldiers on the battlefield, the partisanship of journalists reporting in the United States potentially provided terrorists and repressive regimes with yet another reason why journalists could not be seen as impartial and unbiased providers of information.[42]

During the war in Afghanistan in 2001, the Taliban originally barred journalists from entering the country. In support of this ban, the Taliban Intelligence Chief Mullah Taj Meer was reported by the Afghan Islamic Press as saying, "Any journalists entering illegally into Afghanistan will be treated like an American soldier." The statement was a breach of Article 79 of the Geneva Convention, which states that "journalists who fulfill professional missions in armed conflict areas will be considered as civilians" and "enjoy general protection against the dangers resulting from military operations."[43] It gave a strong indication that the Taliban equated journalists, whether American or not, with the allied military.

Although the Taliban leadership belatedly realized the importance of the media, eventually holding daily press conferences, other groups may have decided to punish members of the media for the successes of the American military. On November 19, 2001, Maria Grazia Cutuli, special envoy for the Italian daily *Corriere della sera*; Julio Fuentes, special correspondent to Afghanistan for the Spanish daily *El Mundo*; Harry Burton, an Australian TV cameraman for Reuters; and Azizullah Haidari, an Afghan photographer for Reuters were taken from their cars and killed. According to reports made at the time, the four journalists were traveling in a press convoy. Two hours outside of Jalalabad, the convoy was halted by six men armed with automatic weapons. The armed men chased away the Afghan driver and translator and forced the journalists to follow them. All the journalists were then shot dead. The remainder of the press convoy managed to make its way back to Jalalabad. Despite Northern Alliance claims that the four journalists were murdered by bandits, it is likely that the journalists were executed by pro-Taliban forces.[44] Evidence of this contention can be seen in the way the journalists were separated from their driver and translator; there are also reports that the armed men shouted slogans in support of the Taliban.[45] A number of the murdered journalists were shot in the back, and at least one of them was attacked with a rock, possible telltale signs of both a summary execution and hatred. Moreover, although the area had a new governor, it had not been fully secured by the anti-Taliban coalition and was still considered dangerous with reports of al-Qaeda fighters roaming the area.[46]

It is difficult to prove beyond a reasonable doubt that the four journalists were killed because of their profession. Nonetheless, their deaths provided a worrying scenario for the future in which the shield of a war correspondent's impartiality has become so tattered and frayed, due to the failure of his or her colleagues at home to remain objective, that journalists are unable to report. In such a scenario, media outlets face the choice of either not sending journalists to the conflict zone or asking the military to provide protection for them. The former would prevent reporting on the conflict, while the latter might render the media a mere adjunct of the military.

Even in the aftermath of September 11, many of America's media organizations were already being accused of relying too heavily on military experts and government spokespersons for their news. The inevitable result of this slow drift toward "patriotic news" would be to force journalists into the arms of government. As a consequence, journalists would become little more than information officers responsible for spreading the official version of events.

By seeking to secure an increased audience share and by playing to the views and emotions of the majority, a number of television news networks sacrificed their own long-term future for a very short-term gain. Jingoistic reporting may well have allowed the news organizations to sail safely through the experience of September 11, but what about the relationship between government and the media once the war on terrorism is over? Will the media return to their traditional role of exposing scandals in the political and corporate life of the United States, or will the expressions of patriotism have irreparably damaged the media? For all intents and purposes the ramifications of this patriotic impulse appears to have been ignored.

A number of these arguments have also been discussed in relation to the vicious, senseless murder of *Wall Street Journal* reporter Daniel Pearl, who was kidnapped on January 23, 2002, in Karachi, Pakistan. Working as the South Asia bureau chief, Pearl had arrived in Pakistan with the hope of finding further information on "shoe bomber" Richard Reid, who attempted to blow up a commercial airliner with explosives packed into one of his shoes. On January 28, 2002, a group calling itself the National Movement for the Restoration of Pakistani Sovereignty claimed responsibility for kidnapping Pearl and said that it wanted better conditions for the prisoners held in Cuba. An e-mail message was also sent to American news outlets with a photograph showing a gun being held to Pearl's head.

After protracted and unsuccessful negotiations, one of the perpetrators of the kidnapping, Omar Sheikh, was arrested by Pakistani police. During the early part of February there were several false claims and leads relating to the kidnapping, but on February 21, 2002, the American government announced that Pearl had been murdered. The proof came in a horrific videotape showing Pearl being killed. Immediately before his death, the journalist had been forced to state that both he and his parents were Jewish. Sheikh was later prosecuted and found guilty of murdering Pearl by the Pakistani authorities.

As with the murder of the four journalists in Afghanistan, it is difficult to reach a settled conclusion about the reasons for Pearl's appalling murder. Indeed, the kidnappers' motivation appears confused. Originally, it appeared that Pearl was accused of spying for both the Israeli secret services and the Central Intelligence Agency (CIA). On hearing the accusation, the CIA took the unusual step of denying the claim. Based on the video evidence, it appears likely that the journalist was killed for his religious beliefs, and possibly for his profession.

An article in the *St. Louis Post* said that Pearl's death highlighted the disturbing trend that journalists were being murdered for the policies of their governments. The article quoted the Paris-based press freedom organization Reporters Sans Frontières as saying that journalists were being made into "scapegoats" for these policies. Aidan White, secretary-general of the International Federation of Journalists, added that Pearl "was targeted and killed because of who he [was] and where he came from."[47]

Writing in *USA Today*, Steve Bell said that Pearl's death might provide an insight into how American journalists perceive themselves and how they invite others to see them. In Bell's opinion,

Pearl was seen by the kidnappers as a symbol of America and, in particular, as a symbol of American Jewry. Therefore, Pearl was killed not because of anything personal, but because of what he represented. According to Bell, journalists can still undertake good reporting without losing their sense of national identity.[48]

Others, though, saw a more direct link between the domestic media and Pearl. While Bell's view that support for one's country can be expressed by questioning the actions of government, it fails to acknowledge how strong the pull of patriotism was on the media during the aftermath of the attacks. The effects of September 11 were immediate. Journalists who sought to practice Bell's type of journalism quickly found, first, that, there was virtually no audience for such news and, second, that journalists faced intense pressure from an alliance of groups within American society that included politicians, corporate sponsors, the public, the conservative media, and even publishers and media executives.

There were other views. A letter to the Poynter Institute's Media News page from Ken Denney, formerly of the *Augusta Chronicle and Daily News*, stated that "the kidnappers of Mr. Pearl insist that he is a political tool, a spy for some foreign government (one day the U.S., the next day Israel). Where could they have possibly gotten the idea that journalists are not the dedicated professionals they claim to be but are instead something else in disguise?" Denney said that the conservative views of the *Wall Street Journal* contributed to the perception of Pearl as a spy for the American government. Alluding to the book *Bias* by Bernard Goldberg, which explores liberal bias in the media, Denney added, "For far too long, the journalistic community has treated conservative criticism of the profession too lightly. False descriptions have dire consequences as we now see."[49]

In contrast to Bell, Denney recognizes some of the risks involved but points the finger of blame in the wrong direction. It is far more likely that the expressions of support for the government by the media, rather than antagonism between the liberal and conservative wings of the media, undermined the perception that American journalists are free of government ties. Moreover, though Denney is right that a connection exists between the home front and the war front, he fails to take into account the fact that, after September 11, journalists well known for their liberal leanings, such as Dan Rather, also professed their support for their country and government.

The true mistake in this period was the failure to realize that the patriotic statements of American journalists at home could jeopardize journalists working abroad because such statements implied that Western journalists, particularly those from the United States, support their governments. This view is affirmed by an e-mail message which was sent by Pearl's kidnappers to the media shortly after the original ransom note. In poor English, the message said, "We warn all amreekan jounlists waorking in Pakistan that there are many in their ranks spying on pakstan under the journlist cover. therefore we give all amreekan journalists 3 days to get out of pakstan. Anyone remaining after that will be targeted."[50] In the eyes of some people in the Middle East, the distinction between the media and government had already been fatally blurred.

It is worth noting that the opinions of journalists and press freedom advocates often differ on this issue. Deputy Director of the press freedom organization Committee to Protect Journalists Joel Simon commented that "if the perception exists that the U.S. media is an adjunct of the U.S. government and people are angry at the U.S. government and its policies then, logically, journalists are in greater danger."[51] This view is supported by BBC News Director Richard Sambrook, who also sees a danger. "I do now think [journalists] are seen as legitimate targets to a greater extent than they were ten or fifteen years ago. . . . I think it is important, therefore, for news organizations to preserve their impartiality as best they can."[52]

In contrast, former Independent Television Network (ITN) Editor-in-Chief Richard Tait sounded a forthright warning note regarding the link between patriotism and the targeting of journalists. "I think this is a dangerous area. I think some journalists have always been opinionated and editorialized. There has always been a gap between factual reporting and comment. I'm reluctant to go down the road that if journalists were objective they would not be targeted by men with guns. My experience is that journalists are not killed because people think a television program or a news program isn't objective." On the question of al-Qaeda, he said, "If you're a member of al-Qaeda then you probably don't think there is much difference between the values of Fox News and ITN. Also, I think the danger of [making this connection] is that it might be used as a reason for attacking journalists."[53]

The patriotic statements of journalists on the home front also reinforced the Middle Eastern perception that some Western journalists had an anti-Arab bias. Using the analogy of a mirror, a number of Arabic media organizations allege that the Western tendency to characterize the Middle East's media as biased in fact reflects the Western media's own bias. Reports in the Middle Eastern media allude to a series of alleged press freedom violations, such as the Mullah Omar interview by the Voice of America, the Condoleezza Rice network call over the bin Laden videotapes, the attempt by the secretary of state to pressure Al-Jazeera, the comments not to focus too closely on civilian casualties, and allegations of bias when reporting on the Israeli-Palestinian conflict.

An examination of Middle Eastern journalism after the September 11 attacks, particularly in opinion pieces, reveals constant references to these events.[54] A number of conspiracy theories add to the mixture that forms both Middle Eastern opinion and its expression in the media. One of these beliefs is that the Americans deliberately bombed the offices of Al-Jazeera in Kabul.

Another source of Middle Eastern anger is the purported failure of the Western media to report on the reason why bin Laden was waging war against America. In the eyes of the Middle Eastern media, the media in the West has repeatedly failed to properly investigate issues like the Israeli-Palestinian conflict, the death of children in Iraq due to the sanctions, the fight to remove American military bases from Middle Eastern soil, and the fact that the United States provides economic support for so-called puppet states in the region.[55] However unpalatable to the Western taste, these views form part of the Arab mindset. As such they can be disagreed with but not ignored.

In an article written by reporter Ranil Mendis, the Western media stood accused of abdicating its responsibility to report facts and opinions. According to Mendis, the Western media have "reduced themselves to a propaganda tool of the government." His article reveals the belief that American foreign policy in the Middle East is stacked in favor of Israel and that American lives on September 11 were being sacrificed so that Israel could gain a few miles of real estate.[56] In the Indian *Milli Gazette*, Ramzy Baroud argued that the media have failed to inform the American public of the realities of the Middle East. He contended that "coverage of the [Israeli-Palestinian] conflict . . . is misleading, and that every mainstream newspaper, or TV network or radio station is often colored with a certain political leaning that not only influences the overall media perception of a certain issue, but every report written, word uttered, image broadcast, type of individual interviewed, or report cited."[57] If such views exist in the Middle East media, they are also likely to reflect the views of many Muslims.

Skepticism toward the Western media was, therefore, already deeply ingrained in the Middle Eastern mindset before September 11. After the attacks, the existing bias made the American government's attempts to explain to a cynical Middle East population why it was invading Afghanistan and embarking on the war against terrorism more difficult. It is interesting to note that, according to a Gallup poll of 9,924 people taken in nine Muslim countries five months after the attacks, only 18 percent of Arabs believed that the perpetrators of the attacks were also Arabs.[58] This poll seemed to provide undeniable proof that the public diplomacy efforts of the United States were simply not working. Perhaps the question to be answered by the Bush administration and some parts of the American media is whether government pressure, the patriotic comments of journalists, and the castigation of others brave enough to speak out helped, in some way, to create this false perception of the events of September 11.

On the issue of skepticism, both Sambrook and Tait point out the dangers for the way the West is viewed in the Middle East. "The concept of an independent media is pretty alien to most societies that we are talking about [in the Middle East]. Therefore, they start with the point of view that journalists are partisan," said Tait.[59] Sambrook acknowledged the possibility that patriotism among the

American media reinforces skepticism in the Middle East and commented, "I think that's why it is important for us to be scrupulous as far as possible because certainly for an international broadcaster like the BBC and CNN your journalism has to have credibility across geographical and ideological boundaries."[60]

In the middle of 2002, journalists, including Dan Rather, started having second thoughts on how the media should behave and whether it should be patriotic. Appearing on the BBC's current affairs program *Newsnight*, Rather said, "I worry that patriotism run amok will trample the very values that the country seeks to defend." On the question of the war on terrorism, the CBS anchor and editor commented, "In a constitutional republic, based on the principles of democracy such as ours, you simply cannot sustain warfare without the people at large understanding why we fight, how we fight, and have a sense of accountability at the very top." He described the impulse to be patriotic in terms of having a "flaming tire" around one's neck: "One finds oneself saying, 'I know the right question but you know what? This is not exactly the right time to ask it.'"[61]

Rather's words imply that journalists may have been waking up to the fact that the government was not being held accountable. Unfortunately, they also echoed Rather's own behavior during the first Gulf War. In a news broadcast with Connie Chung aired during the war, Rather said, "Connie, I'm told that this program is being seen [by the troops] in Saudi Arabia . . . and I know you would join me in giving our young men and women out there a salute." The journalist then saluted toward the camera.[62] However, speaking to author John R. MacArthur after the first Gulf War had ended, Rather said, "I'm not the vice president in charge of excuses here. . . . But some of what happened was because there was a lack of will, a lack of guts to speak up, to speak out, speak our minds, and for that matter to speak our hearts."[63]

It is tempting, on the basis of his behavior, to say that Rather's words the second time around convey little meaning. But they provide a powerful example of the gravitational pull of patriotism during times of crisis. His comments illustrate an emotional arc that many journalists must have experienced. During the war in

Afghanistan, many journalists felt compelled to make jingoistic statements (Rather: "George Bush is the president. He makes the decisions.") and then, after the war, once the giddiness had worn off, they made unconvincing statements of contrition (Rather: "I worry that patriotism run amok will trample the very values that the country seeks to defend.").[64]

The impact of September 11, on the media, like its effect on government and the American public, cannot be underestimated. The attacks overwhelmed media that had never had to encounter anything on this scale before, particularly in their own country. For Tait this unprecedented situation presented the American media with an ethical dilemma—how to report on terrorism when the terrorism is "actually causing mayhem in your own community."[65] Rohan Jayasekera put the attacks in perspective when he said, "September 11 was a game that [the media] had not planned for, [indeed] it was a game they did not even recognize."[66] Echoing these views, Sambrook said, "This was the biggest attack since Pearl Harbor, America had never suffered attacks like that, never really suffered from domestic terrorism and I am not surprised that it produced an extraordinary reaction."[67]

Like a sudden change in the weather, the change of mood in America after September 11 took many journalists by surprise. Journalists received a second surprise when many publishers and network executives failed to support them when they expressed criticism of the Bush administration's actions. The result was a profession that felt extremely vulnerable to the charges of failing to support the war on terrorism and the war in Afghanistan. Instead of fighting against these changes, many journalists either acquiesced to the wishes of public opinion, providing Americans with a steady diet of patriotic rhetoric, or they lapsed into silence on the subject. The risks to an American journalism that had previously been willing to ask the big "why" questions or challenge the prevailing views went unheeded.

A tacit recognition of these problems came from CNN Chairman Walter Isaacson, who, speaking at a dinner on November 7, 2001, said, "In this environment it feels slightly different. . . . If you get on the wrong side of public opinion, you are going to get into trouble."[68] CNN, however, had not been brave enough to withstand the pressures. Caught between the patriotism of domestic audiences and the skepticism of its foreign audiences, CNN created a twin-track news system, opening up the possibility of a future in which specific news is prepackaged and developed in order to be acceptable to certain biased audiences.

The effects of wrapping news in the American flag have not been fully investigated. Outside the United States, the comments of domestic news anchors and talk show hosts, buttressed and supported by their news executives, television and radio networks, and corporate sponsors, reinforced the overwhelming impression that the American media were biased. This view, already held in much of the Middle East, became further entrenched after September 11, helping to foster prejudicial views of both America and its media.

At the moment, it is impossible to tell how much damage has been done to the journalism profession by government pressure and the vocal patriotism of some media outlets and journalists. Within journalism there are renewed fears that journalists are increasingly being seen as legitimate targets on the battlefield and that the erosion of the media's independence and objectivity may further this process. Instances of this type of targeting appeared to be taking place in Afghanistan. In the future, many more such instances may occur.

NOTES

1. James W. Carey, "American Journalism on, before, and after September 11," in *Journalism after September 11*, ed. Barbie Zelizer and Stuart Allen (London: Routledge, 2002), p. 72.

2. Rush Limbaugh, quoted in Howard Kurtz, "Peter Jennings in the News for What He Didn't Say," *Washington Post*, September 24, 2001.

3. Paul Friedman and Peter Jennings, quoted in ibid.

4. Carey, "Journalism on, before, and after September 11," p. 75.

5. Tim Rutten and Lyn Smith, "When the Ayes Have It, Is There Room for Naysayers?" *Los Angeles Times*, September 28, 2001.

6. Bill Maher, quoted in Celestine Bohlen, "In the New War on Terrorism, Words Are Weapons, Too," *New York Times*, September 29, 2001.

7. ABC News, "Maher Apologizes for 'Cowardly' Remark," September 20, 2001, http://www.ABCNews.com (accessed September 9, 2003).

8. Steve Gorman (Reuters), "Maher Sorry for Politically Incorrect Statement," *Chicago Tribune*, September 9, 2001.

9. Paul Farhi, "WJLA's Correction: Pull Maher," *Washington Post*, September 22, 2001.

10. Maureen Dowd, "We Love the Liberties They Hate," *New York Times*, September 30, 2001.

11. Ibid.

12. "Maher Cancelled, Kimmel Lands Slot at ABC," CNN.com, May 14, 2002, http://www.cnn.com (accessed December 5, 2003).

13. Editorial, "Be Careful What Gets Stifled," *Los Angeles Times*, October 12, 2001.

14. Les Daughtry Jr., "Bush Leadership Has Been Superb," *Texas City Sun*, September 23, 2001.

15. ABC News, "Profile: Watch What They Say as America Fights Back: Debate on Limits of Free Speech in America in Times of Crisis with Susan Sontag, Todd Gauziano, Ed Gillespie, and Tom Gutting," *Nightline*, October 3, 2001.

16. Tom Gutting, "Censoring Dissenting Voices Is a Danger to Us All," University of Wisconsin-Oshkosh, October 5, 2001, http://www.uwosh.edu (accessed December 2, 2003).

17. Howard Rosenberg, "A New Kind of War of Words," *Los Angeles Times*, September 26, 2001.

18. Howard Rosenberg, telephone interview, December 10, 2002.

19. David Westin, quoted in Howard Kurtz, "Objectivity Lesson: ABC News Chief Apologizes," *Washington Post*, November 1, 2001.

20. Kurtz, "News Chief Apologizes."

21. Peter Hart and Seth Ackerman, "Patriotism and Censorship: Some Journalists Are Silenced, While Others Seem Happy to Silence Themselves," *Extra!* November/December 2001.

22. David Bauder (Associated Press), "Reporters Caught in Debate about Patriotism, Objectivity," *Chicago Tribune*, September 22, 2001.

23. Jennifer Harper, "Reporters Struggle to Balance Patriotism, News Judgement," *Washington Times*, September 28, 2001.

24. Robert Sandler, "MU 'Deeply Regrets' that Policy Banning KOMU Reporters from Wearing Patriotic Symbols May Have Caused Offense," *Missouri Digital News*, October 4, 2001, http://www.mdn.org (accessed December 2, 2003).

25. Ibid.

26. Teresa Barton, "Dissent Healthy for Nation," *South Bend Tribune*, November 7, 2001.

27. Scott Lucas, "How a Free Press Censors Itself," *New Statesman* (London), November 12, 2001.

28. "What's Relevant, What's Not," *Investor's Business Daily*, September 25, 2001.

29. James V. Plummer, "TV Host Stepped over the Line with Comments," *Albany Times Union*, November 5, 2001.

30. Kathleen Parker, "It Isn't Censorship," *Milwaukee Journal Sentinel*, November 23, 2001.

31. Danny Schecter, telephone interview, December 12, 2002.

32. David Talbot, "Democracy Held Hostage," Salon.com, September 29, 2001, http://www.salon.com (accessed December 2, 2003).

33. Rohan Jayasekera, telephone interview, December 15, 2002.

34. Schecter telephone interview, December 12, 2002.

35. Rena Golden, quoted in "CNN Exec Claims War Coverage Is 'Censored,'" *Quill* 90, no. 8 (October 1, 2002).

36. Sylvio Waisbord, "Journalism Risk and Patriotism," in *Journalism after September 11*, ed. Zelizer and Allen, p. 211.

37. Ellen Goodman, "Balancing Journalism, Patriotism," *Baltimore Sun*, December 9, 2001.

38. Mohammed El-Nawawy and Adel Iskandar, "The Minotaur of Contextual Objectivity: War Coverage and the Pursuit of Accuracy with Appeal," Transnational Broadcasting Studies, http://www.tbsjournal.com (accessed December 2, 2003).

39. Geraldo Rivera, quoted in Peter Hart and Jim Naureckas, "Fox at the Front," Extra! Fairness and Accuracy in Reporting, January/February 2002, http://www.fair.org (accessed December 2, 2003).

40. Joel Simon, telephone interview, March 18, 2003.

41. Michael Kudlak, IPI Death Watch, http://www.freemedia.at (accessed December 2, 2003).

42. Ciar Byrne, "Journalists Face Increasing Danger, Warns CNN Chief," *Guardian* (London), November 20, 2002.

43. Barbara Trionfi, "Afghanistan Report," *World Press Freedom Review* (Vienna: International Press Institute, 2001), p. 104.

44. On the previous day, November 18, 2001, three Radio France International journalists had been robbed on the same road.

45. Associated Press, "Bodies of Four Slain Reporters Recovered in Afghanistan," November 20, 2001.

46. "Slain Journalists Had Big Story," CBSNews.com, November 21, 2001, http://www.cbsnews.com.

47. "Pearl's Killing Sheds Light on a Disturbing Trend," *St. Louis Post*, February 23, 2002.

48. Steve Bell, "On Being an American Journalist," *USA Today*, July 1, 2002.

49. Bernard Goldberg, *Bias: A CBS Insider Exposes How the Media Distort the News* (Washington, DC: Regnery Publishing, 2002).

50. Jack Shafer, "Full Metal Junket: The Myth of the Objective War Correspondent," *Slate*, March 5, 2003, http://www.slate.msn.com.

51. Simon interview.

52. Richard Sambrook, telephone interview, December 19, 2002.

53. Richard Tait, interview, January 10, 2003.

54. Rime Allaf, "Qatar's Al-Jazeera Is Not Pro-Zionist Enough for Faoud Ajami's Taste," *Daily Star Online* (Beirut), http://www.dailystar.com (accessed December 2, 2003).

55. Ranil Mendis, "The Bias of the Western Media," *Island* (Colombo), Sunday edition, October 28, 2001.

56. Ibid.

57. Ramzy Baroud, "About Bias in the Media," *Milli Gazette*, http://www.milligazette.com (accessed December 2, 2003).

58. Andrea Stone, "Many in Islamic World Doubt Arabs behind 9/11," *USA Today*, February 27, 2002. The poll asked 120 questions but some were banned in certain countries.

59. Tait interview.

60. Sambrook interview.

61. Reuters News, "Newsman Rather Tells Americans Ask More Questions," May 16, 2002.

62. John R. MacArthur, *Second Front: Censorship and Propaganda in the Gulf War* (Berkeley: University of California Press, 1993), p. 101.

63. Ibid., p. 213.

64. Jim Lobe, "Media-U.S.: TV Networks Fall in Line and Salute," Inter Press Service, October 11, 2001; Reuters News, "Newsman Rather Tells Americans Ask More Questions," May 16, 2002.

65. Tait interview.

66. Jayasekera interview.

67. Sambrook interview.

68. Alessandra Stanley, "Opponents of War Are Scarce on Television," *New York Times*, November 9, 2001.

Chapter 5

DEZINFORMATSIYA*
AND OTHER
PATRIOT ACTS

The problem of defense is how far you can go without destroying from within what you are trying to defend from without.

—Dwight D. Eisenhower

A BODYGUARD OF LIES

On October 10, 1990, a fifteen-year-old girl nervously took her seat in front of the Congressional Human Rights Caucus Committee and gave eyewitness testimony to the atrocities committed by Iraqi soldiers during the invasion of Kuwait. In an often tearful statement, the girl, who for security reasons could only be referred to as Nayirah, told the Caucus Committee that she had gone to Kuwait with her mother to visit her sister who had recently given birth.

---

*Russian word for "disinformation"

Speaking of the invasion of Kuwait by the Iraqis, Nayirah said, "I only pray that none of my tenth-grade classmates had a summer vacation like I did. . . . What I saw happening to the children of Kuwait and to my country has changed my life forever, has changed the life of Kuwaitis, young and old." The girl told the dramatic story of the invasion, her sister's escape across the desert and her decision to remain in Kuwait as a volunteer at the Al-Idar Hospital. Describing the actions of Iraqi soldiers when they came to the hospital, Nayirah said, "While I was there, I saw the Iraqi soldiers come into the hospital with guns. They took the babies out of the incubators, took the incubators and left the children to die on the cold floor. It was horrifying. I could not help but think of my nephew who was born premature and who might have died that day as well."[1]

Repeating a claim first made on September 5, 1990, by the *London Daily Telegraph* and subsequently carried by Reuters and in the *Los Angeles Times*, the testimony shocked the public and outraged politicians. CNN and the major television networks aired Nayirah's testimony, and a number of other newspapers published the story. Further credence to the baby-killing story was given when, on October 15, 1990, President Bush reported that the emir of Kuwait had informed him that babies had been taken from their incubators and left to die. Bush later repeated the story in a series of television interviews.[2]

Additional support for the story came later the following month. On November 27, 1990, the United Nations Security Council heard testimony from a Dr. Issah Ibrahim, who said that the "hardest thing was burying the babies. Under my supervision, 120 newborn babies were buried the second week of the invasion. I myself buried 40 newborn babies that had been taken from their incubators by soldiers." The story appeared to be validated when the New York human rights group Middle East Watch and the London-based group Amnesty International (AI) were both quoted as sources in reports confirming the story.

Final confirmation of the story's legitimacy came when a leading Democrat on the House Committee on Foreign Affairs, Stephen Solarez, quoted the story from the AI report and Vice President Dan

Quayle said on February 15, 1991, "There are pictures Saddam doesn't want us to see. Pictures of premature babies in Kuwait that were tossed out of the incubators and left to die."[3]

The only problem with the story was that Nayirah's testimony was utterly false. Instead of being the brave volunteer that she claimed, Nayirah was, in fact, the daughter of Kuwait's ambassador to Washington, Saud Nasir al-Sabah, who had attended the hearing in Washington. There had been no visit to Kuwait, no pregnant sister, and no work in a hospital. Both Nayirah and the people who had coached her had taken advantage of the fact that, as a non-Congressional body, the Congressional Human Rights Caucus Committee was not bound by laws covering false testimony. Moreover, there were reasons why this body may have had a vested interest in the girl's stories.

Regarding the Human Rights Caucus Committee, appearances were also deceiving. The body was chaired by California Democrat Tom Lantos and Illinois Republican John Porter, who also chaired the Congressional Human Rights Foundation, a separate organization that received rent-free accommodation in the offices of the Washington headquarters of Hill and Knowlton.[4] One of the largest public relations firms in the world, Hill and Knowlton had been hired by the Citizens for a Free Kuwait, an organization made up of influential Kuwaitis created to make the case for American military intervention against Iraq.

The evidence given before the United Nations Security Council was also tainted. Dr. Issah Ibrahim turned out to be a pseudonym for a dentist named Dr. Issah Behbehani, who along with a number of other key witnesses had received coaching for his appearance before the Council from a Hill and Knowlton public relations team.[5] Once again, none of these witnesses was under oath, and as a result, they could say what they pleased. After the hearing, the United Nations Security Council passed a resolution authorizing members to use military force to dislodge the Iraqi army in Kuwait.[6]

It was to be a similar story in the United States Congress. On January 12, 1991, the Senate voted to support the Bush administration in what amounted to a declaration of war. Victory for the resolution was secured by a narrow margin of six votes. According to John R. MacArthur in his editorial for the *New York Times* in January 1992, the baby-killing story "likely influenced the seven senators," who cited it when backing the resolution.[7] Afterward, when asked if people should have known about the allegation about Nayirah, the cochairman of the Congressional Human Rights Committee, Senator Porter, conceded, "Yes, I think people . . . were entitled to know the source of her testimony."

Nayirah's story was a classic disinformation operation aimed at influencing both politicians and the public. Her story became a shorthand means of expressing the cruelty of Hussein's regime while at the same time justifying the need for armed intervention in Kuwait. However, before it could be readily accepted, it had to go through a process of legitimization. Step one was to create a story that sounded plausible. Given the fact that Hussein had undoubtedly been guilty of a series of horrendous human rights abuses against his own people, the idea that he might engage in brutality against the people of Kuwait was accepted without hesitation. Furthermore, there is no doubt that atrocities were committed, although the murders of the children in Nayirah's story were not among them.

Step two was to choose a believable and sympathetic witness such as Nayirah, who, with her youth and her gift for display of emotion, was the perfect person to deliver the message of Hussein's barbarity to the world. Step three was to present the statement in a respectable forum—in this case, a human rights hearing that had all the trappings of a congressional hearing and that traded on the names of the politicians associated with the body. The effect was to create an environment in which people were unwilling to question the testimony.

Step four was to affirm its legitimacy by disseminating the story through the media, capitalizing on their reputation for exposing the truth. At this stage, the president also helped by repeating the story in numerous interviews. The final step was to dupe credible human rights organizations such as Amnesty International into supporting the lie.

Confronted by public opinion, blanket media coverage of the

invasion of Kuwait by Iraq, the evidence of responsible human rights organizations, and the belief of their own president, politicians from both parties were bound to accept the story's veracity. The lie about the Iraqi soldiers who murdered babies had been laundered, cleansed of its impurities, and presented to the public as fact.

The case of Nayirah demonstrates that the media are pivotal to the success of any disinformation program: The further the tainted information is removed from its original disseminator, the greater its chance of being believed. False information fed to the media is often repackaged, attached to a so-called hook, and presented to the public surrounded by quotations from politicians and the opinions of experts. In this way, it gains the patina of respectability and, with each appearance in the media, becomes more believable. When all the major news outlets are carrying the story, the public has little chance of finding contrasting opinions. At this stage, the truth of the story is shown by the number of times it appears in different media—the story itself becomes the evidence for the story.

One of the fundamental problems in such cases is the process that the media use in checking their stories. If the sources used to verify the information are also corrupted, whether intentionally or not, the overall effect is merely to reaffirm the disinformation. A glance at the Nayirah story reveals this process at work. While the Caucus Committee and United Nations Security Council lent authority to the stories, it was the repetition of the story in the reports of two highly reputable human rights organizations that actually convinced the media that the baby-killing story was true.[8]

Another serious problem arises over government participation in propagating disinformation. If it is true that modern governments have come to rely on the media as a bridge between the political and public spheres, then it is equally true that the media have come to rely on administration officials for some of their stories. Implicit in this relationship is the belief that journalists are being told the truth at press conferences and briefings and in interviews. But what if a government chooses to be disingenuous?

While the American media have never really faced a government that was totally flexible in its attitude toward disinformation—previous administrations have preferred to stonewall the media—a number of events after September 11 persuaded many that the Bush administration was at least willing to blur the divide between information and disinformation. On September 20, 2001, addressing a joint session of Congress, President Bush said that Americans should expect a long campaign against the terrorists and not just a single battle. This war, he said, would be unlike those that had gone before it and "[might] include dramatic strikes, visible on TV, and covert operations, secret even in success."[9] Although Bush appeared to be addressing the need for secrecy regarding covert operations, his emphasis on "secret" conjured up the possibility of a secret war without government accountability.

This fear was heightened at a press conference given by Defense Secretary Donald Rumsfeld. Speaking to journalists on September 25, 2001, Rumsfeld fielded a series of questions on whether he had halted a government information campaign to disprove the Taliban's assertions that it was unaware of the whereabouts of Osama bin Laden. After commenting that no campaign against the media existed, Rumsfeld was asked whether there were any circumstances in which the Defense Department would be authorized to lie to the media. Paraphrasing Winston Churchill, he said, "Sometimes the truth is so precious it must be accompanied by a bodyguard of lies," and added that he did not recall ever lying to the press and could not imagine a situation where he would do so.[10] His words were not reassuring; indeed, the comment appeared to be a tacit admission that Rumsfeld believed that some circumstances might necessitate lies.

Adding to these worries were the administration's ambiguous statements regarding President Bush's activities on the day that the terrorist attacks took place. On September 11, Bush was speaking to a class at an elementary school in Sarasota, Florida, when he was informed of the attack. After being briefed, he returned to inform the assembled media of the events and left for the airport. At approximately 1:00 P.M. eastern time (EDT), Bush delivered a speech at Barksdale Air Force Base in Louisiana before flying to Offutt Air Force Base in Nebraska. The president returned to the White House at 6:54 P.M. (EDT).

Given the fact that the September 11 attacks were seen as the worst perpetrated on American soil since the 1941 attack on Pearl Harbor, the president was widely criticized for not being visible and for appearing indecisive at a time when the American people were in need. On September 12, the *New York Times*'s William Safire said in an editorial, "Bush should have insisted on coming right back to the Washington area, broadcasting—live and calm—from a facility not far from the White House."[11]

Reacting to this criticism, advisors for Bush hastened to explain the president's failure to return immediately to Washington. At a briefing on September 12, Fleischer said that a credible threat had been made by telephone stating that Air Force One would be attacked next. The message was apparently passed on to the president's staff by the Secret Service. Fleischer's comments were later supported by Vice President Dick Cheney, who said of the threat, "I think it was a credible threat, enough for the Secret Service to bring it to me." In the *New Yorker* on September 28, 2001, Bush's leading strategist, Karl Rove, was quoted as saying, "We . . . [had] specific information that the White House and Air Force One were also intended targets of these attacks."[12]

The media campaign appeared to succeed, and by the afternoon of September 12, 2001, stories of the "credible threat" were being published by Reuters. However, within two weeks, the story of the threat was disproved. On September 26, 2001, a senior official said in an obscure and ambivalent statement that the administration had determined the threat was not real: "What was said about Air Force One was said because it was accurate at the time."[13]

Against this background, the media feared that the war in Afghanistan and the constant threat of terrorism might lead to disinformation being planted in the media. Further evidence for this view came with a February 19, 2002, story in the *New York Times* revealing the creation of a body called the Office of Strategic Influence (OSI). According to the article, the Pentagon was prepared to develop news items containing disinformation for foreign media organizations. The effort was part of a new military public diplomacy initiative designed to influence public opinion and policy makers in "friendly and unfriendly countries." The article reported that the OSI, with a staff of fifteen headed by Brig. Gen. Simon Worden of the air force, had been opened shortly after the September 11 attacks in direct response to the Bush administration's worries over the loss of overseas support, particularly in Islamic countries, for its war against terrorism. Regarding the type of operations that the organization would oversee, the article quoted an unnamed official who said, "It goes from the blackest of black programs to the whitest of white."[14]

Another official said that news would be planted in foreign media organizations using "outside concerns" with no discernable ties to the Pentagon. Connected to the issue of appearing at arms length from the government, there was an associated idea for sending the media and civil leaders e-mail messages promoting America or attacking unfriendly governments. "The return address will probably be a dot.com and not a dot.mil," said an unidentified senior Pentagon official, implying that the recipients would be unable to determine whether the message was a Pentagon-generated e-mail.[15]

The *New York Times* article alleged that the Pentagon, in a move that replicated the hiring of Hill and Knowlton by the Citizens for a Free Kuwait, had hired the Rendon Group, a consulting firm based in Washington with an apparent history of working with the CIA and the Kuwaiti royal family. By coincidence, the Rendon Group, like Hill and Knowlton, had denounced atrocities during the invasion of Kuwait. Other private companies would also be hired to develop information strategies to be used by the OSI.[16]

Once the story broke, it caused a storm of criticism among the media. Critics of the new disinformation policies pointed out that the organization would undermine the country's relationship with its allies. More worrisome, information placed in foreign media outlets might be picked up by local media. Known as "blowback," this situation would make nonsense of the administration's argument that the OSI would make a distinction between domestic and foreign media.

At a time when advertising guru Charlotte Beers was still finding her feet as under-secretary of state for diplomacy and, as such, had yet to make inroads into Middle Eastern cynicism toward America, the creation of a body devoted to spreading rumors and untruths would not make her job any easier. On the contrary, her task would be made much more difficult as news of the OSI's existence reinforced long-held suspicions in the Middle East that the Western media were tools of the U.S. government.

In a letter sent to Defense Secretary Rumsfeld, the Paris-based press freedom organization Reporters Sans Frontières (RSF) said that the OSI "could ruin the image of the United States and discredit information provided by the Secretary of Defense." On the subject of OSI, Robert Menard, secretary-general of RSF, said, "How can the United States explain its use of propaganda and disinformation after they strongly denounced the 'propaganda' of Osama bin Laden and the media that broadcast it?"[17] The *Palm Beach Post* also heavily criticized the OSI in an article dated February 26, 2002: "The country that lies abroad in the name of truth is capable of becoming the country that lies at home in the name of security."[18]

Abroad, the criticism was equally damning. The French newspaper *L'Humanite* said, "The fact that it has been announced officially is telling of the scorn that the American administration has for its own public's opinion and that of the rest of the world." Also in France, *Le Figaro* commented, "The game for the media of the world will consist of being able to distinguish the truth from lies. Those who bluff best will win the most." The Italian newspaper *Il Sole* lamented, "This is a strategy that, in order to achieve its goals, will not exclude the release of false information . . . ," while *Komsomolskaya Pravda* in Russia blasted the Pentagon for its decision to "launch a campaign to brainwash the world."[19]

In the face of strong criticism, the Pentagon and the State Department sought to distance themselves from some of the claims regarding the OSI's potential disinformation programs. On February 20, 2002, Under Secretary of Defense for Policy Douglas Feith, the man in overall control of the OSI, attended a breakfast meeting of the media's Defense Writers Group. Opening the discussion, Feith said that Defense Department officials always speak the truth when they speak to the public. When questioned on the subject of disinformation programs, Feith said that the OSI would not endanger the military's public affairs program but that it was important to use information to facilitate the mission of the military. He went on to deny that the military ever undertook covert operations in the field of information: "The Defense Department doesn't do covert actions," he said. Later in the briefing, Feith stated, "We're going to preserve our credibility and we're going to preserve the purity of the statements that defense officials make to the public. . . . We're not going to have defense officials lying to the public." Toward the end of the meeting, the undersecretary said that officials also would not lie to the media.[20] What Feith did not say, however, was that the answer to this thorny problem could be found in the February 19 *New York Times* article, which had stated that information would be fed to the media via "outside concerns" with no "obvious ties to the Pentagon." This strategy would allow the Defense Department to tell untruths to the world, while allowing officials to preserve their "purity."

That same day, when talking to the media, Secretary of Defense Rumsfeld rejected the possibility that the Pentagon would use disinformation; however, he refused to rule out the use of "tactical manipulation." His words increased the confusion as there appeared to be little difference between the two concepts. In a February 24, 2002, interview with Tim Russert on NBC's *Meet the Press*, Rumsfeld provided an example of "tactical manipulation" when he explained that the concept involved the possible use of army maneuvers to confuse the enemy. He said that the press might report on the activities and these reports might fool the enemy into thinking that an attack might occur at a certain time or in a certain way. Regarding the question of the OSI's future, the Secretary of Defense said, "I think the person in charge is debating whether it should exist in its current form, given all the misinformation and adverse publicity that it's received."[21]

According to Press Secretary Ari Fleischer, who was speaking to the media on February 25, 2002, the president had also made it known that he was not in favor of the new organization: "The president would be troubled by any office that does not as a matter of public policy disseminate the truth and the facts." Fleischer also stated that the president had not been aware of the body's existence until it was reported in the media.[22]

Finally, on February 26, 2002, Rumsfeld announced that the OSI would be closed down. "I met with Under-Secretary [of Defense for Policy] Doug Feith this morning, and he indicated to me that he's decided to close down the Office of Strategic Influence," Rumsfeld told reporters. Commenting on the OSI's demise, Rumsfeld later said the OSI "was so damaged, that it's pretty clear to me that it could not function effectively."[23]

It is difficult to give definitive answers to the question of the OSI's role. As one would expect with an organization tasked with spreading disinformation, the OSI itself was also swathed in disinformation. It is entirely possible that the Bush administration created the OSI with the idea of using it as a vehicle for a broad range of public diplomacy initiatives, including the spreading of disinformation among foreign news outlets. Alternatively, it is possible that the OSI's existence was leaked in order to see whether the public and the media would find it acceptable. It could also have been used as a means of reinforcing the perception that top officials—those in charge of the war on terrorism—did not lie and would not countenance lies. In other words, the OSI was a tool in a very slick public relations campaign aimed at ensuring that everyone involved looked good.

The *Washington Times*, however, had other ideas. In an article by Rowan Scarborough dated February 25, 2002, the newspaper said that the OSI had made no plans to falsify stories and that the reason for its existence was to "get the truth" to places like Iran and Iraq. Why, Scarborough asked, did the Pentagon and, in particular, Assistant Secretary of Defense for Public Affairs Victoria Clarke fail to defend the OSI?[24] A number of critics, including Scott Shuger in *Slate* magazine, said it was because the Pentagon spokeswoman feared that the OSI would interfere with her own department's attempts to provide information.[25]

In an article in *Insight on the News*, Paul Rodriguez asserted that Feith and Deputy Defense Secretary Paul Wolfowitz prepared a press release, which was to be signed by Assistant Secretary Clarke, in response to the *New York Times* article. The press release quoted Rumsfeld's February 20 statement that he would not lie and ended with, "Neither I nor any other responsible Department of Defense official have knowledge of, have proposed or have entertained plans which would have violated the secretary's [February 20] statement." Both Feith and Wolfowitz drew back from pressuring Clarke into signing the press release.[26]

When announcing that the OSI was being disbanded, Rumsfeld remarked, "It's over. What do you want, blood?" However, it was likely that some of the functions of the defunct organization would be unloaded onto another agency. Given the fact that disinformation is as old as war itself, this was a largely phantom victory for the media.

Irrespective of the reasons for establishing the OSI, the entire episode was a total public relations failure for the Bush administration, which had once again undermined its own attempts to win hearts and minds in the Middle East. Following, as it did, the Al-Jazeera and bin Laden video tape incidents, the OSI fiasco could only do further damage to the reputation of the United States. Sworn into her new job in early October 2001, Under-Secretary of State for Diplomacy Charlotte Beers, who was given the delicate job of transforming the United States' image abroad, must have winced at the negative publicity her country received around the world.

In a telling postscript to the OSI story, a December 2002 *New York Times* article said that the Defense Department was considering issuing a secret directive telling the military to devise covert operations with the specific intention of influencing public opinion and policy makers in friendly and neutral countries. The OSI had been reborn.[27]

THE PHANTOM OF LOST LIBERTY?

The horror and sheer scale of the September 11 attacks exposed the vulnerability of the world's only superpower within its own borders. Once the Bush administration recovered from its initial shock from the attack, it calmly set about gearing both itself and the country for a war against the Taliban regime that shielded bin Laden and his criminal associates and a wider war against the al-Qaeda networks, wherever they were based. At the same time, on the home front, the government conducted a thorough review of all security measures in an attempt to prevent any further attacks on America's civilian population.

Such a sweeping reevaluation of the country's domestic security involved an in-depth analysis of its information laws. In this post-September 11 world, the Bush administration expressed continual fears that information leaked to enemies would have disastrous results. As Attorney General John Ashcroft wrote in a memorandum, "It is only through a well-informed citizenry that the leaders of our nation remain accountable to the governed," but he added, "The Department of Justice and this administration are equally committed to protecting other fundamental values. Among them are safeguarding our national security [and] enhancing the effectiveness of our law enforcement agencies."[28] In these two sentences, Ashcroft summed up the dilemma of the United States: how to strike a balance between preserving much-cherished civil rights, such as freedom of the press, and securing and protecting the country.

Although at this time much of the American public might well have argued that "life" came before "liberty," others argued equally passionately that holding on to the rights guaranteed by the Constitution showed that the terrorist attacks would not change American society. Otherwise, they argued, individual rights and liberties would become so devalued that there would be little difference between those who would protect American society and those who had perpetrated the attacks.

While this debate continues in the United States, it is undoubtedly true that, almost immediately after the attacks, the Bush administration started to turn off some of the taps through which information flowed. Moreover, with the administration's emphasis on secrecy in the war against terrorism, and with officials displaying an increasing reticence to disclose information, institutions such as the media found it difficult to investigate the government's activities.

One of the first examples of the Bush administration's desire to control information came with its attack on the most fundamental weapon in an investigative journalist's arsenal, the Freedom of Information Act (FOIA). The FOIA was first enacted by Congress and signed into existence by Lyndon Johnson in 1966, but it was not given any real substance until 1974, when Congress passed the Privacy Act 1974, setting aside the veto of President Gerald Ford. Since then, the FOIA has often been described as "[journalism's] post-Watergate reward" and "one of our greatest democratic reforms."[29] By virtue of the act, journalists can make official requests for politicians and government agencies to reveal their public records and documents. The FOIA is pivotal in allowing citizens, journalists, and civil society organizations to investigate the activities of government in all their different guises.

Within the postwar history of the media, a number of examples show the true power of the FOIA and the way in which the media has applied it. In one case, the *Charlotte Observer* used the FOIA to show how the Duke Power Company used questionable accounting rules to avoid breaching defined profit limits. Similarly, *USA Today* used the legislation to expose financial and sexual scandals among the National Guard.[30]

On October 12, Ashcroft issued a memorandum on the FOIA that at first sight may not have appeared particularly damaging, but, according to a number of different organizations, announced a sudden sea change in the way government would handle requests for information. In the memorandum, Ashcroft first reminded the heads of all government departments and agencies of exemptions that existed under the FOIA, then asked them to consider whether "institutional, commercial, and personal privacy interests could be implicated by disclosure of the information." If they could be, Ashcroft continued, "when you carefully consider FOIA requests and decide to withhold records, in whole or in part, you can be assured that the Department of Justice will defend your decisions unless they lack a sound legal basis or present an unwarranted risk of adverse impact on the ability of other agencies to protect other important records."[31]

Ashcroft's decision reversed the directive supporting disclosure issued by President Bill Clinton's attorney general, Janet Reno. The earlier directive instructed departments and agencies not to use "discretionary exemptions" unless an element of "foreseeable harm" could be derived from the disclosure. The Ashcroft memorandum made it clear that the burden had been reversed: The new directive was expressed negatively rather than positively, meaning that where a sound basis for refusal existed, it should be exercised. Ashcroft's statements announced a return to the standard once used by Attorney General William French Smith, a Reagan appointee.[32]

On October 18, 2001, the Office of Information and Privacy (OIP) held a follow-up meeting with agency staff members. At the closed-door session, the OIP referred to a 1989 statement that an exemption connected "solely to the internal personnel rules and practices of an agency" should be used to halt requests relating to "vulnerabilities." With the emphasis now on withholding information, a memorandum by Chief of White House Staff Andrew Card Jr. in late March 2002 told all agencies to review their safety procedures for sensitive information.

Card's memorandum also encompassed records, informing agencies that they should keep classified those types of information that were already excluded under the rules and that could "reveal information that would assist in the development or use of weapons of mass destruction." It said that this guideline should be adhered to even when the information is more than ten years old. In addition, Card stated that loopholes in the FOIA should be exploited if the information is more than twenty-five years old.[33]

With FOIA rules restricted and with fears of further attacks still occupying the minds of the Bush administration, it came as no surprise that a number of government agencies withdrew or altered their Web sites. These agencies included the Department of Energy, the Federal Aviation Administration, the NASA Glenn Research Unit, and the International Nuclear Safety Center. In one instance, the Nuclear Regulatory Commission (NRC) closed its Web site, but had restored a number of pages by March 2002. Most of the Web sites were altered owing to worries that they contained information that might assist terrorists, but the *Nation* claimed that the Environmental Protection Authority had removed information on "the dangers of chemical accidents and how to prevent them."[34] Here was a sign that, in the early days, little thought had been given to what would assist the terrorists and what would benefit the public.

In the early part of 2002, the Bush administration began withdrawing more than 6,600 technical documents from the public sphere. According to an article in the *New York Times*, the administration was also asking "scientific societies" to limit what they published in research reports.[35] While scientists generally saw this request as an attempt to keep harmful information about weapons of mass destruction out of the hands of terrorists, a number of others viewed the withdrawal as unnecessary. The article quoted a doctor from the American Society of Microbiology as saying, "There is very little that comes out of University labs that could conceivably be sensitive." He also said that the publication of basic research furthers important discussions on matters such as the bioengineering of viruses. If this discussion failed to take place, he concluded, it might hinder the production of vital vaccines. In response to the criticisms, the government said that it was reviewing the federal documents and would decide later whether they could be made public again.[36]

Additional proof of this change in attitude toward the FOIA and the free flow of information in general came with Ashcroft's testimony before the Senate Judiciary Committee on December 6, 2001. In his opening statement, Ashcroft said,

> We need honest, reasoned debate, not fear mongering. To those who pit Americans against immigrants, and citizens against non-citizens; to those who scare peace-loving people with phantoms of lost liberty; my message is this: Your tactics only aid terrorists—for they erode our national unity and diminish our resolve. They give ammunition to America's enemies, and pause to America's friends. They encourage people of good will to remain silent in the face of evil.[37]

By equating critics with those who aid and abet terrorists, Ashcroft intimated that the period after September 11 was not a time for criticism. In his words, critics "erode" unity and "diminish" resolve. Using portentous and overblown language, the attorney general appeared to suggest that there is something malicious and unpatriotic about criticizing your country. The underlying implication was that "we," meaning the amorphous conjunction of government and country, were above being censured.

Meanwhile, those who would disparage the government, and by this it was obvious that Ashcroft meant the media and civil society organizations, risked the security of the nation. In this morality tale, such groups were evil tempters at a time when Eden faced its greatest trial. Significantly, it is possible to see links between this express view and the narrowing of the rights previously enjoyed under the FOIA. To hold government accountable, it was necessary for journalists to request documents, but in the eyes of the Bush administration, doing so amounted to criticism and, to borrow Ashcroft's phrase, risked "giving ammunition to America's enemies." By cutting off the free flow of information, the government was able to silence its critics in the name of security.

Replying to Ashcroft's comments, civil society organizations vigorously rebutted the idea that it was wrong to dissent from the views of the government. Ralph G. Neas, president of People for the American Way, said, "Smothering dissent is not the American way" and accused Ashcroft of attempting to intimidate his critics into silence.[38] A barrage of criticism also came from two of America's top newspapers. In a terse editorial published on the day after the Senate Judiciary Committee hearing, the *Washington Post* argued, "[I]f American political history stands for one solitary point it is that democratic debate makes the country stronger. . . . Mr. Ashcroft may not like the criticism. But his job is to defend dissent, not to use the moral authority of his office to discourage people from participating in one of the most fundamental obligations of citizenship."[39]

Adding its own condemnation, a *New York Times* editorial said, "The attorney general rashly claimed that some critics of the administration 'only aid terrorists' because they 'give ammunition to America's enemies and pause to our friends.' Mr. Ashcroft has that one completely backward."[40]

In a statement that raised more issues than it settled, Justice Department spokesperson Mindy Tucker defended Ashcroft. After saying that Ashcroft did not want misinformation and misstatements to be spread, Tucker commented, "Anyone who reported this morning that he criticized anyone who opposed him was absolutely wrong and in doing so became part of the exact problem he was describing."[41] However, this comment failed to adequately explain Ashcroft's extraordinary statement about "those who scare peace-loving people with phantoms of lost liberty," a phrase entirely unconnected to worries about misinformation.

During this period, the Bush administration also chastised Congress for its failure to prevent leaks to the media. On October 5, 2001, in a memorandum on "Disclosures to the Congress" similar to that written on the FOIA, Bush informed the heads of six agencies that only they or a designated officer could brief members of Congress on "classified information" or "sensitive law enforcement information." The memorandum specified those members of Congress who were entitled to receive sensitive information: the Speaker of the House, the House minority leader, the Senate majority and minority leaders, and the chairs and ranking members of the intelligence committees in the House and Senate. All other members of Congress were to be excluded from the information loop.[42]

Expanding on the decision in a press conference on October 9, 2001, Fleischer said, "It's a reflection of the fact that our nation is at war and the rules have changed. . . . It's a reflection of the reality that disclosure of information in a time of war is far different from an inadvertent disclosure at a time of peace. It could literally mean the loss of lives of people who are embarking on missions."[43] Congress reacted by threatening to suspend all legislative hearings. "The defense bill is not moving until we are included," said Alaska Senator Ted Stevens, a Republican on the Senate Appropriations Committee. "I think it's an overreaction," said Alabama Senator Richard Shelby when interviewed on CNN.[44] The new rule was later relaxed in an apparent attempt to mend fences between the executive and legislative branches.

Additional evidence of the government's wish to control the flow of information came in a letter dated October 2, 2001, from Under-Secretary of Defense E. C. "Pete" Aldridge, who wrote to all defense contractors on behalf of the Pentagon. In the letter, Aldridge reminded contractors that it was important to use discretion "in all the public statements, press releases, and communications made by your respective companies." Another memorandum from Aldrige to

Pentagon staff members responsible for acquisition forbade them to speak with the media: "Effective immediately, I don't want anyone with the Air Force acquisition community discussing any of our programs. . . ."[45] While it is understandable that some information regarding military acquisitions should remain secret for operation reasons, the two letters together provide an insight into the administration's tactics. Outside contractors were to be cowed by reminders of "[the] national emergency," but military personnel could be ordered to obey.

With concerns over the possibility of an "information lockdown," twenty-one journalism groups, including the Society of Professional Journalists (SPJ), released a statement on October 13, 2001, saying that, while it was acceptable for governments to take "unusual measures" during war, such restrictions "pose dangers to American democracy." Al Cross of the SPJ was quoted as saying that the media were "finding it increasingly difficult to fulfill their role as watchdogs."[46]

Controversy once again flared over access to information with the revelation in the *Guardian* (London), on October 17, 2001, that the National Imagery and Mapping Agency (NIMA) had purchased exclusive rights to the images taken by the commercial satellite Ikonos. Owned by the Denver-based company Space Imaging, the satellite was capable of producing highly accurate photographs of Afghanistan. Significantly, the NIMA contract did not appear to be tailored toward any specific need; the American military had seven satellites in orbit, named keyholes, which were estimated to be "six to ten times better than the resolution available from Ikonos."[47] By law, the U.S. Defense Department had the right to exercise "shutter control"—meaning that it could prevent photographs from being taken—over all civilian satellites launched from American soil. The law was introduced as a means of preventing enemies from using the pictures during a war with America.

However, had the government elected to exercise "shutter control," the consequence might have been an outcry from the media. Speaking to the *Guardian*, Dr. John Pike of Global Security, a U.S. Web site that publishes military satellite pictures, said, "If they had imposed shutter control, it is entirely possible that news organizations would have filed a lawsuit against the government arguing prior restraint censorship."[48]

There may have been other reasons for purchasing the exclusive rights—reasons related to the military strategy of the war. During early October, newspapers began to report increased numbers of civilian deaths caused by the allied bombing campaign. Indeed, six days before the Ikonos story was published, there were reports of civilian casualties during the bombing of al-Qaeda camps near Darunta, northwest of Jalalabad. As in the first Gulf War, the Pentagon briefings back home often failed to reflect this side of the war and, with journalists often far from the scenes of destruction, it was difficult to confirm such stories. The removal of satellite images allowed the military to use the briefings as a means of highlighting the successes and downplaying failures, including injuries to civilians. The military's own views went unchallenged and potentially embarrassing images were avoided.

Moreover, the incident was reminiscent of an event in the first Gulf War that went straight to the heart of what can happen if the media are deprived of independent information sources. The incident showed how much easier it is to sell a story when a vacuum of information exists in the media. Before the Gulf War in 1991, the American government claimed that by mid-September 1990 some 250,000 Iraqi troops were massing on the border between Kuwait and Saudi Arabia and awaiting orders to invade its second Gulf state. Much of the talk in this period revolved around the number of tanks that Saddam's army owned and the fighting qualities of the Iraqi Republican Guard. At the time, only one media organization challenged the view that this information was a major factor in Bush's decision to intervene—Florida's *St. Petersburg Times*. On January 6, 1991, the newspaper revealed that satellite pictures taken on August 8, 1990, by a Soviet company called Soyuz Karta showed no evidence of the massive Iraqi troop build-up claimed by the U.S government. The images originated from a Japanese newspaper whose edition had approached an expert on satellite imagery to decipher their meaning. Photographs taken on September 13 by the same company also showed no Iraqi installations.[49] Throughout the war, the government claimed that one of the main reasons for intervening in Kuwait was to prevent a further assault on Saudi Arabia. If there was a military threat, the satellite pictures failed to prove Hussein's intent.

With Gulf War veterans Cheney and Powell advising President George W. Bush on the war in Afghanistan, it seems likely that the decision to purchase the Ikonos images may have been motivated by the Soyuz Karta experience. New legislation also had an impact on the media. During the period after the attacks, Congress came under pressure to pass new laws capable of preventing further acts of terrorism in America. One such law was the hastily enacted Uniting and Strengthening America by Providing Appropriate Tools Required to Intercept and Obstruct Terrorism Act—the USA Patriot Act.[50] Signed by the president on October 26, 2001, barely six weeks after the attacks, the new law widened the Foreign Intelligence Surveillance Act, by giving the government new powers over immigrants, libraries, and the Internet. A new section labeled dissent as a terrorist activity, raising the spector of "guilt by association" normally forbidden by the First Amendment.[51]

Under the USA Patriot Act, the Federal Bureau of Investigation (FBI) can demand access to anyone's business or personal records including medical, student, bank, and library records—"to protect against . . . clandestine intelligence activities."[52] The new law has had a particularly detrimental effect on libraries. For the first time, America's security agencies have the power to examine the reading habits of individual citizens. In accordance with the act, librarians are prevented from informing the person or anyone else that such a procedure has been activated. As Judith Krug, the American Library Association's Director for Intellectual Freedom, has said, "[T]hese records and this information can be had with so little reason or explanation. It's super secret, and anyone who wants to talk about what the FBI did at their library faces prosecution. That has nothing to do with patriotism."[53]

Regarding the notion of "guilt by association," section 411 of the act authorized the secretary of state to designate certain domestic or foreign groups as "terrorist groups" if they have engaged in violent activities. Members of these groups who are not American citizens may be detained and deported unless they can prove that they did not know or could not have known that they were assisting a terrorist activity. The section shifts the burden of proof away from the state and places it firmly with the individual. This requirement amounts to the resurrection of laws such as the old McWarren-Walter Act, which barred people who, in some form or other, had advocated communism from entering America. In the past, these laws have been struck down by the courts.

In this new war against terrorism, capturing information from the Internet is also a fundamental priority. By virtue of section 216 of the USA Patriot Act, the FBI can examine Internet addresses without needing to guarantee that the information will remain confidential. The new law removes the probable cause requirement and limits the ability of the judiciary to review the internal decision-making process. Where the FBI needs prior approval, applications to the courts are to be made *ex-parte*. As a result, the suspect is deprived of the right to argue against the application.

The new law also allows for the increased use of new surveillance equipment, such as the notorious "Carnivore," or as it is now known, DCS1000. The equipment may be used at the headquarters of an Internet service provider to track a suspect's e-mail. Perhaps more worryingly, it can also be used to download files and Web pages from the suspect's computer and, if the need arises, to reconstruct e-mail that has been deleted. With the removal under the Act of the traditional need for judicial authorization and "probable cause," there were concerns from freedom of expression groups that the law could be used against innocent users of the Internet.

Many critics of the new law have argued that, whereas in the past, proof was needed before searches were authorized, the USA Patriot Act has lowered the standard to the degree that an FBI employee can merely theorize a need for a search. A number of journalists fear that the new powers could be applied to them—a fear exacerbated by the pre-USA Patriot Act case of Associated Press journalist John Solomon.

On August 20, 2001, Solomon received a letter from U.S. Attorney Mary Jo White informing him that the U.S. Attorney's Office had obtained the records of his incoming and outgoing telephone calls between May 2 and May 7, 2001. The decision had been made by the office after Solomon quoted an unidentified law official who confirmed that a certain senator was under investigation. Under U.S. law, it is illegal for a law enforcement officer to disclose information obtained by a federal wiretap. The U.S. Attorney's Office obtained Solomon's telephone records in an attempt to discover the identity of the officer.[54]

Although the Solomon case occurred before the enactment of the USA Patriot Act, it serves as a serious warning on the matter of federal power. The case proved that the federal government was capable of building a legal case by using a journalist's personal phone records without informing him until after the fact. The USA Patriot Act would allow investigations similar to Solomon's to be conducted in the name of the war against terrorism. Furthermore, such investigations would be conducted without showing probable cause, implying as it does the traditional oversight of the judiciary, and might also involve an examination of library and Internet data. Solomon's case also promoted a worry that investigative reporters would be used unwittingly by the security forces to track down potential criminals.

Recognizing the assault on a journalist's right to confidential sources, a number of press freedom organizations accused the federal government of abusing its powers. Writing on September 10, 2001, about the Solomon case, Johann P. Fritz, director of the International Press Institute, invited Attorney General Ashcroft to take note of the following statement by Justice Byron White in the case of *Branzburg* v. *Hayes*: "[We] do not hold . . . that state and federal authorities are free to annex the news media as an investigative arm of the government." Fritz also said in the letter that "the decision . . . will also have an inhibiting effect upon press freedom. . . . In seeking retribution . . . the government is hindering the [free] flow of information. . . ."[55]

Troubling issues were also raised by the announcement of the Total Information Awareness (TIA) system. At present, the TIA is only a potential research project under the direction of the Defense Advanced Research Projects Agency (DARPA).[56] A second agency—the Office of Information Awareness (OIA)—was created to house the system. With an initial budget of approximately $200 million, the OIA was to be headed by retired Rear Admiral John Poindexter, who was convicted in 1990 of five felony counts of misleading Congress. This conviction was later overturned by an appeals court, which held that Congress had awarded him immunity from prosecution for his evidence.

Using the latest information-storage technologies and computer recognition techniques known as "data-mining," the TIA will allow intelligence analysts to gather and view information in databases and find links "between individuals and groups, respond to automatic alerts, and share information efficiently."[57] According to William Safire of the *New York Times*, the information will be drawn from a number of different sources, including every magazine subscription you buy and medical prescription you fill, every Web site you visit and e-mail you send or receive, every academic record you receive, every bank deposit you make, every trip you book and every event you attend."[58] If successful, the TIA system will create an information dossier on almost everyone living in America.

In effect, the TIA is a highly sophisticated tracking system that traces the electronic footprints left by individuals and hopes to combine this information with photographs from cameras featuring the latest picture-recognition technologies. Once the information has been received, the TIA will be able to make informed connections among the various types of information, flag certain activities as being terrorist in nature, and recommend appropriate action.

Admiral Poindexter spoke about the system in 2002, saying, "We must become much more efficient and more clever in the ways we find new sources of data, mine information from the new and old, generate information, make it available for analysis, convert it to knowledge, and create actionable options."[59] His words held the threat of a massive cyber-net trawling through American society, searching for personal information, improving the government's knowledge of terrorists and their intentions.[60]

An example of the way that TIA would work can be seen in the behavior pattern of the terrorists that carried out the September 11 attacks. A number of the terrorists took flight lessons in the United States, rented apartments, hired rental cars, visited bars, withdrew money from bank accounts, flew in and out of the country, and purchased one-way tickets on the day of the attacks. Many of these activities were carried out with the use of a credit card. The future TIA system would examine this blizzard of electronic information, piece it together with additional information from other agencies, and flag their activities for an immediate response from the FBI or another agency. While such information appears to be of enormous help in the war against terrorism, it could also be used for more malign purposes that have nothing to do with terrorism.

Using the Solomon case as the foundation for a hypothetical example, the TIA system could have been used to track Solomon's movements in order to trace the identity of the federal official who provided the journalist with information. All the TIA system would need to do is triangulate the information of all federal officers with the activities of Solomon. This process would involve examining federal officers' phone calls, their use of credit cards, and pictures from hidden cameras, and then tying this information to Solomon's movements and activities. If Solomon had a telephone conversation with the official, met him or her for lunch and paid with his credit card, it would be possible to carry out a similar check with all the officials in that area to see who might have made mobile telephone calls at the same time, who paid for a meal at the same restaurant on the same day, etc. As a consequence, a journalist could be co-opted into carrying out the work of the FBI.

Using another example, if four journalists in New York make the same FOIA requests for documents, then three of the same journalists purchase airline tickets to Chicago with their credit cards and make phone calls on Lake Shore Drive and one of them has a meal at a Chicago restaurant, once again paying with his or her credit card, the TIA could correlate this information with data on a federal official who made phone calls at the same time and was filmed by security cameras entering the same restaurant on the same day.

By correlating the information, the program would flag when certain agencies were being investigated by journalists, when certain types of documents were being requested, and when journalists were meeting certain people. Instead of being used to fight terrorism, the TIA could be used by the government as an early warning system against investigative journalism. In such an unequal struggle, the government would always have the upper hand over the media. As a result, the government could quickly prepare information campaigns to combat breaking news, or, perhaps more worryingly, it could act to prevent the information from coming to light. George Orwell's Big Brother would then be a reality.

In a powerful editorial, the *Washington Post* said, "Because the legal system designed to protect privacy has yet to catch up with this technology, Congress needs to take a direct interest in this project, and the defense secretary should appoint an outside committee to oversee it before it proceeds."[61] Lee Tien, a civil liberties spokesperson for the Electronic Frontier Foundation, said, "What I don't want to see is a system . . . unable to predict acts of terrorism . . . but perfectly attuned for intimate spying on regular citizens and activists like Martin Luther King [Jr.]."[62]

Another worrying development in the United States was the passage of state laws limiting access to information after September 11. Commenting on security at the state level, the editor and publisher of *Access Reports*, Harry Hammit, said, "Everybody is scrambling to do something that they believe somehow shows they are tough about fighting terrorism."[63] In Florida, for example, the rules committee of the state senate voted to give the senate president powers to close meetings and keep ballots secret, including all votes on bills and any subsequent amendments.[64] The trend was also followed in Idaho, where the attorney general said that it would be advisable if the legislature empowered the governor to withhold documents or records "when necessary for the security of the state." The attorney general also suggested that government employees closely question individuals requesting information. Lawmakers in Iowa discussed a proposal to force journalists to use electronic ID cards to enter the legislature building. Journalists without cards would be prevented from entering the building after the end of the working day and talking to government employees. All journalists applying for a card would be subject to background checks, raising the possibility that journalists might be excluded for reasons other than mere security. In Virginia, lawmakers wished to exclude the freedom of information laws so that they could discuss the threat of terrorism in private, and in South Carolina the state senate government organization committee proposed an amendment to create a homeland security commission exempt from state FOI laws. Many other states also proposed or introduced legislative changes in response to the attacks, and they were a sign that the security concerns of the federal government were broadly reflected at the state level.[65]

After September 11, the Bush administration approached the problem of the flow of information in two different ways. First, it allowed the military to discuss the possibility of disseminating disinformation to foreign media organizations and retreated from this idea only after the clamor for the disbanding of the OSI had become overwhelming. The very public discussion damaged America's image abroad and undermined the public diplomacy efforts of other government agencies.

Second, while the government was forced to confront real security fears, it used them to actively block the free flow of information in America. Perhaps the most egregious examples were the contract for the images from the Ikonos satellite and the aforementioned creation of the TIA. Quite aside from these considerations of information lock-down, there was also the question of information lock-out, when, in the days after the attacks, the movement of journalists was restricted.

LOCKING OUT THE INFORMATION GATEKEEPERS

At a joint press conference with Russian President Vladimir Putin, President Bush was asked about press freedom in America. Bush responded, "[W]hoever thinks I have the capability, or my government has the capability of reining in this press corps, simply doesn't understand the American way."[66] But, in the aftermath of September 11, journalists found the area around the World Trade Center towers cordoned off, a number of journalists were arrested for criminal trespass, and prohibitions on the use of aircraft were enforced against the media.

Immediately after the attack, *Newsweek* sent its journalists onto the streets of New York to obtain eyewitness accounts of the events and to interview those who had managed to escape from the Twin Towers. One such journalist was Arian Campo-Flores, who was stopped by a police officer and told to go back. Unlike many other journalists, Campo-Flores was undeterred, merely retracing his steps and finding another way of getting to the scene of the devastation. "The police weren't organized to keep people out," he said later. "It was a bit easier to move around. If you were stopped at one block, you could kind of work your way around the blocks and maze of downtown, find an opening and find your way around. There was much more serious things than keeping reporters away."[67]

Although the confusion and shock on September 11, as well as fears of another attack, meant that the police had better things to do than shepherd the media, in the days that followed journalists found it increasingly difficult to gain access to the site, and a number were arrested and jailed, while others had their film and press passes confiscated.

On September 15, *New York Times* photographer Tyler Hicks found himself arrested and charged with criminal trespass. The journalist had managed to enter the restricted area but had been caught by two officers, who were escorting him from the area when a ranking police officer told the officers to arrest Hicks, impound his cameras, and confiscate his film. "I was handcuffed on the spot," said the photographer. Hicks spent the night in jail but the charges against him were thrown out by a judge. However, his film was not returned to him on his release from custody.[68]

Ian Austin, a sports photographer, received much the same treatment at the hands of the police. After driving from Maine to New York in the early morning of September 14, Austin walked around the cordon and managed to gain entrance within fifteen blocks of the World Trade Center. "At most of the checkpoints, they turned me away, but one [guard] let me through," he said. Once inside, the photographer was caught by police, who asked for identification and press credentials. "I produced an I.D. but I was not a resident [of New York] and could not produce credentials," said Austin. The sports photographer was told to leave, but as he was walking back he was told to stop. "They handcuffed me, and went through all my camera gear. Between my notebook, my map of New York City and address book, they were very suspicious. So they took me to a captain who said, 'Put him away.'" Like Hicks, Austin was charged with criminal trespass, and he spent three days in jail. The charge was later dropped, but his camera equipment, worth $5,000, was not returned. Speaking of his arrest and incarceration, Austin said, "The atmosphere was ugly. . . . The police told me they were going to make an example of me."[69]

Photographer Emmanuel Dumont and liaison photographer Stephen Ferry were also arrested and jailed. Ferry's story reflects the attitude of the police immediately after the attack, particularly when they believed Ferry was impersonating a firefighter. His resulting criminal prosecution by the city of New York is also significant. Finding himself at the scene of destruction, Ferry, who was on assignment for *Time*, put on firefighter gear to protect himself from the fire and smoke. Later, when a worker handed him a toolbox, the photographer used it to store his camera equipment. For the next two days, he used the toolbox when returning to what became known as Ground Zero. On September 13, Ferry was confronted by police officers and asked to identify himself. As proof of his identity, he produced a New York driver's license that had been altered. Police later charged him with several misdemeanors, including criminal impersonation for possessing the hardhat, work boots, coveralls, and toolbox of a firefighter, and a felony for forging an official document. In his defense, Ferry claimed that he had lost his driver's license while working in Colombia and had altered the expiration date on an old license while he waited for a new one to be sent by the New York Division of Motor Vehicles.

Twenty-eight rolls of film and his camera were also confiscated at the time of the photographer's arrest. Ferry spent four days in jail before being released. He rejected an opportunity to plead guilty to the felony in return for probation. The rolls of film were not included in the offer—they were to be kept by the city. The matter subsequently went to criminal trial and, during pre-trial preparations in February 2002, Ferry started a motion to recover his film from the authorities (by this time his camera had been returned to him). In court, Assistant District Attorney William Beesch argued that Ferry should not be allowed to profit financially or professionally from photographs taken while he was committing a crime. Replying for his client, Ferry's lawyer said that the journalist was prepared to donate money made from the sale of the pictures to charity. Regarding freedom of the press, Ferry's lawyer argued that by refusing to release the film the city was guilty of prior restraint and in violation of the First Amendment. However, the trial judge refused to grant the motion because the photographs were merely evidence of a criminal act and not the subject of the trial and consequently there was no breach of the First Amendment. Despite the decision, Ferry was given access to the photographs in order to prepare his defense.

It is probable that Ferry's case, and in particular the charge of impersonating a firefighter, heightened tension at Ground Zero between the police and the media. Ferry himself was quoted as saying, "At the moment when I put on that fireman's garb, I had no idea that the fire department had taken all those losses. . . . If I had known that, I wouldn't have put the stuff on. Knowing that they'd lost lots of people, it's pretty insensitive."[70]

Journalists faced similar difficulties in Washington, D.C., Pennsylvania, and elsewhere around the country. In Pennsylvania, at the scene of the United Airlines plane crash near Shanksville, William Wendt and assistant Daniel Mahoney were arrested by police for "defiant trespass." According to Wendt, who was on assignment for the New York Times, the two journalists were told by police to register in a tent specially set up for the media and await a bus taking journalists to the crash site. Unable to find the tent, the two wandered into a restricted area and were promptly arrested. Speaking of the incident, Wendt said, "I was worried about being thrown in jail, having to call someone to bail us out, and not getting a picture, so we plead[ed] guilty." Both paid fines and costs amounting to approximately three hundred dollars.[71]

In the nation's capital, Jason Pierce, a staff writer for CNSNews. com, said that when he asked for a good position to take photographs at a White House function nearly three days after the attack, he was told by a policeman not to take pictures. The policeman told Pierce that all people taking photographs would be questioned. Mary Beth Byrd of WTSP/Channel 10 in Tampa, Florida, found herself being questioned by security officers while working on a story examining the mood at an Air Force base. Security officers also seized a camera and videotape, which were later returned with an apology. At Boston's Logan Airport, where two of the hijacked flights originated, television crews were initially asked to park their vans several miles from the airport. The rule was later relaxed.[72]

Sensitive government sites, especially those with a nuclear or military purpose, were also protected from prying eyes by security. On November 28, Jason Henske was arrested while taking photographs of a southern Vermont nuclear power plant for an article in the *Brattleboro Reformer*. He was released after being detained for two hours. Henske had been arrested under Section 3481 of the Vermont Statute, Title 13, which carries a penalty of up to ten years for taking a picture of a nuclear power plant in time of war. Ironically, the Web site for the power plant, even at that time, carried a picture of its own control room.[73]

For several days after the attacks, the Federal Aviation Administration (FAA) shut down the skies over America as a precaution against further attacks using commercial airlines. While a number of restrictions were later removed, the ban on small aircraft, including those used for news gathering and weather reports, continued for a number of days. Restrictions also prevented flights over stadiums and congested city areas. Although a spokesperson for the FAA cited "national security" as the reason, the decision was heavily criticized by the media. The president of the Radio-Television News Director's

Association, Barbara Cochran, wrote letters to the FAA and the Department of Transportation protesting the decision. "Many [journalists] were deeply disturbed by this unprecedented action which limits their ability to serve their communities because they are not able to use news helicopters or other aircraft," Cochran said.[74] She then stated that the government could not show good reason why certain aircraft are allowed to fly while news-oriented planes and helicopters have been grounded: "This comes at a time when people are watching their stations more than ever, looking for news and wanting to be reassured that everything is safe."[75]

Bearing in mind the terrible events of September 11, it is improbable that the restrictions on the movement of journalists were anything other than the reactions of a police force reeling from the considerable loss of life and needing to impose security measures to prevent further attacks. Commenting on the arrests and restrictions, Cochran said, "I've heard of some of the things that happened, but 'sporadic' is exactly the right word to use."[76]

Nevertheless, stories of the media impersonating fireman, which in all likelihood stemmed from the arrest of Ferry, created bad feelings between the police and the media. For this reason, the police were perhaps harsher with journalists than they needed to be. Moreover, as people adjusted to the enormity of the attacks, the situation improved. "If anything, after some of the nervousness in the early days, officials and journalists worked through these issues," declared Cochran.[77] It is interesting to note that, at the site of the Pentagon attack, where security was probably at its highest, there were no reports of journalists being harassed by security agencies.

Although the arrests of journalists immediately after the September 11 attacks did not appear to be part of a government-inspired attempt to prevent the media from reporting, the changes the Bush administration made to the "information environment" at this time were deeply prejudicial to free and fair reporting. Rather than approach the subject of security from the perspective of what should or should not be shielded from the media, the Bush administration sought to impose a blanket ban on many aspects of reporting. The result of this action was to push the journalists to the threshold of a new media environment in which security claims outweighed freedom of the press. Inevitably, this pattern of behavior would be observed by other countries that had much to gain from the events of September 11 and the war on terrorism.

NOTES

1. Kathy Kelly, "What about the Incubators?" Emperor's New Clothes, http://www.emperors-clothes.com (accessed September 17, 2003).

2. John Stauber and Sheldon Rampton, *Toxic Sludge Is Good for You: Lies, Damn Lies, and the Public Relations Industry* (Monroe, ME: Common Courage, 1995), chap. 10.

3. Dan Quayle, quoted in Bill Gallagher, "Baby Killing Hoax Led to First War in Iraq, Now Comes the Rematch," *Niagara Falls Reporter*, September 24, 2002, www.niagarafallsreporter.com (accessed December 2, 2003).

4. Stauber and Rampton, *Toxic Sludge Is Good for You*, chap. 10.

5. John R. MacArthur, *Second Front: Censorship and Propaganda in the Gulf War* (Berkeley: University of California Press, 1993), p. 65.

6. Ibid.

7. John R. MacArthur, "Remember Nayirah, Witness for Kuwait," *New York Times*, January 6, 1992.

8. MacArthur, *Second Front*, pp. 66-67.

9. G. W. Bush, "Address to a Joint Session of Congress and the American People," White House, September 20, 2001, http://www.whitehouse. gov (accessed December 5, 2003).

10. "U.S. Admin, Media Struggle for Rules in War vs. Terrorism," *Dow Jones International News*, October 12, 2001.

11. William Safire, "New Day of Infamy," *New York Times*, September 12, 2001.

12. Bennett Roth, "Aides Claim Attackers Targeted President," *Houston Chronicle*, September 13, 2001.

13. Elizabeth Bumiller, "The New Slogan in Washington: Start Watching What You Say," *New York Times*, October 7, 2001.

14. James Dao and Eric Schmitt, "Pentagon Readies Efforts to Sway Sentiment Abroad," *New York Times*, February 19, 2002.

15. Ibid.

16. Ibid.

17. "RSF Calls on Donald Rumsfeld to Reject the Use of Propaganda," Enduring Freedoms, February 21, 2002, http://www.enduringfreedoms.org (accessed December 2, 2003).

18. Editorial, "Governments Exploiting Fear to Increase Security," *Palm Beach Post*, February 26, 2002.

19. "Pentagon's OSI Plans Unleash Indignation in Foreign Media," Global Security, February 22, 2002, http://www.globalsecurity.org (accessed December 7, 2003).

20. Douglas Feith, quoted in "Undersecretary Feith Breakfast with Defense Writers Group," Federation of American Scientists, February 20, 2002, http://www.fas.org (accessed December 2, 2003).

21. Mike Allen, "White House Angered at Plan for Pentagon Disinformation," *Washington Post*, February 25, 2002.

22. Ari Fleischer, quoted in Charles Aldinger, "Bush-U.S. Will Not Lie to World on Defense Policy," Reuters News, February 25, 2002.

23. Editorial, "True or False? The Pentagon Says It's Closing Its Office of Strategic Influence, We Hope It's Not Lying," *Newsday*, March 2, 2002.

24. Rowan Scarborough, "Rumsfeld Expresses Doubts on New Propaganda Office," *Washington Times*, February 25, 2002.

25. Scott Shuger, "The Artifice of War," *Slate*, February 22, 2002, http://www.slate.msn.com (accessed December 2, 2002).

26. Paul M. Rodriguez, "Disinformation Dustup Shrouded in Secrecy," *Insight on the News*, May 6, 2002.

27. Tom Schanker and Eric Schmitt, "Pentagon Debates Propaganda Push in Allied Nations," *New York Times*, December 16, 2002.

28. John Ashcroft, Memorandum for Heads of All Federal Departments and Agencies. Subject: The Freedom of Information Act, October 12, 2001.

29. Ruth Rosen, "The Day Ashcroft Foiled FOIA," *San Francisco Chronicle*, January 7, 2002.

30. Ibid.

31. Ashcroft memorandum to heads of federal departments and agencies.

32. "Homefront Confidential," Reporters Committee for Freedom of the Press, http://www.rcfp.org (accessed September 17, 2003).

33. Ibid.

34. Bruce Shapiro, "Information Lock-Down," *Nation*, November 12, 2001.

35. William J. Broad, "U.S. Tightening Rules on Keeping Scientific Secrets," *New York Times*, February 17, 2002.

36. Ibid.

37. John Ashcroft, testimony before the Senate Judiciary Committee, December 6, 2001.

38. Neil A. Lewis, "Ashcroft Defends Anti-terror Plan and Says Criticism May Aid Foes," *New York Times*, December 7, 2001.

39. Editorial, "The Ashcroft Smear," *Washington Post*, December 7, 2002.

40. Editorial, "John Ashcroft Misses the Point," *New York Times*, December 7, 2001.

41. Reuters News, "U.S. Justice Department Blasts Reports on Ashcroft Hearing," December 7, 2001.

42. Memorandum, Disclosures to the Congress, Federation of American Scientists, October 5, 2001, http://www.fas.org (accessed December 5, 2003).

43. "Bush Restricts Lawmaker Access to Classified Info," Federation of American Scientists, October 10, 2001, http://www.fas.org (accessed December 2, 2001).

44. Ibid.

45. "Aldridge Drops 'Discretion' in Dealing with the Media; Air Force Goes Further," Federation of American Scientists, October 9, 2001, http://www.fas.org (accessed December 2, 2003).

46. Joel Eskovitz, "Journalism Groups Critique Security," Associated Press, October 13, 2001.

47. Duncan Campbell, "U.S. Buys Up All Satellite War Images," *Guardian* (London), October 17, 2001.

48. John Pike, quoted in Joseph Fitchett, "Two Countries to Aid U.S. with Planes for Spying: French and British Jets Will Provide Detailed Images of War Zone," *International Herald Tribune*, October 20, 2001.

49. MacArthur, *Second Front*, pp. 173–78.

50. The House of Representatives vote was 356 to 66 and the Senate vote was 98 to one. No committee report was provided with the act and there was little or no public debate on the subject.

51. H.R. 31462, Uniting and Strengthening America by Providing Appropriate Tools Required to Intercept and Obstruct Terrorism Act.

52. Anita Ramasasty, "Why the ACLU Is Right to Challenge the FBI's Access to Library, Bookstore and Business Records under the USA Patriot Act," Modern Practice, September 2003, http://www.practice.findlaw.com (accessed December 5, 2003).

53. Judith Krug, quoted in "FBI Checks Out Libraries," CBSNews.com, June 24, 2002, http://www.cbsnews.com (accessed December 2, 2003).

54. Johann P. Fritz, director, International Press Institute, letter to United States Attorney General John Ashcroft, September 10, 2001, http://www.freemedia.at (accessed December 2, 2003).

55. *Branzburg v. Hayes* 408 U.S. 665 (1972); ibid.

56. At the time this note is being written, funding for the project has been suspended. Senator Ron Wyden (D-OR) and Senator Chuck Grassley (R-IA) successfully attached an amendment to a budget bill, which was passed on January 17, 2003. The amendment freezes funding for TIA until the Bush administration provides a detailed explanation of the project to Congress and prevents the TIA from being used against U.S. citizens without the express consent of Congress.

57. John Markoff, "Pentagon Plans a Computer System That Would Peek at Personal Data of Americans," *New York Times*, November 1, 2002.

58. William Safire, "You Are a Suspect," *New York Times*, November 4, 2002.

59. Markoff, "Pentagon Plans."

60. John M. Poindexter resigned on August 14, 2003, from his position at the Defense Advanced Research Projects Agency (DARPA) after the controversy surrounding a futures market on Middle East developments.

61. Editorial, "Total Information Awareness," *Washington Post*, November 16, 2002.

62. Eliot Borin, "Feds Open 'Total' Tech Spy System," *Wired News*, August 7, 2002.

63. Mimi Moon, "States Also Limit Access in Wake of 9/11," *News Media* and the Law 26 (winter 2002): 28.

64. Ibid.

65. Ibid.

66. George Bush, joint press conference with Vladimir Putin, November 13, 2001.

67. Philip Taylor, "Journalists Confront Sporadic Restrictions in Aftermath of Sept. 11 Terrorist Attacks," *News Media and the Law* 25 (fall 2001): 11.

68. Ibid.

69. Ibid.

70. "Judge Refuses to Release Confiscated Film to Photojournalist," Reporters Committee for a Free Press, February 15, 2002, http://www.rcfp.org (accessed December 2, 2003).

71. Taylor, "Journalists Confront Sporadic Restrictions."

72. "Judge Refuses to Release Confiscated Film."

73. "News Photographer Detained under Treason Law," Reporters Committee for a Free Press, December 4, 2001, http://www.rcfp.org (December 2, 2003).

74. Barbara Cochran, letters to Federal Aviation Administration and Department of Transportation.

75. Ibid.

76. Ibid.

77. "Helicopter Ban in Wake of Attacks Frustrates Broadcast Journalists," Reporters Committee for Freedom of the Press, September 21, 2001, http://www.rcfp.org (accessed November 5, 2002).

Chapter 6

TRADING LIBERTY FOR SECURITY
The Coalition against Terrorism

We have ignored or condoned abuses in nations that support our anti-terrorism effort...

—Former President Jimmy Carter

HUMAN RIGHTS EXCUSES:
NEW FRIENDS, NEW ALLIANCES

T he siege at a Moscow theater began shortly after nine on Wednesday, October 23, 2002, when fifty-three Chechen rebels burst into the auditorium just as many theater goers were returning to their seats after an intermission. Dressed in camouflage uniforms and armed with heavy weaponry, some of them with explosives attached to their bodies, the attackers took to the stage and announced that they were taking everyone hostage. "We are at war here," one of them allegedly said. The masked hostage takers then attached explosive devices to seats, pillars, and the sides of the theater. After the initial shock of the attack, Russian authorities made a series of attempts to negotiate a peaceful settlement for the release of over eight hundred hostages, including many Americans, Australians, Austrians, British, Dutch, and Germans. However, attempts at negotiation were swiftly rejected by the rebels. In return for the safety of the hostages, the rebels demanded an end to the war in Chechnya; if the Russian army failed to withdraw from the breakaway republic within seven days, the rebels said, the theater and hostages would be blown up. There was to be no deviation from this single demand. Facing a growing crisis, President Vladimir Putin cancelled trips to Germany and Portugal.

Further evidence of the rebel's single-minded resolve came on the morning of Thursday, October 24, 2002, when the Qatar-based television network Al-Jazeera broadcast a message from a man claiming to be one of the hostage takers. Speaking on the videotape, the unnamed man said, "I swear by God we are more keen on dying than you are keen on living. . . . [E]ach one of us is willing to sacrifice himself for the sake of God and the independence of Chechnya."[1]

As the siege dragged on, a group of hostages was released, including several children, but rebels refused to release other children and continued to make threats.[2] Those leaving the theater told stories of the growing agitation among the hostages, some of whom were fatalistic about escaping from the theater alive. Further attempts were made to negotiate with the rebels. Indeed, the *Washington Post* went so far as to describe the proceedings as a "wave" of potential negotiators.[3] Among them were a member of parliament for Chechnya, a journalist critical of Russia's occupation of Chechnya, former Russian Prime Minister Yevgeny Primakov, and foreign diplomats attempting to secure the release of the foreign hostages. "They reject any negotiations," said film director Sergei Govorukhin, after returning from a meeting with the rebels.[4]

With the authorities frustrated by the apparent stalemate, the end of the siege came early on Saturday morning. It was precipitated by an unnamed male hostage who threw a bottle at one of the rebels, leading to gunfire that killed another man and injured a woman. Fearing that the rebels had begun executing the hostages, the Russian authorities decided to end the siege by force. Using the theater's ventilation system and a series of drilled holes, the authorities pumped sleeping gas into the auditorium in the hope of knocking out the rebels and preventing them from setting off their explosives. After the successful application of the gas, a large team of anti-terrorist forces worked their way through the theater, engaging in a fierce firefight with those rebels still able to resist. Within forty minutes of the soldiers' arrival, fifty rebels lay dead while the three survivors were captured. According to *Time*, more than 750 hostages, among them 30 children and 75 foreigners, were released.[5] At the time, the rescue was declared an unqualified success. However, it was later revealed that more than 100 hostages were killed, many of them from the effects of the sleeping gas. There were also disturbing claims that some of the rebels had been murdered extrajudicially while unconscious. Such news trickled out slowly after the attack as the Russian authorities reverted to massaging the available information—Soviet style.

In the days following the rescue, the question of the type of gas used in the theater became an open source of friction between the media and grieving relatives, on the one side, and the Russian authorities, on the other. At first, the Russian authorities refused to discuss the sleeping gas with members of the local and international media. Significantly, it appeared that such secretiveness also extended to the American government: "We have only been given general information that it was an incapacitating or calming agent but we do not know specifically the nature of the substance," said American Ambassador Alexander Vershbow.[6]

Asked to reveal the exact nature of the gas, Deputy Interior Minister Vladimir Vasileyev, speaking on October 26, 2002, would say only, "You ask me if we used gas or not. Well, I am authorized to say that special means were used. . . . That allowed us . . . to neutralize the kamikaze women who were strapped with explosives and held their fingers on the detonators."[7]

However, news reports criticizing the Russian authorities for their failure to arrange proper medical facilities for the injured began to appear. There were claims that security forces left unconscious hostages on the sidewalk; that foreign doctors who offered their services to the Russian authorities were refused access to the scene, even though at the time few medical staff were in attendance; and perhaps most worryingly, that medical staff at local hospitals were unprepared for survivors who had inhaled the gas. Indeed, some families of the hostages claimed that doctors at the hospitals were also kept in the dark as to the nature of the gas. As a result, individuals and some human rights organizations alleged that many of the hostages suffered unnecessarily.[8]

With speculation about the gas increasing toward the end of October, Russian health officials admitted that the mystery gas was fentanyl, an opiate-based pain killer used as an anesthetic. This information was later confirmed by Public Health Minister Yuri Shevchenko, who was quoted by the TASS news agency. The admission was, however, disputed by pharmacologists in America, who said that the experiences of the survivors failed to match the known aftereffects of the drug. A class of gas known as halogenated anesthetics was thought to be a far more likely candidate. Schevchenko also sought to dispel the idea that doctors had not been informed about the type of gas used. He said they had been told to use naloxone, which is often given to heroin addicts, to revive the hostages. Despite this statement, it is believed that many of the hostages choked on their own vomit after having a severe reaction to the gas. The question of the execution of many of the unconscious rebels was also deflected.

Government film taken shortly after the rescue showed rebels in theater seats either slumped forward or with their heads thrown back, indicating, according to the *Chicago Sun-Times*, "that they may have been shot while unconscious." The *Sun-Times* also claimed that bullet wounds could clearly be seen in the heads of the rebels.[9] A *Time* article also stated that the anti-terrorist forces had shot the unconscious suicide bombers in the head. The article quoted a member of the assault team as saying, "When a person wears two kilos of plastic explosive, we didn't see any other way of neutralizing them."[10]

The allegations of extrajudicial killings were enough for both Human Rights Watch (HRW) and Amnesty International to write to

President Putin with their concerns about the rescue mission. While the human rights organizations condemned the hostage taking, they called for the creation of an independent commission of inquiry to answer key questions about the rescue operation. HRW's executive director for Europe and Asia, Elizabeth Andersen, commented, "The Russian government should have made sure that medical doctors with knowledge of the exact gas used and equipped with sufficient quantities of antidote were at the theater at the time of the operation. . . . The lack of an appropriate plan for this aspect of the operation is an inexcusable violation of the right to life." Regarding the murders, HRW said that a future inquiry should determine whether some of the rebels were executed while unconscious.[11]

Against this background of nagging fears that human rights breaches might have been committed, foreign heads of state were nonetheless effusive in their support for Putin. A spokeswoman for British Prime Minister Tony Blair said that, while he deplored the loss of innocent life, the prime minister was pleased that the "Russian authorities were able to bring a swift end to this terrible incident."[12] Indian Prime Minister Atal Bihari Vajpayee phoned Putin to congratulate him on his courageous handling of the siege. In the United States, President George Bush said, "Any time anybody is willing to take innocent life for a so-called cause, they must be dealt with and [Putin] made some very tough decisions. . . ."[13] Not one of the leaders saw fit to mention the possibility that innocent people had died needlessly or that the so-called courageous effort might have included the disturbing sight of anti-terrorist soldiers calmly going about the business of executing rebels.

Interestingly, the work of Amnesty International and HRW has often been used by Western governments claiming that certain countries have poor human rights records; a good example occurred during the first Gulf War when both the American and the Kuwaiti governments used Amnesty International reports to reveal the appalling human rights record of Saddam Hussein (see chapter 5, page 136). Why then, on this occasion, were the legitimate concerns of Amnesty International and HRW so willfully ignored?

The answer lay in the new alliances made after September 11, together with a growing awareness among the international community of the dangers of terrorism, almost to the exclusion of all other issues. Ever since the al-Qaeda attack had brought home the truly awful realities of a terrorist attack in the United States, the Bush administration had made terrorism, and the eradication of Osama bin Laden and his al-Qaeda network, in particular, the central feature of its foreign and domestic policies. Faced with an amorphous and sophisticated enemy prepared to use the most modern technology and financing arrangements, as well as more traditional methods, the Bush administration acknowledged early on that it needed assistance.

With Vice President Dick Cheney, Defense Secretary Donald Rumsfeld, and Secretary of State Colin Powell as his brokers, President Bush was able to create an alliance of diverse countries. At the same time as the North Atlantic Treaty Organization (NATO) invoked its Article 5, which states that an attack on one NATO member is an attack on all of the members, Bush was making tentative overtures to the country NATO was created to defend Western Europe against—Russia.

Needing army bases close to Afghanistan, America courted Russia in the hope that Russia would use its influence on the former Soviet republics of Tajikistan, Turkmenistan, and Uzbekistan. Another country bordering Afghanistan, Pakistan, was also convinced to join the international coalition, as were several other Middle Eastern countries, among them Egypt and Saudi Arabia. In order to offset the alliance with Pakistan, and in recognition of the possibility of war between the two countries, India was also brought into the fold.

Having already gained the support of Russia and its vital vote on the United Nations Security Council, America turned to another permanent member of the council, namely, China. Coming shortly after an international incident involving the collision of American and Chinese planes, the agreement between the superpower and the emerging superpower took longer than that between the United States and Russia, but China eventually agreed to support the global war against terrorism. Outside of these pivotal relationships, other countries also agreed to ally themselves with the United States.

Such assistance was given at many levels, from cooperation regarding the tracing of companies and funds, the exchange of intelligence information, and political support and leverage, to the offer of military bases and even military and logistical support. Without such assistance, the overthrow of the Taliban and the destruction of the al-Qaeda bases in Afghanistan would have been made more difficult.

But what had gone unrecognized at the alliance's creation could be seen clearly after eighteen months of its existence. This was no one-way street; the entanglement of relationships involved a degree of reciprocity. Many of the countries claimed to have terrorist problems of their own and called for mutual support. Taking into account the support offered to America after the September 11 attacks, it was a call that the Bush administration found difficult to ignore. Nowhere were these strands of international policy more evident than in the reactions to the Moscow theater siege.

An examination of these responses to the United States' calls for assistance reveals the tremendous changes that occurred after September 11, 2001. Many of the old divisions, even the old enmities, had been swept away to be replaced by a new political reality, at the heart of which was the view that almost everything could be subordinated to the fight against terrorism. The principle was perhaps best articulated in President Bush's address to Congress on September 20, 2001, when he said, "Every nation in every region now has a decision to make: Either you are with us or you are with the terrorists." His words also carried a threat: "From this day forward, any nation that continues to harbor or support terrorism will be regarded by the United States as a hostile regime."[14]

Responding to this stark statement, a number of countries were quick to identify with the United States by pointing to their own domestic terrorism problems. The result of this support was a curious blend of domestic and international terrorism, with Islamic fundamentalism providing the often tenuous link between both. The call to arms against terrorists opened the door for a number of repressive regimes to use the campaign for their own purposes, especially against groups fighting for independence.

Distracted by its thoughts on coalition building, the war in

Afghanistan, and homeland security, America appeared to give little heed to the nuanced difference between terrorists and those fighting for independence. President Bush's statement to countries that they are either "with us or against us" appeared to be a "one size fits all" approach, offering the chance of a fresh start with the world's only superpower that was accepted enthusiastically by many countries.

The Moscow siege became a litmus test for the new friendship and alliance between Russia and the United States. Moreover, it handed the Bush administration a wonderful opportunity to publicize the continuing dangers of terrorism both at home and abroad as it rushed to the defense of a friend who had provided valuable assistance during the war in Afghanistan.

Regarding the U.S. reaction, Secretary of State Colin Powell showed a willingness to use the Moscow siege to justify the Bush administration's own fight against terrorism. Speaking on October 26, Powell said that the siege was proof that "terrorism can strike anywhere, and we have to be on guard." Appealing directly to his domestic audience, Powell continued, "There's no country that is not a potential victim of terrorism. And that's why it has to be an international crusade of the kind that President Bush launched after 9/11 and is now leading."[15]

A November 12 meeting between President Putin and German Chancellor Gerhardt Schroeder was even more remarkable. Long known for his support of human rights and its criticism of Russian abuses, particularly in Chechnya, Schroeder issued a statement that set aside these differences in order to focus on the global issue of terrorism. "Solidarity with Russia and its president in the fight against terrorism was, is, and remains a matter of course for us," Schroeder said. "It was interesting to hear from the president how the political process is organized and promoted with regard to Chechnya. This mainly means the constitutional process. I can see good approaches which, I find, deserve our support."[16] Schroeder's comments amounted to a complete renunciation of European and American criticism of Russia over the breakaway republic of Chechnya. In effect, Germany was backing Russia's war, irrespective of human rights abuses.

Russia also sought to capitalize on the siege by asking America to label rebel groups fighting in Chechnya as "foreign terrorist organizations." This designation would have frozen bank accounts and prevented members of these organizations from traveling to the United States. Showing a keen awareness of the new international environment, Russia said that if the United States agreed, it would be displaying solidarity in the joint "international war on terrorism."

Asked about the request, State Department spokesperson Richard Boucher responded, "We're always looking at groups that might be included, that might be listed, but I don't have any new decisions at this point one way or the other. . . . The process of determining this sort of legal determination to put a group on a list involves a collection of a lot of information and the careful analysis of the group and its record."[17] Although the State Department was noncommittal, the idea of Russia nominating groups to be placed on a U.S. list of terrorists previously would have previously been dismissed out of hand. The fact that it was even considered was a further sign of how much had changed.

After the Moscow siege, Russian Defense Minister Sergei Ivanov announced a new crackdown on militants to prevent acts of terror in Chechnya. In order to find the militants, the Russian military began to "lock down" villages, urban areas, and refugee camps. Once this process was completed, the army arrested large numbers of Chechens, who were taken into custody for questioning. These so-called mopping-up operations have consistently been condemned by human rights organizations because they are often a pretext for torture and, occasionally, the murder of Chechen men. With the terrorist outrage in Moscow still fresh in the minds of many people, there was little or no international outcry.

For many governments, the fight against terrorism clearly transcended other concerns, particularly those of human rights, and could be adapted to many different situations and causes. During the Moscow siege, the terrorists had made purely domestic demands, namely, the removal of the Russian military from Chechnya. However, this limited demand did not prevent the Russian authorities from portraying the attack as broadly similar to that which occurred on September 11. By blurring the distinction between domestic and international terrorism, Russia could ask for the support of its new allies. Caught between the push of the new alliance in the war against terrorism and the pull of Russia's historic lack of concern for human rights, many countries chose to ignore the latter, allowing Russia to use the impetus and the capital gained in the theater siege to perpetrate fresh attacks in Chechnya. Like the possible human rights abuses in the theater siege itself, these attacks could be undertaken without criticism by the international community.

Although world leaders appeared largely acquiescent during this period, they had not always been so willing to remain quiet on the subject of Chechnya. Comparison with the attitudes of the international community in former times further attests to the changes regarding human rights abuses after September 11.

Beginning under the presidency of Boris Yeltsin in 1994, the first Chechen war, which lasted two years, almost led to Yeltsin's political demise. After initial successes, the Russian army found itself involved in a guerrilla war that quickly dissolved into a bloody stalemate. The Russian army withdrew in 1996, leaving the republic virtually independent. Some three years later, a series of bomb attacks in Moscow that killed more than 300 people was blamed on Chechen rebels, leading to a resumption of the war. This time, Putin promised that the armed insurgency would be destroyed and that Russia would regain full control of the region.

Since the beginning of the second war, there have been constant allegations by international organizations of human rights abuses in Chechnya. Civilians have allegedly been robbed, tortured, raped, and murdered by Russian soldiers, often conscripts, who have acted barbarically in the face of an equally savage opponent. One of the main targets of the Russian army is the youth of Chechnya, who have been arrested and subjected to detention and beatings. There are also claims that stiff rebel resistance has led the Russian military to institute a scorched-earth campaign. Many of the human rights abuses have been substantiated by the independent reports of Russian and international nongovernmental organizations (NGOs), which have continued to investigate the situation.

Stung by these reports, the Russian government has done its best to prevent the outside world from knowing what is happening. To this end, heavy restrictions have been placed on the movement of journalists, who are often accompanied by government representatives determined to keep the media on a tight leash. But the controls on reporting have not stemmed the flow of horrific stories from Chechnya. In a telling sign of the Russian military's behavior, an unnamed Russian commander even went so far as to describe the overall situation as "lawless."[18]

Before September 11, 2001, the reports of human rights abuses in Chechnya caused outrage among the international community and led to condemnation of Russia in organizations such as the Council of Europe (CoE) and the United Nations. Criticism of Russia's policies was at its height in the year 2000 when State Department spokesperson James Rubin used a press briefing to highlight a number of reports by human rights organizations that the Russian army had beaten, raped, and summarily executed civilians for providing aid to Chechen rebels. Describing the reports as "credible," Rubin said that they warranted investigation by the Russian authorities. He also highlighted the restrictions placed on the movement of journalists, which he said were hindering information from reaching the outside world. In reply, the Russian Foreign Ministry said that Rubin's words amounted to cooperation with the terrorists in their information strategy.[19]

Writing in the *Washington Post* in March 2000, Secretary of State Madeleine Albright provided insight into the Clinton administration's approach to Chechnya. Albright said that where human rights abuses have occurred, the Clinton administration had not minced its words. Reflecting on the start of the second Chechen war, she said that the United States had issued a warning that the war should not be a pretext for abridging civil liberties and that "pulling our punches on Chechnya would be contrary to American principles and interests."[20] Similar views were expressed in Europe, and pressure also came from the United Nations.

Before becoming president, George W. Bush had also used different language to describe events in Chechnya. Speaking at the

Ronald Reagan Library in November 1999, when Putin was prime minister and the second Chechen war had only recently begun, then-governor Bush said, "We cannot excuse Russian brutality." He went on to argue that "Russia cannot learn the lessons of democracy from the textbook of tyranny." Issuing a warning, Bush said, "The Russian government will discover that it cannot build a stable and unified nation on the ruins of human rights." Sadly for the citizens of Chechnya, Russia was to learn that it could escape censure if it traded on its support for America's war on terrorism and blurred the distinction between different types of terrorism.

Before the attacks on the World Trade Center and the Pentagon, it was possible to see the international community working on many levels to pressure Russia into halting the human rights abuses in Chechnya. At the intergovernmental level, organizations such as the CoE had brought Russia to the brink of isolation, while the United Nations Human Rights Commission (UNHRC), working with the European Union, added to this pressure by passing a strong resolution urging Russia to halt the abuses. At the national level, the U.S. State Department and the president continued to criticize the Russian government at meetings and through press briefings. The effect of this criticism was to leave the Russian government in no doubt as to how the international community viewed its activities in Chechnya.

Since the September 11 attacks, however, a vacuum has formed. The siege at the Moscow theater is only one example of a far wider problem that has seen human rights take a back seat to other issues. For the present, it appears that these universal rights, which are the very foundation of democracy, have been superseded by the urgent need to protect the world against terrorism.

In effect, the congratulations that rained down on Putin after the hostages were released were not only a recognition of this subtle transition but also proof that, through its support for the United States, Russia had joined a select club that gave it a certain license regarding human rights abuses. This unspoken license allowed the abuser to ignore the warnings of NGOs while other members of the club who had previously upheld human rights failed to support Amnesty International and similar organizations. Perhaps the saddest aspect of this new club is that democratic governments are now acting in concert with repressive ones. The danger is that they may well become accustomed to this arrangement. Seen from this perspective, to paraphrase President Bush's words uttered in the Reagan Library, the lesson of the new friendships and alliances is that you cannot learn democracy from tyranny, but by sidelining democracy, you may learn a little tyranny.

In the aftermath of September 11, a relative quiet has descended on many intergovernmental organizations regarding human rights issues. While the secretariats of these organizations continue to warn of the need to safeguard liberties and to argue that security should not become the overriding policy concern, much of the vitality and sense of urgency has disappeared. The primary reason for this quiescence is that the countries that provided the real teeth in these bodies are now engaged elsewhere, attending to other issues, particularly terrorism and the attendant worry of home security. Sadly, the warnings of the secretariats have been to no avail: security has now toppled human rights from the agenda.

Nowhere is this attitude more prevalent than in the United States. While the country may continue to espouse these principles occasionally, its policy-making institutions are engaged in other matters and are focusing on different problems—far from the everyday matter of ensuring that countries all over the globe stick to their democratization programs or continue to work on human rights issues. Such a dramatic reorientation has left a gaping hole in the international community's approach to human rights. It also marks a significant departure for the foreign policies of the United States.

SERVING THE NATIONAL INTEREST: HUMAN RIGHTS AND AMERICA

Ever since the end of World War II, the United States has been calling on countries around the world to accept democracy, assert the rule of law, and uphold human rights. Indeed, successive administrations have emphasized that these principles are the keystone on which any nation should be built and are essential to any thriving society. But, from where does a country's focus on human rights derive? American policy appears to entertain three main considerations.

The first consideration is the belief that repressive governments cannot withstand the internal pressure for democracy and must eventually change or face being removed by their own people. This view is perhaps best expressed by President George W. Bush when he said in May 2001, "History tells us that forcing change upon oppressive regimes requires patience. But history also proves, from Poland to South Africa, that patience and courage and resolve can eventually cause repressive regimes to fear and then to fall."[21] Democracy is therefore an engine for introducing change that is almost impossible for even the most repressive of regimes to ignore.

Second is the belief that it is in the national interest of the United States to promote human rights. As the dominant economy in the world, the United States needs stability to prosper and stable partners with which to trade. As Under Secretary of State for Global Affairs Paula Dobriansky said in her testimony before the Senate Foreign Relations Committee in May 2001, "The strongest, most stable, tolerant, and prosperous countries are precisely those which respect universal human rights. For that reason, we have long made the promotion of human rights a focus of our foreign policy and our foreign assistance programs."[22] Another strand of the national interest argument is that America has been wearied by two world wars that undermined international stability. Prompting human rights and democracy, in this view, reduces the risk of war.

Finally, the United States believes that international human rights reflect the values and morals upheld within its own society. This view sees America's commitment to human rights dating back to the foundation of the country and the Declaration of Independence. As a result, the desire to bring democracy to other parts of the world is merely an extension of the battles that have already taken place within America to promote individual liberties and provide adequate protection from a powerful government. Seen from this perspective, universal human rights are an embodiment of American principles. With this perceived commingling of human rights and

American values, successive administrations have found it easier to convince domestic critics who have questioned foreign policy initiatives of the need to introduce these rights around the world. Using this argument, the "American way" has become the way of international human rights.

With the prevalence of these views in American foreign and domestic policy, it is possible to see how America, in the words of Paula Dobriansky, has become one of the "world's leading advocate[s] for democracy and human rights."[23] These prevailing beliefs also help to explain why the United States has been one of the leading forces in the postwar creation of institutions that support human rights.

In his State of the Union Address on January 6, 1941, President Franklin D. Roosevelt outlined four essential freedoms on which he believed that a future world should be founded: freedom of speech, freedom to worship, freedom from want, and freedom from fear. He ended his speech by expressing the belief that these freedoms were attainable in the present rather than the future.[24] Roosevelt's words defined not only his own world view but that of the United States, and it incorporated an understanding that nations should be prevented from waging war on one another. These views were to appear in one form or another in many subsequent treaties and accords, including the United Nations Universal Declaration of Human Rights.

Despite the widespread perception of the United States as an insular and inward-looking nation, a number of polls questioning Americans on their attitudes have revealed considerable public support for human rights. In 1997, a Hart research poll asked, "Do you believe that every person has basic rights that are common to all human beings, regardless of whether their government recognizes those rights or not, or do you believe that rights are given to an individual by his or her government?" Seventy-six percent of the respondents said that every person has such rights, while only 17 percent said that such rights were granted by governments.[25]

Data from polls also shows that the American public supports foreign policy that promotes human rights. In a 2002 poll by the Chicago Council on Foreign Relations (CCFR), 90 percent of the respondents said that "promoting and defending human rights in other countries" should be an important goal for foreign policy. The CCFR has asked this question every four years since 1974, and, on every occasion, more than 80 percent of the people polled have said it is important. Moreover, the percentage stating that it is very important has climbed from 34 percent in 1994 to 47 percent in 2002.[26]

Questionnaires such as those by Hart and the CCFR reinforce the notion that Americans care deeply about human rights both within America and for other countries. Given this view, in conjunction with the role played by the United States in promoting international institutions that uphold human rights, it is disappointing to see the U.S. government working with other nations whose human rights records are truly appalling.

By seeking to contend with terrorism almost to the exclusion of all other issues, the Bush administration has reduced the importance of human rights. But terrorism appears to thrive in repressive countries. Physical abuse, disenfranchisement, and inequality can lead to hatred. In ignoring human rights abuses in the allied countries and elsewhere, the international community is running the risk of creating future terrorists. In the introduction to its Country Reports on Human Rights Practices for 2001, the U.S. State Department explicitly accepted this view: "[A]long with the need to defend ourselves came the growing awareness that terrorism has been gaining adherents for some time in countries where human rights are denied and civil liberties are repressed."[27]

A real danger for the United States and the international community is that they will find themselves involved in a vicious cycle of seeking to eliminate terrorists while, at the same time, creating a whole new generation of terrorists because they have failed to tackle the root causes of terrorism itself. Moreover, by drawing repressive regimes into the alliance against terrorism, the United States and its allies are in danger of having their own war against terrorism diluted by the desire of these regimes to include their own insurgents on the list of those to be rooted out. Frustrated by the denial of civil liberties, these groups are often fighting for independence in the face of governments bent on suppressing them. Where once the United

States could have helped to solve the problem by calling for democratic reforms and increased human rights, it is now caught on the same side as these governments. As a result, an important avenue for enhancing human rights may be lost. Already this loss of influence appears to be happening with Chechnya and in China with the people known as the Uighurs.

With the end of the clear distinction among different types of terrorism and the weakening of the United States' ability to press for democratic change comes an additional danger that the distinction between countries that uphold human rights and those that do not will be lost. The Moscow siege exposed this possibility. In congratulating President Putin for the operation against the Chechen rebels, the likes of Tony Blair, George W. Bush, and Gerhardt Schroeder became identified with the human rights abuses committed by Russia. As the recipient of such support, Russia felt justified in carrying out further human rights abuses in Chechnya, while the leaders of countries that have, in the past, argued for greater civil rights appeared to undermine their own democratic positions. The act of accommodating and supporting repressive regimes in the alliance against terrorism has only further encouraged these countries to ignore human rights.

STRATEGIC PARTNERS: THE COUNTRIES SURROUNDING AFGHANISTAN

The countries that border Afghanistan were strategically vital in the war against terrorism. Several of the former Soviet republics in Central Asia—Tajikistan, Turkmenistan, and Uzbekistan—had military bases that could be used by U.S. forces in the war to overthrow the Taliban and destroy the al-Qaeda network. To the south of Afghanistan, Pakistan, with its volatile Muslim population, controlled essential airspace that could be used to fly sorties from American aircraft carriers based in the Arabian Sea. Working with the Pakistan army, U.S. special forces could also be flown into nearby tribal areas of Pakistan to engage retreating Taliban and al-Qaeda forces. With little expertise in the area, American intelligence also wanted to pool information with their better-informed Pakistani counterparts.

Concerning Iran, which has no political contact with the "Great Satan," America used its ally the United Kingdom as a bridge to engage diplomatically with the fundamentalist government and convince it to acquiesce to the war in Afghanistan. Fortunately for the allies, Iran's hatred of the Taliban regime, which it had been undermining for years, far outweighed its fears of U.S. hegemony in the region.

Although years of Muslim fundamentalist rule have left the conservative elements in Iran with little or no interest in engagement with the outside world, the other countries surrounding Afghanistan, particularly the former Soviet states, had their own good reasons for wanting to rebuild relationships with the outside world. This is also true of Pakistan, which, since the military overthrow of Prime Minister Nawaz Sharif in 1999, had been isolated by the international community.

Cozying Up to Dictators: Pakistan

Speaking on September 11, Pakistani President Pervez Musharraf condemned the attacks on the United States: "We strongly condemn this most brutal and horrible act of terror and violence. The world must unite to fight against terrorism in all its forms and root out this modern day evil." The president then offered his sympathies and condolences to President Bush.[28] Musharraf could not have known on that day just how quickly he would be asked to act on his words.

The self-proclaimed chief executive of Pakistan, Musharraf came to power in 1999 in a bloodless coup that ousted the democratically elected Sharif and led the country back to the bad days of military rule. In a curious and ironic turnaround, Sharif, the legitimate head of Pakistan, was later tried on a spurious charge of treason and subsequently exiled from the country, leaving Musharraf to govern with the support of the military.

In Washington, the Clinton administration shed few tears over the removal of Sharif, but some officials expressed condemnation of the coup, which was echoed by the European Union. Moreover, an important loan from the International Monetary Fund (IMF) was suspended. But the September 11 attacks would provide Musharraf with a perfect opportunity to return to the international fold.

In the face of violent street opposition and supposed rumblings among the military, some of whom expressed religious sympathies with the Taliban, Musharraf announced his support for the war in Afghanistan in a televised address to the nation. Choosing his words carefully, the president said that Pakistan's integrity and security would be threatened if it did not make the right choice, and he hinted that if the country denied the international community, it could face attack. He also appealed to nationalist sentiment by arguing that the United States could turn to Pakistan's rival, India, for help. Confronted by these challenges, Musharraf said there was no other choice but to provide assistance to America.[29]

Behind the reasons given to the Pakistani people, however, were other motives. Before he went on television, Musharraf had received heavy hints from America that his country would be rewarded for its assistance. We "stand by our friends who stand by us," said the U.S. Ambassador to Islamabad, Wendy Chamberlain.[30] Despite Chamberlain's denials that a deal had been reached between the two countries, there were rumors of a financial package that included the easing of sanctions and a reduction in Pakistan's international debt. Later in 2002, Musharraf would see his greatest reward for supporting the U.S. war on terror.

Heartened by the United States' support, in October 2002 Musharraf held elections that were deeply flawed. According to Human Rights Watch (HRW), the military government used a range of tactics to ensure the outcome of the vote. These tactics included a series of constitutional amendments that effectively sidelined the leaders of the two most popular opposition parties, Benazir Bhutto and Sharif, both of whom were exiled, and sought to prevent their parties from gaining the popular support of the people. Retaining the power to dismiss the heads of constitutional offices, as well as an elected parliament and government, Musharraf kept a tight hold on the reins of power.[31]

During the elections, there were widespread accusations of vote rigging and intimidation. Opposed by the parties of the two former prime ministers, the military government swung its weight behind the Pakistan Muslim League Quaid-e Azam (PML-QA). There were claims made by election monitors that polling booths were being moved at the request of the PML-QA and that the party was choosing its own polling officers. Amid allegations that the other main parties were being harassed by the police, the chief election commissioner was forced on September 21 to issue a statement asking the police to respect the candidates and their parties. To meet these challenges, a large European Union delegation flew into the country to observe and monitor the election process.

On October 10, 2002, the elections were held, and while they did not go entirely as Musharraf may have intended—a large Muslim vote protested the alliance with America—the twin tactics of constitutional amendments and apparent vote rigging at the ground level were enough to assure him victory. The unelected president had managed to push through a largely superficial attempt at meeting outside standards of democracy which was confirmed by an initial report from the European Union monitors, who said there were "serious flaws" in the election process. The monitors also raised concerns over Musharraf's decision to retain power in the National Security Council, the ultimate decision-making body in Pakistan, thereby preventing a true transfer of power from the military to civilian institutions.[32]

Before the election, Brad Adams, executive director of the Asia Division of HRW, articulated the view of many observers when he said, "In the three years since the coup, Pakistan has witnessed a consolidation of military power rather than a transition to democracy. Pakistan's international partners cannot ignore the fact any longer. They need to insist on progress toward democracy in Pakistan."[33] These words were well chosen; unfortunately, Adams was wrong: the international community could and would ignore Pakistan's lack of democracy.

Speaking before the election result had been confirmed, U.S. State Department spokesperson Richard Boucher said, "[The United

States] would accept this result as a credible representation of the range of opinion in Pakistan if these initial impressions are borne out."[34] Boucher's words amounted to an elaborate shell game played out before the international community. As long as Pakistan was seen to be inching its way toward democracy, it could be described as a country in transition and not a dictatorship. Applying the logic that any attempt at democracy was a positive development, it could be argued that the elections, no matter how flawed, were an advance over what had previously existed. As long as Pakistan moved incrementally in the right direction, it was always possible to congratulate the country on its improvements. However, this argument failed to take into account the accusation, put forward by a number of NGOs, that Musharraf was merely consolidating his power beneath the veneer of a flawed democracy and that he had no intention of making way for an elected government. Given Pakistan's strategic importance, the Bush administration apparently had no wish to look too deeply into this matter.

Outside the political sphere, the impact of the flawed elections was keenly felt in the media. According to the human rights reports of the U.S. State Department, Pakistan maintained a lively media environment but journalists were inclined to practice self-censorship, particularly when writing stories concerning the military; in the broadcasting field, wary of television's power, the government maintained a "closely controlled" monopoly.

Broadly speaking, these impressions are correct, but they fail to take into account the media's lack of access to Pakistan's ruling institutions. As noted in the State Department's reports, journalists are often deterred from writing about the military, but they are also hindered in their attempts to write about the government and, in particular, the coup. Lack of access increased dramatically after September 11, with journalists being prevented from attending high-profile court cases. The trial of Daniel Pearl's murderer is just one example of a high-profile court case from which the media were excluded by the authorities.

Beginning with Musharraf's decision to join the war against terrorism, the 2002 elections showed that the Pakistani media, like many other institutions in the country, would continue to be stifled until genuine democracy was introduced. The elections were merely the end of a process that had started with Musharraf's helping to overthrow Pakistan's former client state, the Taliban, and destroy the al-Qaeda bases. In return for his support for the anti-terrorism effort, Musharraf received an end to international isolation, relief from debt, and, perhaps the most prized possession of all, an aura of legitimacy.

A Tale of Two Countries: Tajikistan and Turkmenistan

Beset by economic and social problems, the former Soviet republics of Tajikistan and Turkmenistan have terrible human rights records and a history of suppressing the media. Both governments have intimidated political opponents to the point at which there is little open debate and the law is persistently abused by the police and security services. Terrorism is also a problem, particularly for Tajikistan, where the Islamic Movement of Uzbekistan (IMU) is calling for the creation of a separate Muslim state in the Ferghana Valley and using Tajikistan to launch attacks against neighboring Kyrgyzstan and Uzbekistan. Members of the Hizb-ut-Tahir Ferghana (Party of Liberation), which has its origins in the Middle East, are also moving through the valley. Although the Hizb-ut-Tahir, according to Amnesty International, also wants to create a separate Muslim state, it does not believe in the use of violence to meet this end.[35] Groups like the IMU and Hizb-ut-Tahir present a serious problem for the country, and the government has continued to restrict comments on these issues.

When the September 11 attacks occurred, the leaders of the two countries reacted very differently to the crisis. In Tajikistan, President Emomali Rakhmonov condemned the September 11 attacks and pledged his support for the war on terrorism; Turkmenistan's president, Saparmurad Niyazov, offered his condolences but tried to steer a neutral course by refusing to use the words "terrorist act." Some days after the attack, the Turkmenistan foreign ministry said that the government approved of the alliance against terrorism but would not be an active participant.[36]

After the war on terrorism had begun, Tajikistan allowed the allied forces to prepare bases at the airports at Dushanbe and Kulyab and opened up its airspace to allied airplanes. In a change of heart that contradicted its earlier neutral stance, Turkmenistan subsequently allowed America to use its airspace to deliver humanitarian aid to Afghanistan. It also allowed American planes to land and refuel at Asgabat airport.

Curiously, after the overthrow of the Taliban, the relationship between Tajikistan and the alliance against terrorism rose to even greater heights. With its views on international terrorism forged out of its own difficulties, Tajikistan continued to seek political capital out of the September 11 attacks. Addressing a conference of law enforcers in May, President Rakhmonov said, "After September 11, the world community finally realized how ominous the threat [of] international terrorism [is]. . . . Tajikistan warned about [the threat of terrorist organizations] years ago."[37]

The United States and Tajikistan exchanged letters of congratulation in March 2002, on the tenth anniversary of the establishment of diplomatic relations between the two countries. These exchanges continued on the first anniversary of September 11, when Rakhmonov sent a message to President Bush stating that the close relationship formed by the two countries should be used as the foundation for further cooperation in the fight against terrorism. Describing terrorism as "evil," the president reassured the United States that Tajikistan would continue to collaborate in the hope of achieving these goals.

The ardent support appeared to have paid off when, in October 2002, Tajikistan began receiving financial aid from its new friend. According to *Asia Pulse*, which contacted the American embassy in the capital, Dushanbe, the U.S. State Department increased its assistance to Tajikistan and Central Asia after September 11. On October 29, 2002, the State Department airlifted medicines worth $4 million—the first delivery of a financial package worth $20 million—to hospitals in the capital.[38] Unwilling to be outdone, America's ally the European Union (EU) announced that the September 11 attacks had led to a new plan for cooperation in the region and that it was doubling its funding to the country. The director-general of the European Commission's External Relations Directorate Kurt Jul also said that the EU would help Tajikistan join the World Trade Organization.[39]

Reticent at first but finally made agreeable through a mixture of cajoling and inducements at the diplomatic level, Turkmenistan arguably received more benefits from the allies, and the United States in particular, than its neighbor Tajikistan. A fundamental reason for this difference is the existence of natural gas fields in Turkmenistan and the possibility that the income from this source could be used to stabilize Afghanistan. During July 2002, the question of natural gas led to the discussion of a pipeline being extended to Pakistan, which needs large amounts of fuel. The proposal raised the specter of the United States creating synergies throughout the region by encouraging repressive regimes to work with each other to increase oil production. With an eye on the potential for American companies in the region, U.S. Ambassador to Turkmenistan Laura Kennedy expressed the hope that some American firms would also take part in the pipeline project.

Bolstered by this new relationship with the United States and the economic support that flowed from it, Tajikistan and Turkmenistan felt secure enough to continue their respective programs of repressing the media, apparently seeing a new understanding after September 11 between those countries that upheld democracy and the "helpful" abusers of it. A rather cynical political dance ensued in which the State Department dutifully criticized these countries in its Human Rights Reports while President Bush wrote letters to the countries' leaders on the anniversary of their independence from the Soviet Union thanking them for their contributions to the war on terrorism. The extreme divergence between the two modes of behavior encouraged these repressive countries to ignore any words of criticism.

Indeed, this was particularly true in Turkmenistan. Made president for life of Turkmenistan in 1999, President Niyazov rules over one of the most heavily controlled societies in the world. His leadership can be seen everywhere, from decisions over whether opera and ballet have a role in Turkmen culture to the destruction of history books that provide an alternative to the official history of the country. The print media, under the petty domination of President Niyazov, are fearful of reporting on news without his consent. As the cult of Niyazov has grown, much of the news has been dedicated to the president's alleged achievements and his speeches.

Information from outside the country has been reduced to a slow trickle, and citizens are forced to read Russian newspapers (when these are not suspended) or watch Russian television. During 2002, even this avenue was closed when government authorities imposed heavy restrictions on the cable networks relaying foreign broadcasters. Elsewhere, the authorities have banned Turkomans from accessing foreign Internet sites and any discussion of politics is suppressed.[40] Given these problems, real press freedom is nonexistent.

In neighboring Tajikistan, the problems are similar but differ in degree. On the eve of World Press Freedom Day, May 3, 2002, the Tajikistan newspaper *Asia Pulse* described the situation in the country as "lots of rights, but little freedom," a phrase that adequately sums up the situation for the media in recent years. Restrictions in the country are far more subtle than those in Turkmenistan and derive from the severe penal code, which carries a number of clauses that prevent independent reporting by the media. Journalists are routinely harassed and intimidated by officials in power, and access to information is hindered at almost every step. Although outside institutions provide funding, journalists are poorly trained and self-censorship is prevalent. Printing remains in the hands of the government, which can use its monopoly to stop articles from being printed.

It would be inaccurate to argue that the human rights abuses in both countries stem from their support of the alliance against terrorism. Rather, for both Tajikistan and Turkmenistan, sins of omission as opposed to commission are at the root of the problem. Before the attacks, the two countries were being told to expand democracy and introduce new rights; pressure was being applied through local intergovernment organizations, such as the OSCE. America's development agency, the United States Agency for International Development (USAID), was also working to provide assistance. An examination of the situation now would probably reveal little tangible difference from before September 11 except that these countries, having assisted the United States, can now ignore the criticism without fear of retribution. The international desire to bring about meaningful change has given way to a desire to stem terrorism.

Uzbekistan and the "Evil-Doers"

A country that made even greater use of the aftereffects of September 11 than either Tajikistan or Turkmenistan was another former Soviet republic, Uzbekistan. Although other countries stretched the definition of terrorism to include their own domestic terrorists and used the tragedy to introduce new laws suppressing political dissidents, the government of Uzbekistan went even further in distorting its own problems.

The president of Uzbekistan, Islam Karimov, said in his call for increased vigilance after the September 11 attacks, "Above all, we should look directly at the ugly face of the terrorist threat. . . . [T]hose with evil intentions who are spreading various fabrications, handing out leaflets, committing theft and sedition in some neighborhoods, and . . . spreading propaganda on behalf of religion should be recognized as being supportive of these evil-doers."[41] According to Karimov, almost every criminal was connected to terrorism. Indeed, criminality in itself was terrorism. In joining the allied effort, it was clear that Karimov would not only seek financial support but would expect the United States, a long-time critic of the regime, to look the other way while it dealt with the criminals, the dissenters, and its own brand of Muslim fundamentalist terrorists, the IMU. Significantly, even before the September 11 attacks, there were problems with terrorism in Uzbekistan, particularly in the Ferghana Valley, which also runs through the country.

In late 1997, a number of law enforcement officers were murdered in the Namangan region, resulting in a vicious retaliation by the government against the Muslim population. The police arrested hundreds of ordinary Muslims on the pretext of looking for the Islamic terrorists who were thought to have carried out the murders. Two years later, in 1999, sixteen people were killed in bomb explosions in the capital, Tashkent. Once again, the Muslim population was heavily suppressed. Karimov banned a number of organizations, including political movements, religious groups, and human rights monitoring groups. Amnesty International documented an increase during this period "in the number of arbitrary detentions, ill-treatment, and torture."[42]

Desperate for airbases from which to launch attacks on Afghanistan, the United States saw Uzbekistan as a linchpin in its war. After preliminary talks, Karimov quickly opened up Uzbeki airspace and allowed U.S. airbases to use its Khanabad airbase for military search-and-rescue missions.

The new relationship between the two countries enabled the Uzbeki authorities to feel justified in acting against the country's own citizens. Talking to a Radio Free Europe reporter in September 2002 about the changes, the HRW representative in Tashkent, Matilda Bogner, said, "The difference now, after September 11, in Uzbekistan is that the United States is a lot closer to the Uzbek authorities, and a lot more money is flowing into Uzbekistan from the United States. And the United States is not really using its new leverage to ensure that there are improvements in human rights, the United States is pretty much closing its eyes."[43] This pessimistic view appeared justified when the U.S. government publicly linked the IMU to Osama bin Laden and the al-Qaeda network.

As an example of how these views permeated the various government institutions in Uzbekistan, in October 2001, Ravshan Haidov died in police custody after being arrested for alleged membership in the banned Islamic group Hizb-ut-Tahir. In seeking to vindicate the policemen charged with his death, a spokesperson said that Hizb-ut-Tahir was responsible for the September 11 attacks.[44] Haidov's death should not have surprised the international community because, as the United Nations Rapporteur on Torture Theo van Boven reported, the authorities systematically torture those held in detention.

The independent media are also suppressed in Uzbekistan. Much of the media is under the direct control of the authorities, as evidenced by the reaction in the press to the war on terrorism. In late 2001, the media focused on two essential themes: first, that the U.S. attack on Afghanistan was targeting terrorism and, second, that it did not represent an indiscriminate attack on the Muslim population. According to freelance journalist Ferida Harba, the newspaper headlines at the time reflected these views. "Terrorism: A Threat to All Humanity," one headline said, while another reiterated the goal of the war, "Peace and Stability: Our Common Goal." Moreover, government-controlled media outlets reminded Uzbeks of their own terrorist problems.

The mass arrests of Muslims, Harba believes, have had a chilling effect on media organizations. Journalists are afraid to raise the issue of terrorism in the Ferghana Valley, and residents in the region fear reprisal if they dare criticize the U.S. bombing campaign in Afghanistan. Those journalists brave enough to speak out found themselves the subject of intense scrutiny by the police, while some were physically assaulted. The media, therefore, like many other groups in Uzbekistan, continue to be silenced. This situation is unlikely to change if the West stops applying pressure on President Karimov.

Confirmation of Uzbekistan's new status as ally and friend to the United States came with a visit by President Karimov to Washington and his meeting with President Bush on March 12, 2002. Describing the Uzbeki leader as the United States' new strategic partner in the region, Bush showed the world that an appalling human rights record was no bar to a relationship with the United States. Speaking after the meeting, Karimov quoted President Bush as saying, "Now you know and can convey to your people that Uzbekistan has a strategic partner. And that partner, in the person of the USA, will always be with you."[45] Support for Karimov's version of the meeting came the same day when Secretary of State Colin Powell described Uzbekistan as a "solid coalition partner."[46]

With the administration providing glowing reports of its new partner, it was left to the legislature to add a dose of reality to the visit. Members of Congress criticized Karimov for his failure to halt the suppression of religious and secular groups, and said that the country should uphold its obligations in accordance with its membership in the OSCE. The statements appeared not to worry Karimov, who, before flying back to Tashkent, was polite enough to thank the United States for the $160 million allocated in aid to Uzbekistan.[47]

SUPERPOWERS: PAST AND FUTURE

China in My Hand

The People's Republic of China is a permanent member of the United Nations Security Council and a potential future superpower itself; as such, its support in the war against terrorism was essential for the United States. Despite a tense relationship between the two countries in the past, owing in part to the 1999 bombing of the Chinese Embassy in Belgrade and spying accusations involving a midair crash, the Bush administration had worked hard at promoting a better understanding between the two countries. Once again, however, the bargaining that took place for China's consent to U.S. military deployment in what amounted to its own political backyard was to have an unfortunate consequence for human rights in the region. It led to implicit U.S. support for China in its repression of the Uighur people.

Living in the northwestern Xinjiang Uighur Autonomous Region (XUAR), the mainly Muslim Uighur people are the largest indigenous group in this sprawling Chinese territory, which shares borders with Afghanistan, Kazakhstan, Kyrgyzstan, Pakistan, Tajikistan, and India. The region is blessed with many natural resources, including reserves of coal and oil, yet most of the Uighur people live in abject poverty, with the natural fuel being transported to other regions of China.

Within the XUAR region there have been calls by the Uighurs for the formation of an independent state, East Turkestan, uniting the region with other parts of central Asia where the Uighurs also live. These calls for independence, or "splittism," as the Chinese government calls it, have been forcibly resisted by the Chinese authorities.

To prevent the formation of a breakaway republic, the Chinese government has undertaken a campaign of repression against the Uighur people and encouraged other countries belonging to the Shanghai Cooperation Organization (SCO)—Russia, Kazakhstan, Kyrgyzstan, Tajikistan, and Uzbekistan—to arrest Uighurs and extradite them to China to stand trial. For the last seven years, the Chinese government has placed heavy restrictions on religious and cultural freedoms, held unfair trials, and often executed separatists. According to Amnesty International, in 1997, the Chinese security forces rounded up thousands of Uighurs after protests and a series of bombings.[48]

In their reports on the subject, Amnesty International stated that, in the rush to quell the Uighur separatist elements, the authorities have violated the human rights of many innocent people. Amnesty International has also argued that the Uighur people lack "legitimate channels" to air their grievances, and those Uighurs brave enough to speak out have been tortured or detained for long periods without access to legal counsel. Moreover, Amnesty International has also raised the alarm over post–September 11 antiterrorist arrangements among SCO countries that could lead to suspects being extradited to face possible torture in China.

Against this background of repression against its own people, China was lobbied by the U.S. government for its support in the war against terrorism. Within a month of the September 11 attacks, however, China revealed its own price for acceding to U.S. demands; like most other countries, China was largely concerned with its own internal problems. In what was becoming standard practice, a country with a disgraceful human rights record used September 11 as a bargaining chip to gain international acquiescence for the suppression of its own supposed terrorist problems. The first step in this process was to remove any division between international terrorism and domestic calls for independence.

Losing no time in making the all-important connection, a Chinese foreign ministry spokesperson said on October 11, 2001, that the international community should support China's efforts to destroy the separatists. "We believe that our fight against the East Turkestan is part and parcel of the international effort to combat terrorists," said the spokesperson Sun Yuxi, who went on to say that the West should not have "double standards" on terrorism. According to a report in the *Asian Wall Street Journal*, Sun's words were the most "explicit sign yet that Beijing expects Western governments to mute their frequent criticisms of China's harsh tactics in return for Chinese support."[49]

Responding to the comments of Chinese officials, Amnesty International said that the country had failed to distinguish between the activities of terrorists and separatists. It also accused China of attempting to silence the claims for a separate state: "Separatism . . . covers a broad range of activities[,] most of which amounts to no more than peaceful opposition or dissent. . . ."

At the same time that China was making its tendentious links with international terrorism, President Bush was preparing to visit the country. In his first foreign engagement since the September 11 attacks, President Bush met Chinese President Jiang Zemin in Shanghai on October 19, 2001. The trip also gave President Bush the opportunity to address other Asian leaders who were attending the Asia-Pacific Economic Co-operation Forum (APEC) in Shanghai. At the press conference held shortly after their meeting, both leaders stressed their countries' willingness to cooperate and alluded to the common interests they shared. On the subject of terrorism, President Bush thanked China for its quick response to the September 11 attacks and said, "There was no doubt that [China] would stand with the United States and our people during this terrible time." He spoke of a "common understanding" between the two countries and stressed the importance of the cooperation being offered by China in intelligence matters. For his part, President Jiang said that there was a need to work together with the international community to combat terrorism.

On the same day as the meeting, and as a counterpoint to the discussions on cooperation, the Hong Kong–based Information Center for Human Rights and Democracy made public a letter from two Chinese dissidents, Wang Dang and Wang Juntao, asking President Bush to pressure China on the subject of human rights. While accepting the right of the United States to strengthen ties with China, the letter that said human rights in the country had steadily worsened and there was a real need for reform. Acknowledging that the United States had a certain amount of leverage over China, the letter asked President Bush to continue with the pressure that had led to the release of a number of dissidents during the critical period when China was engaging with the globalized economy.[50]

Admittedly, President Bush made some mention of China's human rights record during his trip to Shanghai; however, the comments failed to meet the high standards set by the rhetoric of the administration at the start of the year. In February 2001, Secretary of State Colin Powell warned China that the Bush administration would continue to raise the issue of human rights and do it "frankly," often the diplomatic code word for "forcefully." In a meeting with China's ambassador to the United States, Li Zhaoxing, Powell said that "China needed to follow the rule of law. . . ." The meeting came one day after members of a banned religious group, Falun Gong, set themselves on fire in Tiananmen Square to protest the government's suppression of their activities.[51]

Since the September 11 attacks, China has continued its crackdown on all forms of freedom of the press and freedom of expression. Indeed, within two months of the October meeting between the two presidents, China was announcing an intensive "strike hard" campaign on the "three forces" of religious extremism, ethnic separatism, and terrorist violence. As in Chechnya, there were press restrictions on reporting in the region, with a press secretary claiming that the media were being used as a primary method of "infiltration and sabotage."[52] In an article from the Hong Kong news agency Zhongguo Tongxun She, China said it was ready and willing to intensify its cooperation with the United States and Russia. The United States, therefore, found itself allied with two countries in its war against terrorism claiming that the forces fighting for independence within their own borders were also terrorists. The Bush administration would find these unsubstantiated claims difficult to ignore.

Making a claim similar to the one made in Uzbekistan, the Chinese government stated that al-Qaeda terrorist Osama bin Laden had aided the separatists in the XUAR region. In a statement issued by the Chinese State Council, the government said that bin Laden had schemed with the "heads of Central and West Asian terrorist organizations . . . to help the East Turkistan terrorist forces in [the] XUAR [region] to launch a holy war. . . ."[53] The comments came after an admission by U.S. officials that "Chinese Uighurs" had apparently participated in Taliban missions in Afghanistan.

Fulfilling an earlier promise, President Bush returned in late February 2002 to visit China. With the war in Afghanistan virtually over, Bush risked offending his hosts by calling for religious freedom and a freer, more open society. He also provided Chinese officials with an example of American democracy in action by allowing students to question him on any subject at a televised meeting. Significantly, Bush administration officials put pressure on their Chinese counterparts to ensure that the "townhall" gathering was broadcast live on air.

Despite serving as evidence that the administration was beginning to understand the need to mention human rights abuses when visiting repressive regimes, the mere fact of the president's visit took away much of the force of his remarks. As with other countries in the region, being rewarded with a visit by the president of the United States or an invitation to the White House sent a mixed message. The dual signal appeared to highlight a considerable distance between word and deed.

Later in the year, there was evidence that China's persistence had finally paid off. On August 19, 2002, a little known group, the East Turkestan Islamic Movement (ETIM), was added to the State Department's list of foreign terrorist organizations. The decision followed a State Department meeting with Chinese officials on the subject of terrorism in the XUAR region. Speaking of the decision, Deputy Secretary of State Richard Armitage said, "[A]fter careful study, we judged . . . that [the ETIM] committed acts of violence against unarmed civilians without any regard for who was hurt." After the meeting the Chinese government expressed their satisfaction at the decision. However, a spokesperson at the East Turkestan Information Center in Sweden said that the decision would now be used to justify Chinese suppression of the Uighur people.[54]

Concerning the Chinese media, journalists in the country are some of the most heavily restricted in the world. The Chinese government continues to pressure journalists to censor themselves, there are numerous examples of prior restraint at newspapers, and long jail sentences have been handed out to those seeking to express themselves on religious and political issues. One of the most worrying post–September 11 changes has occurred in the Special Administrative Region of Hong Kong, where proposed security legislation threatens freedom of expression and other fundamental rights. Under the new law, journalists fear that they could be charged with treason if they disclose leaks from government officials. Moreover, democracy activists may face criminal charges for peaceful protest.[55]

Because of its new relationship with the United States, China has been able to use the tragic events of September 11 to garner support for its own terrorist cause. Its immediate offer of help to the United States, particularly with its influence over other countries in the region, gave it a privileged position that was used to convince the State Department that the ETIM should be banned. The likelihood of the State Department adding the ETIM to its list of terrorists was greatly improved when China argued that links existed between its own terrorist groups and al-Qaeda, a claim for which the evidence is tenuous at best. As a result, China continues to suppress the Uighur people while arguing that it is fighting a war on terrorism.

Russia and the "Common Foe"

On September 12, 2001, Russian President Vladimir Putin not only gave his unconditional support to the United States in its time of need but also said that the two countries shared a "common foe," a view based on the fact that "bin Laden's people are connected with the events currently taking place in Chechnya."[56] The assertion that September 11 is connected to the war in Chechnya has been a constant mantra for Russian officials who want the international community to see the repression of the Chechen people as an aspect of the wider war on terrorism. Toward the end of September 2001, President Putin returned to the theme when he claimed that the war in Chechnya should have alerted the West to the dangers of Islamic fundamentalism. In March 2002, the U.S. State Department released its human rights report on Russia, and the Russian Foreign Ministry responded to it by saying, "One gets the impression that its writers simply used old drafts, as if nothing had happened in either Russia or the United States in recent years, as if the events of September 11, 2001, had not occurred and the international community had not closed ranks in the battle against terrorism."[57]

With the connection between the two events made to the satisfaction of the Russian government, it was perhaps inevitable that the authorities would want a special waiver to pursue the country's war in Chechnya unmolested by criticism from its new ally, the United States, or the Western media. Moreover, the Moscow Theater siege would also encourage the authorities to attempt to silence their own media.

The United States has often complained loudly about Russia's behavior, particularly in the State Department's Human Rights Reports. As Tom Malinowski, the Washington advocacy director for HRW, said when complimenting the State Department for not pulling its punches, "[A] human rights report is not by itself a human rights policy."[58] Moveover, even if the reports could be construed as a policy, it certainly failed to discourage the Russian authorities from seeking to silence their critics.

Russia's attitude over Chechnya can be seen in the row over the activities of Radio Free Europe/Radio Liberty (RFE/RL). In the early part of 2002, RFE/RL announced that it would be broadcasting a new radio service aimed at listeners in the north Caucasus. The hour-long daily programs were to be divided equally among the local languages of Avar, Chechen, and Circassian. Responding to the new broadcasts, the Russian authorities protested that Chechen language broadcasts might inflame tension in the breakaway republic. Mikhail Lesin, the Russian information minister, said in an interview that the decision to air the broadcast would be seen as an "unfriendly step" that would undermine the struggle against international terrorism. To affirm his point, Lesin said that the United States was well aware of the number of al-Qaeda fighters trained in Chechnya. He also did not rule out legislation in the Russian parliament preventing the broadcasts. Again linking the Chechen problem to the events of September 11, he said that just as the U.S. Congress took its "emotional decision" on the war in Afghanistan and the war on terrorism, the Russian parliament would undertake to do the same over RFE/RL.

Despite last-minute meetings on April 11 between Lesin and officials from the U.S. Congress, Department of State, and U.S. Under Secretary for Public Diplomacy Charlotte Beers, the radio station went ahead with its plans. True to its promise, the lower house of the Russian parliament voted on April 24 for an inquiry into the status of RFE/RL. The inquiry was also to examine whether any existing agreements would allow Russia to broadcast Spanish and English programs in the United States; if properly pursued the threat could have had some intriguing results.

While rebuffed on the question of the Chechen broadcasts by RFE/RL, the Russian authorities have been more successful at restricting their own media over the question of Chechnya. Even before September 11, journalists had been prevented from traveling to the region on their own; journalists on official visits found themselves tightly controlled by press officers, and journalists have been assaulted by Russian soldiers. Indeed, journalists without the proper accreditation were arrested and held for long periods while other journalists were accused of aiding the rebels. At home, newspaper reporters and television broadcasters who tried to interview Chechen rebels or who departed from the government line found themselves confronted by political pressure, tax raids, and threats of violence. After the September 11 attacks, the Russian authorities felt that these acts could be undertaken with impunity.

During the tense stand-off at the Moscow theater between the Russian security forces and the Chechen rebels holding over eight hundred hostages, the media were in constant contact with the hostages and rebels via cellular phones. Forced to watch interviews with the rebels on Russian television, officials reacted angrily. An Information Ministry spokesman, Yuri Akinshin, warned the media that they should stop airing interviews with the hostage takers. "If this is repeated . . . we reserve the right to take all proper measures, up to the termination of the activity of those media," Akinshin was quoted as saying by the Interfax news agency.[59]

A direct request was also made to the Russian media. The editor of *Ekho Moskvy*, Aleksei Venediktov, confirmed that he had been approached by the Information Ministry to tone down its reporting, but told officials that the station was not breaking Russian law. The ministry also moved to close *Ekho Moskvy*'s Internet site after it carried interviews with the rebels; however, the request was withdrawn after the station removed the offending text. Like *Ekho Moskvy*, the television broadcaster *Moskoviya* found itself caught in the Information Ministry's cross-hairs. On October 25, 2002, Information Minister Mikhail Lesin ordered the closure of *Moskoviya* for apparently promoting terrorism. Initially taken off the airwaves, the station returned to its normal scheduling after a meeting between the station's director general and officials at the Information Ministry. The print media also received warnings. The Moscow daily *Rossiyskaya Gazeta* was singled out after it published a photograph showing the body of a woman killed by the rebels on October 23, 2002. The authorities were also outraged when journalists from the Russian network NTV managed to enter the Moscow theater and interview a number of the rebels. Later, NTV broadcast the images of both the hostages and rebels, but did not broadcast their voices.[60]

After the rescue, the government, incensed by the media coverage, pressed ahead with a new media law designed to hinder reporting on terrorism and Chechnya. Discussed in the lower house of Parliament only hours before the siege had begun, the law, loosely translated as the "Law on Battling Terrorist Propaganda in Mass Media," was given new momentum by the experiences of the authorities during the Moscow Theater siege. Largely viewed by press freedom organizations as a reaction to media reports on the subject of Chechnya, the bill banned the media from printing or broadcasting news on a number of different subjects. According to the Committee to Protect Journalists (CPJ), the bill included sections banning information that might justify the activities of terrorists, support resistance to counterterrorism, hinder operations designed to counter terrorism, or disclose antiterrorist tactics. So wide-ranging as to be applied to almost any subject, the law was an unjustified attempt to control the flow of information from Chechnya. This did not stop it from being portrayed by the government as a necessity in the fight against terrorism. Naturally, among the Russian media and NGOs it caused a tremendous outcry.

Fortunately, although the bill passed in both houses of the Russian parliament, President Putin used his veto to send it back to allow for more consultations with the media. The decision offered

President Putin a chance to be seen as a defender of the press while allowing others to take the blame for introducing such a damaging press law in the first place.[61]

YOUR ENEMY IS MY ENEMY: THE IMPACT OF SEPTEMBER 11 ON THE EUROPEAN UNION AND OTHER ALLIES

The September 11 attacks sent shock waves around the world. Overwhelmed by the number of deaths, and finding the size and scale of the destruction difficult to comprehend, many democratic countries hastily reexamined their own laws on terrorism, security, and secrecy. Intentionally or not, many of these laws impeded civil liberties. As a result, the very freedoms that clearly separated these countries from those that produced the terrorists who committed the heinous acts were undermined.

Indeed, by passing new laws that limited freedom of expression, these democratic countries were ignoring international law stating that freedom of expression may be restricted only when a specific test had been met. This test had three distinctive elements: First, the restriction should be provided by a law and drafted with such precision that an ordinary citizen could "regulate his conduct" accordingly. Second, the restriction should have a legitimate aim. Third, it should be both necessary and proportionate.[62]

Taking into account these three elements of the test, it is clear that the prevention of terrorism and the safety of citizens represent legitimate aims, but that security, where possible, should not be increased by passing new legislation and, if there is a need for new legislation, sections that restrict freedom of expression should be drafted as narrowly as possible. If the changes to legislation fail to meet this three-part test, they cannot be justified under international law.[63]

The European Union (EU), an ally of the United States, acted quickly to develop a common approach on counterterrorism measures. Within a relatively short time after the attacks, the EU had reached a decision over a joint definition of terrorism and was actively tracing terrorist financing in its member states. Regarding the hunt for terrorists, the EU agreed on a common arrest warrant and actively worked with the United States to produce a list of proscribed terrorist groups. At the same time, member states examined their own domestic laws and made changes where necessary. Consequently, a range of new or amended laws affected civil liberties across Europe.

One such example involved the decision by the EU to amend the 1997 European Directive on the Protection of Telecommunications Data and Information. Under Article 15 of the amendment, member states would be empowered to draft legislation giving police, intelligence agents, and customs officials access to e-mail, Internet, and telephone connections. Companies would be required to store the information for a predefined period rather than retaining information for the purposes of charging customers and then quickly deleting it, as was traditionally done. In May 2002, the journalists' union and press freedom organization the International Federation of Journalists (IFJ) vigorously protested Article 15, arguing it would "open the door to the snooping society in which people's private communications will become subject to official monitoring."[64] Other organizations feared that the amendment would jeopardize the right of journalists not to reveal their sources.

On October 9, 2002, the European Union's Council of Ministries put forward additional proposals that worried civil liberties groups. Perhaps the most significant was the decision to amend the definition of what constituted a terrorist offense. By changing the definition to actions that "seriously affect," as opposed to "seriously alter," the institutions of a country and by adding the phrase "international organization" to the list, the Council of Ministers was including organizations such as the World Bank and the World Trade Organization. Responding to this new definition of terrorism, Tony Bunyan, editor of the watchdog organization State Watch, said, "The actions by the European Union are a deliberate attempt to broaden the concept of terrorism to cover [globalization and environmental] protests such as those in Gothenburg and Genoa."[65]

At the domestic level, a number of member states adopted laws that diluted existing freedoms. In the United Kingdom, the government of Prime Minister Tony Blair undertook an array of measures to combat terrorism. Shortly after the September 11 attacks, the government heightened the public's fears by declaring a "state of national emergency" which allowed it to derogate from Article 5 of the European Convention on Human Rights (ECHR). This declaration enabled the United Kingdom to introduce powers to imprison without trial those foreign citizens believed to be engaged in terrorist activities or guilty of expressing sympathies for terrorists. The new power suspended the centuries-old right of habeas corpus that allowed courts to review the legality of the imprisonment.

Aside from antiterrorism laws, the decision of the U.K. government to delay the implementation of its Freedom of Information Act (FOIA) until January 2005 was detrimental to the free flow of information in the country. Announced shortly after the war in Afghanistan had begun, the decision to delay the implementation frustrated the will of a parliament that had adopted the FOIA legislation in November 2000. Claiming that it needed more time to implement the legislation, the government appeared to be backtracking from previous declarations that it wanted an open and responsive government. Disappointingly, at a time when the public needed as much information as possible to understand the momentous events, the U.K. government had sought to deny them information.

Moreover, the claims that the decision to delay the FOIA's implementation had been made for purely domestic reasons appeared disingenuous as it followed an international wave of attempts to retrench secrecy. In the United States, the FOIA had been weakened by Attorney General John Ashcroft's October 12 memorandum, which broadly stated that government departments should exploit loopholes to avoid handing over information. In Canada, the authorities amended their own Access to Information Act by giving the minister of justice the power to issue exemption certificates, a power deemed by many FOIA experts to be totally unnecessary.

The U.K. government's decision regarding the FOIA seemed to follow the same pattern as the previous discussion over the bin

Laden videotapes. First the United States made a decision shortly followed by the United Kingdom. Given the timing of each decision and the subsequent U.K. reaction, it was difficult not to believe that considerable discussion on secrecy matters was going to and fro across the Atlantic.

Meanwhile, across the choppy waters of the Channel, France was also introducing new powers through the enactment of antiterrorist legislation. The attacks in New York and on the Pentagon encouraged a rethinking of the original Information Society Bill that resulted in the inclusion of a terrorism section allowing the authorities to survey and track e-mail messages and Internet sites. Fearing the possibilities of encryption technology in the hands of terrorists, the authorities also wanted to regulate this new computer technology.

The amendments led to outspoken debates in France, and as a result of the criticism, the criminal liability of Internet service providers was quickly dropped from the legislation. As a means of protection for users, an independent regulatory body—the Forum of Internet Rights—was created, but its powers were poorly defined. On the question of the media's portrayal of terrorists, like the U.K. government, the French government and the Audio-Visual Upper Council (CSA) seemed to take their lead from U.S. Secretary of State Colin Powell.

With strong echoes of the Ikonos case in America, Reuters reported in October 2001 that the Defense Ministry had prevented a French satellite imagery service, Spot Image, from selling photographs of Afghanistan to the media. Moreover, seemingly willing to accept the U.S. State Department's views on the Middle East television network Al-Jazeera, the CSA announced in that same month specific recommendations for all radio and television stations on the handling of information "linked to the current crisis." The CSA urged the media outlets to pay particular attention to French values. In early November 2001, it accused Al-Jazeera of broadcasting live images without giving context and providing false information without making later corrections.[66] Not only were the allegations similar to those made by Rumsfeld and Powell in Washington, but they, too, failed to acknowledge that, in France as in the United States, news content was independent of the government. Reporters Sans Fron-tières responded by asking the CSA to ensure that the current crisis did not usher in new controls over the content of information.

In a rare decision among its counterparts, France's neighbor, Germany, did not use the attacks to increase its own antiterrorist powers. With its own large Muslim population, Germany worked to maintain a balance between human rights and national security. Indeed, the aftermath led many German media organizations to reflect on the impact of the September 11 attacks on relations between the Middle East and the West. A report by the IFJ quotes commentator Siegfried Weischenberg as saying, "[Y]ears of efforts toward mutual comprehension have been destroyed in one day," a statement that aptly summed up the mood of the country.[67] Any criticism of the media was also muted.

In the Republic of Ireland, however, other sensibilities were at play. Acknowledging the strong historical relationship between the Republic of Ireland and the United States, the conservative media and the Irish government were extremely sensitive to any criticism of either U.S. or Irish policy in the wake of the attacks. Setting the tone, Brian Cowen, Ireland's minister for foreign affairs, said, "Ireland is not neutral in the struggle against international terrorism."[68]

One of the least tolerant Irish media outlets was the *Sunday Independent*, which attacked journalists such as the U.K.'s Robert Fisk for criticizing American foreign policy in the Middle East. In an article in the *Sunday Independent* titled "Retribution Is Coming," retired U.S. diplomat George Dempsey argued that Ireland should avoid "posturing" and that the anti-American stance taken by parts of the Irish media meant that they should share blame for the attacks.[69] The debates in the Republic of Ireland, conducted in the open, pro-vide some idea of the pressure that much of the Western media were under at the time.

Outside of Europe, one of America's staunchest allies, Australia, also made a number of changes to its laws. The government of Prime Minister John Howard sought to amend the Commonwealth Crimes Act, which made it an offense for a person to receive leaked docu-ments from government or state employees. Under the new provisions, those journalists who breached the law faced up to two years in jail. Cementing its approach to terrorism, the government also proposed a new security bill allowing officials to proscribe organizations that threatened security and to detain suspects as well as intercept e-mails and other communications. In early 2002, the government faced opposition to these new powers from members of the Australian Senate and civil society organizations. As a result, it agreed to reexamine the proposed legislation in light of these criticisms.

A far more disturbing outcome of the attacks was Howard's shameless attempt to win an extremely close election by explicitly linking the country's illegal immigration problems to worries over terrorism. The decision to connect the two promoted fears in an already jittery Australian public and increased racist sentiment. Almost immediately after the attacks, the government openly discussed the possibility of "sleeper terrorists" operating in their midst or trying to enter the country as asylum seekers. This possibility was reinforced by the comments of Defense Minister Peter Reith, who said, "[Illegal immigrants] can be a pipeline for terrorists to come in and use your country as a staging post for terrorist activities."[70] Such comments generated a fierce debate in Australia, with parts of the media accusing John Howard of playing the terrorist card during the elections. In turn, the media found themselves under attack from the government and its supporters, who accused them of failing to understand the gravity of the new situation. When it became clear that the election would be one of the closest in years, the government made terrorism and illegal immigrants the central themes of its reelection campaign.

In the final days of the race, Howard told Brisbane's *Courier Mail* that his harsh policy on asylum seekers was justified by the attacks on September 11: "You don't know who's coming and you don't know whether they do have links or not."[71] As expected, the comments captured the headlines and further fueled fears over terrorism. On November 10, Howard won what was described as a "remarkable victory" with a swing to his government of nearly 2 percent. Like the governments of China, Russia, Pakistan, and Uzbekistan, the government of Australia had discovered that the war on terrorism could bring about a number of political benefits. But, by following the example of repressive regimes, Australia had cheapened its own democracy.

Uncomfortable as the proposition may be, after the attacks, a number of countries actively profited from their relationship with the United States. By virtue of lending their support to the United States, some countries won the right to pursue unmolested their policies of cruelty against their own peoples. Other countries, such as Pakistan, gained the legitimacy they craved, and the willingness of the Bush administration to overlook flawed elections served only to affirm this fact.

Unused to the international attention, countries such as Turkmenistan and Uzbekistan were brought out of the political wilderness to receive increased aid, letters of congratulation, and invitations for their leaders to present themselves on the White House lawn. These meetings were conducted with an international bonhomie not often seen on the international stage.

In the midst of terror, the United States had forged new friendships and new alliances. Thrown together by circumstances, the leaders of democratic countries mingled with their counterparts from repressive regimes grateful to them for agreeing to join in the war against terrorism.

Some political leaders even bravely spoke of a new world order where advantage could be taken of the new relationships to forge a better world. This view was apparently confirmed when British Prime Minister Tony Blair, speaking at his political party's conference in 2001, said, "The kaleidoscope has been shaken. The pieces are all in flux. Soon they will settle again. Before they do, let us reorder the world around us."[72] The only question was: reorder the world for whom? Certainly not innocent Uighurs or Chechens whom Western leaders conveniently appeared to forget in their haste to close ranks with their repressive allies in the war against terrorism. Certainly not for those who aspired to having elected leaders in Pakistan or Turkmenistan. And certainly not for genuine asylum seekers hoping for a better life and a new start in Australia.

The hopes for a bright new future based on democracy and

human rights were hollow. Rather than being upheld, human rights all across the world were being diluted or, in extreme cases, ignored altogether. The grandiose claims that out of the tragedy a better world was emerging quickly floundered on the political realities of the post–September 11 world. However, the new environment had also been noticed by undemocratic regimes that were willing to use the actions of the United States as the justification for their own repressive behavior.

NOTES

1. Susan B. Glasser and Peter Baker, "Blasts Go Off in Russian Theater: Russia Says Two Hostages Killed by Chechen Rebels," *Washington Post*, October 21, 2002.

2. Ibid. According to the *Washington Post* article, a total of eighty-four hostages had been released from the theater by October 26.

3. Ibid.

4. Sergei Govorukhin, quoted in ibid.

5. Johanna McGeary, Paul Quinn-Judge, and Yuri Zarakhovich, "Bloody Drama: His Back to the Wall, Putin Retakes a Moscow Theater from a Chechen Suicide Squad, But the Cost Is High," *Time*, November 14, 2002.

6. Jonathan Thatcher, "Bloody Raid Ends Moscow Theater Siege," Reuters News Service, October 26, 2002.

7. Vladimir Vasileyev, quoted in ibid.

8. "Rough Justice: The Law and Human Rights in the Russian Federation," Amnesty International, October 2, 2002, http://www.amnesty.org (accessed December 5, 2003).

9. Christina Lamb and Ben Aris, "Chechen Rebels' Link to Al-Qaeda Probed: Putin Apologizes for Failing to Save All Hostages at Theater," *Chicago Sun-Times*, October 27, 2002.

10. McGeary, Quinn-Judge, and Zarakhovich, "Bloody Drama."

11. Elizabeth Andersen, "Independent Commission of Inquiry Must Investigate Raid on Moscow Theater," Human Rights Watch, October 30, 2002, http://www.hrw.org (accessed December 2, 2003).

12. Agence France Press, "Britain Welcomes End of Hostage Drama," October 26, 2002.

13. Mike Allen, "Bush Defends Putin in Handling of Siege," *Washington Post*, November 19, 2002.

14. George Bush, address to Congress, September 20, 2001.

15. Colin Powell, press briefing, Inter-Continental Hotel, Las Cabas, Mexico, October 26, 2001, http://www.state.gov (accessed December 2, 2002).

16. Gerhardt Schroeder, quoted in "German Chancellor Backs Russia's Fight against Terrorism," Deutschland Radio broadcast, November 12, 2002.

17. Richard Boucher, quoted in Johnson's Russia List, "U.S. Could Add Chechen Groups to 'Terrorist' List," *CDI Russia Weekly*, November 1, 2002, http://www.cdi.org (accessed December 2, 2003).

18. Editorial, "A Free Pass in Chechnya," *Washington Post*, July 21, 2002.

19. Madeleine Albright, "Clear on Chechnya," editorial, *Washington Post*, March 8, 2000.

20. Ibid.

21. "Bush Signals Support for Sending Aid to Dissidents in Cuba," Washington File, U.S. Department of State, May 18, 2001, http://www.usinfo.gov (accessed December 2, 2001).

22. Paula Dobriansky, testimony before the International Operations and Terrorism Subcommittee, Senate Foreign Relations Committee, May 24, 2001.

23. Ibid.

24. Franklin D. Roosevelt, State of the Union Address, January 6, 1941, australiapolitics.com, http://www.australiapolitics.com (accessed December 5, 2003).

25. "Human Rights, Americans and the World," http://www.americans-world.org (accessed December 2, 2003).

26. John Gershman, "Human Rights: Celebration and Concern," Tom Paine, December 10, 2002, http://www.TomPaine.com (accessed September 30, 2003).

27. U.S. State Department, introduction to *Country Reports on Human Rights Practices for 2001* (Washington, DC: GPO, 2001), www.state.gov (accessed December 2, 2003); "Country Reports on Human Rights Practices for 2001," released by the Bureau of Democracy, Human Rights, and Labor, U.S. Department of State, March 2002.

28. Reuters News Service, "Pakistan Condemns 'Brutal and Horrible' U.S. Attack," September 11, 2001.

29. Pru Clarke, "Musharraf's Delicate Balancing Act," *Financial Times*, October 4, 2001.

30. Trevor Royle, "Stuck in the Middle," *Sunday Herald* (Edinburgh), September 23, 2001.

31. Human Rights Watch, "Pakistan: Entire Election Process 'Deeply Flawed,'" October 9, 2002, http://www.hrw.org (accessed December 2, 2003).

32. "Preliminary Statement: European Union Election Observation Mission to Pakistan," *Asia Pulse*, October 31, 2002.

33. Human Rights Watch, "Pakistan."

34. State Department briefing, Richard Boucher, October 12, 2002, http://www.usembassy.state.gov (accessed December 2, 2003).

35. Amnesty International, "Central Asia: No Excuse for Escalating Human Rights Violations," October 11, 2001, http://www.amnesty.org (accessed December 2, 2001).

36. Galina Gridneva and Valery Zhukov, "Tajik President Calls for Building Up Intolerance of Terrorism," ITAR-TASS World Service and Reuters News Service, May 31, 2002.

37. Ibid.

38. "Tajikistan Hospitals to Receive New Bulk of Assistance Provided by U.S. State Department," *Asia Pulse*, October 29, 2002.

39. Galina Gridneva and Valery Zhukov, "EU Revises Strategy of Cooperation Central Asia," ITAR-TASS World Service and Reuters News Service, December 14, 2002.

40. Karl Ömer Oguz, "Turkmenistan Report," *IPI World Freedom Press Review, 2002* (Vienna: International Press Institute, 2002), p. 142.

41. Islam Karimov, quoted in Amnesty International, "Central Asia."

42. Amnesty International, "Central Asia: No Excuse for Escalating Human Rights Violations."

43. Breffni O'Rourke, "UN: Human Rights Chief Steps Down, Warning of Post-September Rights Crackdown," Radio Free Europe/Radio Liberty, September 11, 2002, http://www.rferl.org (accessed December 2, 2003).

44. "Opportunism in the Face of Tragedy," Human Rights Watch, http://www.hrw.org (accessed December 2, 2003). The policemen were later convicted of Haidov's murder.

45. "USA Will Always Be with Uzbekistan: Uzbek Leader," BBC Monitoring Reports from Uzbek Television First Channel, March 16, 2002, http://www.factiva.com (accessed December 2, 2003).

46. Dana Milbank, "Uzbekistan Thanked for Role in War; U.S., Tashkent Sign Cooperation Pact," *Washington Post*, March 13, 2002.

47. "USA Will Always Be with Uzbekistan."

48. Amnesty International, "Central Asia: No Excuse for Escalating Human Rights Violations."

49. "China to Step Up Its Campaign against Separatists," *Asian Wall Street Journal*, October 11, 2001.

50. Wang Dang and Wang Juntao, open letter to President George Bush, released by the Information Center for Human Rights and Democracy, October 19, 2001, Democracy Now, http://www.pacifica.org (accessed December 2, 2003).

51. David R. Sands, "Powell Lectures China on Human Rights Issues," *Washington Times*, January 25, 2001.

52. Committee to Protect Journalists, "Looking Back, Looking Forward," http://www.cpj.org (accessed December 2, 2003).

53. "China Says bin Laden Gave Xinjiang Separatists Help," *Kyodo News*, January 21, 2002.

54. William Foreman, "U.S.: China Muslims Planned Attacks," Associated Press, August 30, 2002.

55. "Proposed Hong Kong Law Severely Threatens Free Expression," December 19, 2002, Freedom House, http://www.freedomhouse.org (accessed December 2, 2003).

56. Ian Taylor, "Russia and Nato Unite Against International Terror," *Guardian* (London), September 13, 2001.

57. "USA Will Always Be with Uzbekistan."

58. "U.S. State Department Rights Report Critique," Human Rights Watch, March 4, 2002, http://www.hrw.org (accessed December 2, 2003).

59. "Media Face Government Restriction and Pressure on Coverage of Hostage Standoff," press release, Committee to Protect Journalists, October 28, 2002, http://www.cpj.org (accessed December 2, 2003).

60. Ibid.

61. On April 8, 2003, an antiterrorist convention was voluntarily adopted by the Industrial Committee comprising the heads of TV channels and print media. The convention contained clauses that still restricted press freedom.

62. *The Sunday Times* v. *United Kingdom* (Series A No. 30), European Court of Human Rights, (1979–80) 2 EHOO 245, April 26, 1979.

63. Toby Mendel, "Consequences for Freedom of Expression of the Terrorist Attacks of 11 September," Article 19, May 2002 (unpublished report).

64. Aidan White, "Journalism and the War on Terrorism: Final Report on the Aftermath of September 11 and the Implications for Journalism and

Civil Liberties," International Federation of Journalists, September 3, 2002, http://www.ifj.org (accessed December 2, 2003).

65. Ibid.

66. Ibid.

67. Ibid.

68. "Statement by the Minister for Foreign Affairs of Ireland, Mr. Brian Cowen, UN General Assembly Debate on Terrorism," *Irish Times* (Dublin), October 2, 2001, http://www.Ireland.com (accessed December 2, 2003).

69. White, "Journalism and the War on Terrorism."

70. Sonny Inbaraj, "Post Sept. 11 Reportage Fuels Divisions, Stereotypes," Inter-Press Service, July 1, 2002.

71. "Threat Justifies Immigration Crackdown—Howard," Thomas Crosbie Media, November 7, 2001, http://www.tcm.ie (accessed December 2, 2003).

72. Michael White, "Let Us Reorder This World," *Guardian* (London), October 3, 2001.

Chapter 7

"EVERYONE HAS HIS OWN BIN LADEN...."

Freedom knows no borders.... [A] fiery voice of liberty in one country can raise the spirits of another far away.

—Kofi Annan, Secretary-General of the United Nations

THE FIERY VOICE OF LIBERTY

Delivering a speech at the John Fitzgerald Kennedy Library in Boston, United Nations Secretary-General Kofi Annan recalled the story of how a group of freedom fighters in Africa broke into applause on hearing that John F. Kennedy had been elected president of the United States. Annan said he "treasured the story because it reminds us all that freedom knows no borders, that a fiery voice of liberty in one country can raise the spirits of another far away. John Kennedy was that voice for his time, and we will struggle to fill the silence that he left."[1]

Although originally referring to President Kennedy, Annan's words could have also applied in a wider sense to America itself. Its history of supporting individual liberties, its strong Constitution, its powerful Supreme Court with a tradition of independence, and its finely balanced legislative and executive branches make the United States one of the most democratic countries in the world. Furthermore, its economic strength and its general willingness to peg financial aid to the need for democratization and increased human rights make it a powerful force within the international human rights community. For these reasons, the United States can be seen as the "fiery voice" of Annan's speech—an example to many countries around the world of a successful and advanced nation that prides itself on upholding human rights and civil liberties.

However, if it is true that the attacks on September 11 changed the way that Americans lived and how they viewed the outside world, it is also true that they greatly affected the human rights community. The coalition and subsequent war on terrorism deeply damaged this community, as repressive regimes mixed with their democratic counterparts in an alliance that made the two sets of countries almost indistinguishable from each other.

Moreover, America's response to the attacks, including its own internal adjustments to civil liberties, tarnished the country's image abroad, damaging one of the best working examples of a democracy but also denying the United States the higher ground from which it had traditionally encouraged others to bring about change. The result was the inverse of what had previously gone before: after the events of September 11, instead of a "fiery voice" calling for others to tread the road toward liberty, America acted as the justification for repressive regimes all around the world.

Within the United States itself, it is likely that the damage to civil liberties can be undone. The impulse toward human rights is too deeply rooted for it to be otherwise. In addition, the institutions that reinforce this attitude and protect and nourish democracy are too strong to be destroyed overnight. The United States is rather like a large and unwieldy supertanker whose wheel has been sharply turned, but it will be a considerable time before the country changes its course. In the intervening period, institutions within America can act to prevent the new course from being made permanent.

The real problem lies outside America's borders. One of the first journalists to recognize this was Argentinian Horacio Verbitsky. In New York to receive a press freedom award from the Committee to Protect Journalists (CPJ) in November 2001, Verbitsky said that each American violation resonates in countries where democracy is fragile and where press freedom is only one option: "People who defend dictatorships say, 'You see? In America they're talking about dictatorship, too.'"[2] He warned that "repressive regimes will adopt the rhetoric and use it in their own crusades to crush dissent and control the media."[3] Given the later developments, it was difficult not to see Verbitsky's words as prophetic, for both press freedom and human rights in general.

Perhaps the best expression of the consequences arising from the September 11 attacks came from the CPJ, which saw them as having a "ripple effect," implying a series of interconnected violations starting off at a specific epicenter and then widening and extending outward to touch virtually every country on every continent.[4] In Africa, countries as disparate as Benin, Uganda, and Zimbabwe all tried to use the war on terrorism to repress the media. In Europe, Belarus followed other Western countries and hastily enacted an antiterrorism law that was little more than a thinly disguised attempt to protect the state from the intrusion of journalists during times of crisis. In Asia, a number of countries tightened their own repressive laws and attempted to justify them by pointing to the United States' passage of several new laws. In the view of Middle Eastern countries, the U.S. response vindicated their own crushing of dissidents and allowed them to argue that the war on terrorism required new approaches, producing yet another smokescreen to justify repressive and inhumane behavior.

DO DICTATORS READ THE AMERICAN PRESS?

Rippling outward, the wave of violations could be traced back to the concatenation caused by the original attacks and the subsequent actions of the Bush administration, which had provided support to those repressive countries that wished to subdue their own people. The case of Yaser Esam Hamdi in America, who was held incommunicado and without access to a lawyer, provides one of the best examples of the damage that could be done to human rights by an administration that had focused solely on itself and had failed to reflect on the wider implications of its actions.

Captured in Afghanistan by U.S. forces during the Mazer-e-Sharif prison riots in November 2001, Hamdi found himself at the center of some of the most extraordinary legal maneuvers ever undertaken by the executive branch of the U.S. government. On being transferred to Camp X-Ray, Guantanamo Bay, Cuba, investigators discovered that Hamdi had been born in Baton Rouge, Louisiana, and was an American citizen. However, he had spent much of his life in Saudi Arabia.

Fearing the possibility that, as an American, Hamdi might challenge the conditions and status of the prisoners in the camp, authorities quickly transferred Hamdi to a naval brig in Norfolk, Virginia. The transfer set in motion a legal battle of wills between a Justice Department determined to limit Hamdi's rights under U.S. law, for the purposes of security and the protection of sources, and human rights groups worried that individual liberties were being diluted in the war against terrorism. Although it was unclear at the outset, the legal fight would arguably set aside the Constitution, pit the executive against the judiciary, and become a crucial test of the president's right to claim emergency powers.

Speaking of Hamdi's move to Norfolk, Defense Secretary Donald Rumsfeld said:

> At some point the lawyers will decide what they want to do with him. . . . They'll either keep him and try to get information from him, or they'll send him back home because he's not interesting, or they'll try him under one of the alternative opportunities we have: The Uniform Code of the Military Justice, the criminal justice system or a military commission.

On the question of the laws being applied in the case, Rumsfeld would only say, somewhat airily, "The lawyers think about all of those niceties."[5]

On the question of legal niceties, the lawyers for the military and the Justice Department faced the difficult task of ensuring that Hamdi's detention in Norfolk did not afford him the rights of other Americans. Under U.S. law, a prisoner has the right to appoint and see a lawyer and to be charged and brought before the courts within forty-eight hours of his arrest. All of these rights were denied Hamdi. How could the Bush administration justify this denial? The answer would require some light footwork on the part of the Justice Department's lawyers and it would not sit well with their civil rights colleagues and some members of the judiciary.

From the outset, all captured al-Qaeda and Taliban prisoners sent to Guantanamo Bay had been designated as "enemy combatants," a phrase that left the captured men stranded in a legal limbo, untouched by international law. The declaration meant that the prisoners were not prisoners of war for the purposes of the Geneva Convention. Regarding rights under the U.S. Constitution, a Supreme Court decision in 1950 said that enemy combatants who were not held on U.S. soil had no access to the U.S. legal system.[6]

As a result, the detainees could be held for an indeterminate period of time without being charged and without being accorded the normal rights under international law. For all intents and purposes, in Camp X-Ray, the innocent and the guilty alike were ghosts without a definite legal form, stranded together and deprived of any contact with the outside world. But, what about Hamdi, who was not only an American, but also now residing in solitary confinement on U.S. soil? The answer lay in the power that the president possesses as the country's wartime chief.

According to the government, the Constitution gives the executive branch of government both the right and the responsibility to wage war; furthermore, the judiciary, under the separation of powers, has no right to interfere in decisions made by the executive during wartime. Therefore, the Bush administration could treat Hamdi, who was being held on U.S. soil, in the same way as the prisoners in Camp X-Ray. Such a view, however, was heavily contested by civil libertarians, who argued that the right of the judiciary to review the acts of government did not evaporate when the country went to war.

Consequently, the stage was set for a struggle that could be seen as the first stand against the government's attempt to "embed in law a vast expansion of executive authority with no judicial oversight in the name of security."[7] The opening shot of the battle came with the decision by a federal judge in Norfolk to allow Hamdi to see a lawyer, a move precipitated by the refusal of the military to allow public defender Frank W. Dunham Jr. to see the detainee.

In the last week of May 2002, U.S. District Court Judge Robert Doumar ordered that Hamdi be given access to a federal public defender "without military personnel present, and without any listening or recording devices of any kind being employed in any way." The decision came after lawyers from the Justice Department argued that contact with the outside world, including discussions with a legal adviser, would "interfere with the success of the interrogation effort." They also argued that as an "enemy combatant," Hamdi was not entitled to legal representation or any rights under the Constitution. Stating that "fair play" and "fundamental justice" entitled people jailed in the United States to lawyers, Judge Doumar said that the government had been unable to provide the court with one case "where a prisoner of any variety within the jurisdiction of a United States District Court, who was held incommunicado and indefinitely, and who has filed a petition for a writ of habeas corpus, was denied access to [an] attorney or the right to file such a petition."[8] In reply, the government appealed to the Fourth U.S. District Court of Appeals and, on May 31, 2002, filed an emergency petition to stay the judge's ruling, which was accepted by the higher court. The legal move once again prevented Dunham, who had filed a petition on behalf of Hamdi's father, from seeing Hamdi.

Assistant Federal Public Defender Robert J. Wagner, in his brief to the court of appeals on Hamdi's behalf, argued that the executive branch did not have the requisite power to hold a prisoner incommunicado and prevent the courts from examining whether this procedure was indeed proper. If the court failed to be persuaded by this position, Wagner said, "[It] would eliminate any limitation upon [the government's power] to indefinitely detain any American citizen, under a state of war or peace, as long as the military determines that the detainee is an enemy."[9]

In its own submissions to the court, the Justice Department argued that access to the detainee would prejudice future investigations and that it was entitled to use the "enemy combatant" determination in the case. Discussing the role of the courts, the brief said, "The court may not second-guess the military's enemy combatant determination" as it would infringe the president's powers, including his rights with regard to "the capture, detention, and treatment of the enemy and the collection and evaluation of intelligence vital to national security."[10] Hidden behind the legal rhetoric was the assertion that the president had suspended habeas corpus—the historic right of the courts to review imprisonment—in the case of Hamdi.

Already deeply concerned, the *Washington Post* editorialized that the Justice Department's arguments supporting the label "enemy combatant" effectively gave the president the right to an "I-said-so test." If this were to be accepted by the courts, the editorial argued, "any American could be locked up indefinitely, without a lawyer, on the president's say-so. You don't have to believe that Mr. Hamdi is innocent to see grave peril in this."[11]

On June 25, 2002, a three-judge panel of the Fourth U.S. District Court of Appeals heard legal argument from both sides. The result was a partial victory for the government. In its opinion of July 12, 2002, the court advised Judge Doumar that "the political branches are best positioned to comprehend this global war in its full context and it is the president who has been charged to use force against those nations, organizations, or persons he determines were responsible for the September 11 terrorist attacks."[12] However, the court accepted the need for a partial judicial review to take place and asked Judge Doumar to hear more arguments and examine more facts.

Responding to Judge Doumar's request for more information, on July 25, 2002, Michael H. Mobbs, an adviser on enemy combatants for the Defense Department, provided Judge Doumar with a two-page declaration on Hamdi's detention. According to the declaration by Mobbs, Hamdi had traveled to Afghanistan in July or August of 2001 and received training and subsequently joined a Taliban army unit. He was later caught by the Northern Alliance with a gun in his hand. The document failed to set out witness testimony from anyone who had captured Hamdi or interrogated him, nor did it contain Hamdi's own statements. Moreover, Dunham claimed that Hamdi should be given the opportunity to see the statement in order to rebut any of its claims.

Confronted by this document and unable to make a determination in accordance with the higher court's ruling, Judge Doumar asked the Justice Department to provide copies of Hamdi's statements, interview notes, details of the locations where Hamdi had been detained, and the names and addresses of those who had undertaken the interrogation. To allay government fears over security, Judge Doumar said he would review the documents in private.

With breathtaking audacity, the Justice Department ignored the order and filed a motion before the court asking Judge Doumar to drop his request. "Such intrusive discovery is unnecessary in this case," argued the Justice Department. "None of the materials listed in the court's July 31 order is within the scope of a proper inquiry into Hamdi's legal status." Asserting the separation of powers, the motion said that the military did not have to supply the information because the detainee was an enemy combatant captured in time of war.[13]

The motion prompted Stephen Dycus, a legal expert at the University of Vermont, to state that he could not remember a time when the government had ignored a court order: "I don't think the Justice Department has the power to simply defy the court."[14] In mid-August, Doumar ruled that the motion was insufficient and made a second request for the information. This request was again ignored by the Justice Department, which was given permission to appeal to the Fourth U.S. District Court of Appeals.

Whether it was empowered to do so or not, the government appeared to be defying the courts. In the order allowing the appeal, Doumar tellingly stated, "If the Mobbs declaration is sufficient proof of Hamdi's status as an enemy combatant, then the Court of Appeals has indicated that further judicial review of his current detention is foreclosed."[15]

In a fifty-four-page judgment delivered on January 8, the Fourth U.S. District Court of Appeals sided with the government: "Judicial review does not disappear during wartime, but the review of battlefield captures in overseas conflicts is a highly deferential one."[16] The decision was criticized by civil libertarians, who argued that the courts had supported the executive branch in its determination to have the last word and had therefore abrogated their own role in such matters.

As a direct consequence of Hamdi's case, U.S. citizens caught on foreign soil and defined as "enemy combatants" could be held for an indeterminate period of time without charge, without access to a lawyer, indeed, without any rights at all under the Constitution.[17] Perhaps most worrisome, one of the highest courts in the country found this situation acceptable on the basis of a two-page summation written by someone who was not present at Hamdi's arrest or at any of his interrogations.

Although it is to be hoped that the Supreme Court will overturn the rulings of the lower courts and permit a hearing on the merits of his detention, the case reveals the sheer desire of the Bush administration to win. Indeed, this desire was evident at one of the earlier hearings before Judge Doumar when it was argued that because Dunham had not seen Hamdi he was not even entitled to represent the detainee. Based on this argument, it would appear that the administration did not believe that detainees had the legal right to enter the judicial system in the first place. It was no wonder that voices were raised in protest.

However, the media and civil liberty groups were not the only ones interested in the case. Unknown to the Bush administration, the legal maneuvers were also being closely observed in Liberia. Arrested six times previously, Liberian journalist Hassan Bility's seventh time would see him disappear for six months, during which the *Analyst* reporter would face torture and inhumane treatment at the hands of his government captors. Fueled by then–Liberian President Charles Taylor's blatant disregard for human rights, Bility's case would become a focal point for human rights groups concerned that the case represented a new round of suppression in Liberia, with the September 11 attacks, and terrorism in general, as the justification. The case was also to have disturbing parallels with Hamdi's.

Snatched on the streets of the Liberian capital, Monrovia, on June 24, 2002, close to the offices of the headquarters of the Press

Union of Liberia, Bility was taken by plainclothes security officers to the Central Police Headquarters. He was held at the station until early the next morning, when he was driven to President Taylor's residence in Congo Town for a personal interrogation. During the drive to the president's house, he was blindfolded, and the tightly wound cloth covering his nose and mouth interfered with his breathing. According to Bility, "I could not breathe properly and I was yelling. When I told them I could not breathe . . . they said that was okay because they were going to kill me." He was also beaten in the car, causing damage to his left eye.[18]

At the president's residence, Bility was questioned by Taylor, with security officers and government ministers in attendance. During the interrogation, the journalist was informed that technicians and security officials had broken into his computer and discovered e-mail messages showing that Bility was collaborating with the rebel Liberians United for Democracy and Reconciliation (LURD), which was engaged in a vicious war against government forces. Taylor alleged that Bility was working with LURD, the U.S. Embassy, and mercenaries to overthrow him. When Bility protested his innocence, Taylor told him that he would not be released and that a "prison cell would be . . . [his] home for a long time."[19] After two hours, the disoriented and beaten journalist was driven back to Monrovia.

With Bility now among the "disappeared," the Liberian government faced hostile questioning from the international community. Facing their accusers, officials said Bility was involved in terrorism and, in a direct allusion to the Hamdi case in the United States, claimed that he was an "unlawful combatant." Although the use of the military phrase was nothing more than a smokescreen for suppression and cruelty, it showed that the ramifications of the Hamdi legal action in the United States had now spread to one of the most repressive regimes on the African continent.

At the beginning of July, in a move that repeated the earlier legal process in the United States, the National Human Rights Center, the Catholic Justice and Peace Commission, the Center for the Protection of Human Rights, and the Legal Consultant Incorporated jointly filed a writ of habeas corpus before Criminal Court B, inviting the Liberian government to produce Bility for an assessment of his detention. In accordance with the laws of Liberia, the court issued an order to produce the journalist, which was ignored; indeed, on July 2, 2002, the public prosecutors' office denied that Bility was even in government hands.

In Liberia, as in the United States, the struggle between the executive and the judiciary was unequal. On July 8, 2002, Taylor rescinded the court order to produce Bility, saying that the court had no authority because he was in the hands of the military. His failure to appear in court fed fears that the journalist had been tortured and killed. These fears were shared by officials from the Bush administration, who, in a supreme irony, on July 9, 2002, urged Liberia to follow the rule of law and present the journalist in public.

Adding further insult to injury and showing that it was making good use of the lesson in the separation of powers, the Liberian government further embarrassed the Bush administration in a press conference given by Liberian Information Minister Reginald Goodridge. Speaking to the U.S.-based All Africa media outlet, Minister Goodridge said, "This man is being held as an unlawful combatant and it was you guys [the American government] who coined the phrase. We are using the phrase you coined."[20] Goodridge had no need to repeat the phrase; the message had been received the first time.

Later, Judge Wynston Henries ruled that Bility would not be tried by his criminal court but before a military court. Reacting to Henries's decision, the human rights organizations filed another writ of habeas corpus before the military court, which on July 25, 2002, ordered the production of Bility, as the criminal court had done before it. The decision once again prompted the direct involvement of the government, which, through Defense Minister Major General Daniel Chea, declared the decision null and void because the court had not been authorized as the competent authority to hear the case.

Blocked at every attempt in the Liberian courts, the human rights groups sought an appeal to the African Commission on Human Rights in Banjul, Gambia, an organization whose wheels grind agonizingly slowly. Meanwhile, in Monrovia, the government obstinately refused to discuss the Bility case. However, in September, there were signs that Taylor was reconsidering his position. In an interview with the Voice of America on September 19, 2002, Liberian foreign minister Monie Captan hinted that the government would be prepared to release Bility to end the crisis. The offer was made again in October, when Taylor said that Bility would be released if he signed a statement acknowledging that he would be rearrested if he committed further violations. Finally, on December 10, 2002, the government released Bility on the condition that he leave the country and never return. Once released, the journalist was able to talk about the appalling treatment he had received while in jail. His story served only to reinforce the terrible dangers that the local journalists faced when reporting in the war-torn country.

Talking to Musue N. Haddad of the *Perspective*, Bility said that he was transferred to Clay—outside of Monrovia—on July 24, 2002, where he faced questioning from military personnel.[13] Of his prison cell, he said, "I was held in . . . [an] underground prison in the middle of the rainy season with other prisoners. . . . The cell is about three feet high and it is filled with water so I basically squatted."[21] Bility said he was later moved from Clay and must have been taken to at least thirteen different locations during his incarceration. "At some of the prisons, I was basically in the midst of maggots with rains and the maggots were creeping over my body. And I was in another prison where I was in a toilet hole cell," he said.[22]

Concerning his sadistic treatment, Bility said, "They tied me with the rope they called twine. It is a rubberlike rope but very strong and it usually cuts the victims. It penetrated the areas above my elbow where it was tied. There was a deep cut there and I was physically beaten regularly and they electrocuted me with the hope of extracting statements from me. They electrocuted my private parts and all over my body. . . ."[23]

Except for the torture, Hamdi's and Bility's cases were remarkably similar. Each man was arrested in the name of terrorism and accorded the status of "combatant." Each was prevented from seeing a lawyer and from exercising other rights under his country's constitution. Moreover, the governments of their respective countries refused to accept applications for habeas corpus and insisted that the domestic legal system had no right to try them. This view was initially challenged by the judges at first instance, but they were eventually forced as a result of the persistent interventions of the executive branch of government to concede this point. In the United States, the defeat of the habeas corpus applications was achieved with the use of determined and able Justice Department lawyers and the Fourth U.S. District Court of Appeals; in Liberia, which preferred a far more hands-on method, it was attained through the direct intervention of ministers disdainful of the separation of powers.

Given these similarities, what distinguishes the two cases? One answer might be that one case occurred in a freedom-loving country that espouses democracy and the other happened in a repressive regime governed by a tyrannical leader. It might also be said that the overriding sanctity of the U.S. Constitution and the supremacy of its legal system, taken together, provide citizens with an unrivalled set of rights and protections. Yet, Liberia also has a constitution and a legal system which is modeled on that of the United States and is a signatory to the African Charter on Human and People's Rights, all of which provide powerful prohibitions on arbitrary arrest or detention.

On the surface, when confronted with such similarities in the legal landscape though not the same history of upholding the rights of the individual, the difference must surely be in the operation of these institutions. The fact that the judges could not assert their independence and Taylor's belief that democratic institutions could be bent to his will were singular to Liberia. But, and here was the problem for human rights, the institutions which should protect democracy in both countries were acting in a similar manner. Indeed, the results in both countries were the same.

From the outset, both presidents wanted to ensure that the prisoners were not presented before the courts by exerting the supremacy of the executive over the judiciary branch. As a consequence, both presidents managed to prevent writs of habeas corpus from being applied, and they managed to stop lawyers from visiting their respective detainees. In doing so, the rights of Hamdi and Bility were ignored. The only real difference in the cases was that in the United States the decision was reached in the full glare of the media and without the clumsy machinations so beloved of Taylor and his ministers.

Steeped in democratic traditions for over 200 years, the United States is an admirable example of a democratic country in action, but the Bush administration's desire to exclude the Constitution relieved it of the moral high ground from which it could have drawn distinctions between its own treatment of Hamdi and Liberia's treatment of Bility. Furthermore, State Department spokesman Richard Boucher failed even to see the irony of his call for Liberia to produce Bility at a time when Hamdi was sitting incommunicado in a prison cell in Norfolk and prevented from seeing a lawyer.[24]

The Liberian government's treatment of Bility showed that after September 11, repressive regimes were eager to learn new ways to justify the suppression of their own people. Such countries were handed the twin excuses of the war on terrorism, which could be subordinated to their own causes, and the regressive actions of arguably the most democratic country in the world. It was a dangerous concoction that was to have a lasting impact all over the globe.

IN THE NAME OF TERROR

Toward the end of November 2001, the Zimbabwean government released a list of those it accused of "assisting terrorists." Referring to a speech given by President Bush, a spokesperson for the government said, "We agree with President Bush that anyone who in any way finances, harbors, or defends terrorists is himself a terrorist."[25] Despite appearing as an attempt to assist in the global war against terrorism, the list actually contained the names of six persons who were journalists and a South African–based human rights campaigner.

Under the guise of fighting terrorists, President Robert Mugabe had produced a list of major irritants who had persistently criticized his attempts to destroy civil society in Zimbabwe and prevent news of his predations from reaching the outside world. The list prompted a rebuke from State Department spokesman Richard Boucher, who said that "the United States rejects any comparison between the international coalition's fight against terrorism and the deterioration of the rule of law and the state-sponsored violence in Zimbabwe."[26]

Boucher's statement was laudable in its aims. However, Boucher failed to appreciate that repressive regimes would draw their own "comparisons" and were bound to see terrorism through the lenses of their own distorted outlook on the world. President Mugabe was merely one example of this expression of self-interest.

In September 2002, the departing United Nations High Commissioner for Human Rights Mary Robinson voiced her concern that the environment for human rights had worsened since the attacks. In particular, she said that governments were using the campaign against terrorism as an excuse to curtail the legitimate rights of citizens. Robinson's views were supported by the chairman of the Organization for Security and Cooperation in Europe (OSCE), Antonio Martins da Cruz, who argued that human rights should be respected in the fight against terrorism.[27]

Bolstering Robinson's opinion, Human Rights Watch (HRW) wrote an open letter almost one year after the September 11 tragedy stating that many governments had adopted antiterrorist measures that were disproportionate and arbitrary. Many governments, the letter said, were using terrorism "opportunistically" to justify crackdowns and the abuse of their political opponents.[28]

In the aftermath of the attacks, governments were quick to offer their respects to America and then attend to the business of determining their own response to the tragedy. The effect on press freedom was profound. Typically, repressive governments either enacted new terrorist laws or amended existing ones, and they placed a greater emphasis on secrecy. The media also suffered, with journalists being arrested or forced to censor themselves. Described by President Bush as a battle to protect freedom, in an ironic twist, the new measures in many countries actually reduced the freedoms available to their citizens.

Malaysia's response was typical of a number of countries that saw the attacks as a golden opportunity to reduce the importance of human rights within their own borders. Speaking at the end of October 2001, Musa Hitam, the chairman of the Malaysian government's Human Rights Commission, said that the issue of human

rights would have to take a "back seat" following the political and economic crisis caused by the September 11 attacks: "I hope people don't
misunderstand me, but I am nationalistic enough to realize that these
matters dealing with security of the country should be given precedence before we start talking about democracy and human rights."[29]
There is little doubt that the chairman's words were met with enthu-
siasm by the Malaysian government, which was already considering
toughening its draconian Internal Security Act (ISA).

Introduced by the British to help in the fight against communist
insurgents, the ISA allowed the Malaysian police to detain without
trial anyone considered to be a threat to the nation. In the past, it
had often been used by Prime Minister Mahathir Mohamad's government to imprison political rivals, as shown by the arrest of six
supporters of the former deputy prime minister, Anwar Ibrahim, in
April 2001. After the September 11 attacks, sixty suspected Islamic
militants were arrested under the ISA, drawing praise from Washington for the swift action. This praise marked a complete reversal in
the United States' previous position on the much-reviled law.

Local authorities in Malaysia later caused the Bush administration considerable discomfort when, under fire for using the ISA, they
likened the law to the USA Patriot Act, going so far as to say that it
was as fair as this U.S. law. A senior member of the ruling United
Malays National Organization, Tengku Ahmad Rithauddeen Tengku
Ismail, said that Malaysia was pleased that countries like the United
States saw the need for ISA-style legislation.[30] The attempted comparisons caused U.S. Ambassador to Malaysia Marie T. Huhtala to deny
the similarities. "It is fashionable in this country to draw a parallel
between your ISA and the measures that we have put in place since
September 11, but actually there are very few similarities," she said.[31]

Whether accurate or not, the comparison served as additional
evidence that American diplomats around the world were finding it
increasingly difficult to counter the perceived wisdom that the
United States was diluting its freedoms and strengthening its security by passing restrictive laws in order to combat terrorism. These
discussions were further encouraging signs for regimes that cared
little for the rights and freedoms of their citizens.

In December 2001, the former Soviet bloc country of Belarus joined the growing number of countries reexamining their security laws. Traditionally deeply prejudicial against the media, Belarus government officials said that the laws should be revised despite the absence of a large-scale threat in the country. Known as the Law of the Republic of Belarus on Fighting Terrorism, the new legislation permitted those persons undertaking investigations into terrorist activities to "use for official purposes means of communication belonging to citizens, state agencies and organizations, regardless of their form. . . ." This vaguely worded authorization meant that, in addition to private communications, officials might be allowed to take over the media during a terrorist crisis.

The new law also enabled officials to enter private property and stated that they need not inform a prosecutor of their actions until twenty-four hours after the fact. Regarding the media's right to report on terrorism, the law stated that the head of the investigation "regulates the activities of media representatives in the zone of the conduct of an anti-terrorist operation." As a result, the right of the media to pursue news stories independently would be severely curtailed. In a letter to Belarus President Aleksandr Lukashenka, press freedom organization Article 19 said that the law "constitutes a serious restriction on the right to freedom of expression which cannot be justified, even in the context of counter-terrorism operations."[32]

Another country that undertook a careful examination of its terrorism laws was India. After September 11, India, along with Pakistan, benefited considerably from the lifting of sanctions imposed as a consequence of its nuclear weapons testing program. Drawn in from the cold, India sought to strengthen its relationship with the United States and made much of its desire to play a significant role in the international coalition against terrorism. At the same time, the country also produced a draft terrorist act—the Prevention of Terrorism Ordinance 2001 (POTO). With provisions compelling journalists to reveal their sources and making it an arrestable offense for journalists to meet with sources or receive information without permission, the proposed law was immediately attacked by the media and press freedom organizations. Responding to the provisions, the Editors Guild of India said that it was "shocked," particularly by the fact that the government had failed to consult with the media before drafting the law. The organization accused the government of "exercising [a] coercive and extra constitutional power."[33]

The criticism caused the government to go on the offensive by lecturing the media on its supposed responsibilities. Speaking in Lucknow, Arun Jaitley, Union Minister for Law, Justice, and Company Affairs, said that the Indian media should follow the example of the U.S. media after September 11: "The media there did not show dead bodies and there was no public outcry and nobody cursed anybody for the intelligence failure. Instead, people organized mass prayers [and] hoisted the national flag and the media worked for the restoration of the national pride." The minister went on to accuse the Indian media of failing to educate the masses and said that cynicism in Indian society actually stemmed from the media.[34] Jaitley's words disclosed yet another government determined to gain the upper hand over the media after the events of September 11.

Indeed, Jaitley appeared to be hinting that, with the media in the United States as a role model, the Indian media should set aside their willingness to censure the government and support it wholeheartedly. In other words, the first thing the media should jettison in this post–September 11 world was their own independence. Implicit in this statement was the belief that the media have a set role that can be determined by the government. Rather than examining the actions and behavior of the government, the minister argued that the media's role within Indian society was to educate the masses, or, failing that, to educate the masses in what the government wished them to hear. Such a view abdicated the government's own responsibility to explain issues to the people via the media. In essence, Jaitley's words were nothing less than a call for a compliant, malleable media to subordinate themselves to the will of the government.

Nevertheless, the pressure did not stop journalists from continuing to condemn the provisions of the POTO. With complaints about the possible effects of POTO on press freedom growing louder, the government agreed in early December 2001 to make significant amendments to the legislation. In effect, the obligation to provide information on terrorism was dropped, as were the penalties for non-compliance. The decision amounted to a comprehensive victory for the media, which had campaigned vociferously for the changes. But, once again, the long-drawn-out process undertaken by the government, and the comments of ministers such as Jaitley, revealed how eager governments were to force the media to conform.

While the most obvious approach by governments after September 11 was to tighten their laws on terrorism, some countries decided to take a different route. Like Zimbabwe, which had wanted to use the new environment to pursue its war against the media, Jordan saw the chance to amend its own press legislation to persecute the media. Coming as they did only weeks after the September 2001 attacks, the actions of the Jordanian government were purely opportunistic, occurring at a time when many countries and the world's media were focusing elsewhere. On October 8, 2001, the government endorsed amendments to the Penal Code that provided for tougher penalties for press freedom violations. Changes to the 1999 legislation included fines of up to 5,000 dinars (US $7,000) or prison sentences ranging from three months to three years, or both. Toward the end of October 2001, perhaps as an attempt to silence objections to the amended Penal Code, the government announced that, after numerous false starts, it was finally scrapping its Ministry of Information.

In a comment that sought to justify the Penal Code amendments, officials said that the removal of the ministry necessitated new legislation to fill the legal and administrative vacuum. The announcement was further proof of the government's cynical view of the media. Such political maneuvering failed to impress the Jordanian Press Association (JPA), which forwarded a list of its own proposed changes to the law. The changes included halting pre-print censorship, the confiscation of print editions, the suspension of newspapers, the revocation of licenses to print, and the arrest and imprisonment of journalists for their writing. The JPA's list proved to be a far more accurate and detailed view of the media landscape in Jordan.

With Muslim populations of their own, many African governments were also extremely sensitive to the issue of terrorism and the possible existence of al-Qaeda cells in their own countries. Fearing attacks from a vengeful United States, some governments attempted to suppress any talk of terrorism or bin Laden in the media, while other countries passed new antiterrorism laws that repressed freedom of expression. In March 2002, Uganda's parliament passed an antiterrorism bill that was not only a response to the September 11 attacks but also a recognition of its own internal terrorist problems. The bill loosely defined terrorism as "the use of violence or threat of violence with intent to promote or achieve religious, economic and cultural social ends in an unlawful manner, and includes the use, or threat to use, violence to put the public in fear or alarm."[35] Because of the extremely broad definition, journalists feared that the law could be used to suppress groups and individuals who criticized the government, a real likelihood given the fact that the country had suspended political debate in 1986.

Protesting the new law in a letter to Ugandan President Yoweri Museveni, the director of the International Press Institute (IPI), Johann P. Fritz, wrote, "Anti-terrorism laws . . . should be proportionate and measured. Since the tragic events of September 11, there has been a rush to legislate on this issue and IPI is of the opinion that laws enacted in haste are invariably poorly drafted."[36] In April 2002, unbowed by pressure from the international community, the Ugandan parliament adopted the bill and attached the death penalty to the legislation for any journalists caught publishing material in support of terrorism. Overly worried by security issues, the Ugandan government also banned the media from taking photographs of President Museveni, even during his participation in public functions. As the president explained, "I am a useful person, and I cannot allow these people to blow me up."[37]

The government of Benin was also anxious concerning allegations about its terrorist connections. On September 27, 2002, *L'Aurore* newspaper published an inaccurate story alleging that bin Laden and al-Qaeda had links with Benin. Furious at the story, the Benin government released a statement calling on the media to avoid false stories that "tarnish the image of the country." The government asked its media authority, the Higher Authority for Audio-

Visual Communications, to investigate the story. Subsequently, police arrested the publisher, editor-in-chief, and secretary of the newspaper. Detained for a number of hours, all three were later released and no further action was taken against *L'Aurore*.

In the Middle East, the recipient of the second largest amount of U.S. aid, Egypt, reacted to the September 11 attacks by purging its own Muslim extremists. The government tried to make a connection between the cruel treatment of its own extremists and the attacks on the Twin Towers of the World Trade Center. Speaking in the aftermath of the attacks, Egyptian Prime Minister Atef Abeid criticized human rights groups for wanting "to give these terrorists their 'human rights.'" He added that Egypt was at the forefront of the war on terrorism: "After these horrible crimes . . . Western countries should begin to think of Egypt's own fight against terror as their new model."[38] According to HRW, the Egyptian government prosecuted nearly three hundred suspected Islamists before a military court, ignoring the fact that they were civilians. In a foreshadowing of the Hamdi case in the United States, HRW said many of these civilians had been detained for long periods without trial.[39]

The treatment of the detainees did not go unnoticed by U.S. officials. During a press conference on September 27, 2001, Secretary of State Colin Powell said, "We have much to learn from [Egypt]," and commented, "[Egypt is] really ahead of us on this issue [terrorism] and there is much we can do together."[40] As the legal maneuvering in the United States proved, it did not take the Bush administration long to learn from its client. Powell's comments emboldened Egyptian President Hosny Mubarak, who confidently asserted on December 16, 2001, that the actions of the United States after the attacks "prove that we were right from the beginning in using all means, including military tribunals" against terrorists. He argued that the events of September 11 created a "new concept of democracy, that differs from the concept that Western states defended before these events, especially in regard to the freedom of the individual."[41]

Like those of the Malaysian and Liberian leaders, the words of President Mubarak should have been deeply humiliating to the Bush administration. After all, a country that has supported human rights, in one form or another, for much of its history was being forced to take "lessons in democracy" from a country with a deplorable human rights record. Instead of rebuking Mubarak, however, the Bush administration not only implicitly condoned the actions of the Egyptian government, but seemingly applied the lessons of the Egyptian military courts—detention without trial and solitary confinement in the United States.

Aside from the questionable comments of the Bush administration on the subject of democracy, there was disagreement among human rights organizations over the truthfulness of the U.S. State Department's human rights reports for 2001, particularly the report concerning Egypt. On March 4, 2002, HRW said that the reports were "largely candid and accurate," as well as forthright in their acknowledgement that terrorists often find their supporters in countries that deny their citizens human rights. "For the most part, the State Department deserves credit for pulling no punches." HRW, however, sounded a warning note when it said that "a human rights report is not by itself a human rights policy."[42]

Opposing this view, however, the Lawyer's Committee for Human Rights (LCHR), which conducted a thorough comparison of the 2000 and 2001 reports, stated that the 2001 report for Egypt had deleted a number of statements made in the previous year's report. According to the LCHR, the 2001 report had deleted the phrase "The military courts do not ensure civilian defendants due process before an independent tribunal." Another section that said, "[Military judges] are neither as independent nor as qualified as civilian judges in applying the civilian Penal Code" had also been excised. Commenting on the discrepancies, LCHR said, "It appears that the United States' ability to comment objectively and authoritatively on human rights abuses around the world has been compromised by its own disregard for international fair trial standards at home."[43] In effect the LCHR delivered a concise statement of the United States' policy toward Egypt, one now founded on its own treatment of terrorists captured in both the United States and Afghanistan.

The United States' human rights approach was in danger of becoming characterized by contradiction and ambiguity. Although

HRW was correct in saying that many of the reports were unstinting in their criticism, in a number of cases there was a wide divergence between what the Bush administration was saying and what it was doing. Criticism in the form of reports was not likely to be taken seriously by countries that were simultaneously being complimented by the U.S. president and secretary of state alike. This reaction could be seen time and time again with countries such as Russia, China, and Uzbekistan. It was also evident in the Bush administration's support of Egypt, a country so far down the road of repression that its leader's belief that other countries would wish to sit at its feet and take notes on democracy was staggering. Sadly, in this new environment, few countries seemed prepared to come to the aid of democracy by highlighting the damage caused by the decision to allow repressive regimes to join the coalition against terrorism.

One example of this trend was Israel. Describing the September 11 attacks as "a wake up call from hell," former Israeli Prime Minister Benjamin Netanyahu told the House of Government Reform Committee of the U.S. Congress on September 20, 2001, that the United States should be unrelenting in its pursuit of the perpetrators. Speaking of terrorism, Netanyahu said that it was sustained by regimes that "serve as deadly proxies to wage a hidden war against more powerful enemies" and that have carried out a propaganda campaign to "legitimize terror." Informing the members of Congress that a "network" existed, he went on to list its members: Iran, Iraq, Syria, the Taliban in Afghanistan, Yasser Arafat's Palestinian Authority, and several other Arab states including Yemen. With few exceptions, the list was a roll call of the enemies of the state of Israel.[44]

Netanyahu's reaction to the attacks encapsulated Israel's own approach, which was to make an explicit connection between the United States' war on terrorism and its own problems, particularly the horrendous suicide attacks in Israel and the murder of Israeli settlers in the West Bank and occupied territories. If this message had been confusing, Prime Minister Ariel Sharon's comment to Secretary of State Colin Powell that "everyone has his own bin Laden. Arafat is our bin Laden" left little room for doubt. To confirm the impression, a spokesperson for Sharon later added that Arafat had been following the "ideology" of bin Laden in his leadership of the Palestinian National Authority (PNA).[45] Although such comments were combined with offers to join the coalition against terrorism, they revealed a firm strategy of ensuring that the United States appreciated Israel's defense of itself during the Palestinian Intifada. If, at the time, Sharon was saying, "your problem is my problem," he was also implying that the reverse was true.

The tactic was to have profound implications, not only for the coalition being built by the Bush administration but also for any future attempt to resolve the conflict between the Israelis and the Palestinians. The Palestinian Intifada and constant Israeli references to the state sponsors of terrorism in the Middle East region left Arab countries united in the view that they would not participate in the coalition if Israel was also a member. Their stance, which largely reflected the position of the Arab countries in the war against Iraq in the early 1990s, came at a time when the United States badly needed the assistance of these countries. On the question of the Palestinian Intifada, the claims about Arafat served only to push the two parties farther from the peace table, leaving both sides bitter and resentful as the death toll on both sides continued to mount.

At first, the United States attempted to bring about a series of truces between the two sides, but these were broken in an endless bloody cycle of murder and murderous revenge. With the notion of terrorism firmly embedded in the minds of its people after their own recent experiences, Israel could easily justify its own position by showing that it also suffered from terrorist attacks—a claim brought home to the American public night after night on their television screens. Because the Israeli viewpoint was finding countless supporters in America, the Bush administration was unable to apply pressure on Israel. As a result, yet another country benefited from the connections drawn between its own domestic terrorism and the international fight against bin Laden and al-Qaeda.

The Palestinians, however, repeatedly denied the existence of a united terrorist network with al-Qaeda and Palestinian groups as members. Hatem Abdel Kader, a member of the Palestine legislative council, responded to Sharon's and Netanyahu's comments by stating that "the international community needs to make a distinction between terrorism and the legitimate resistance of the people who fight to restore their independence." He accused Israel of a double standard in linking Palestinian resistance to terrorism.[46] Despite the possible legitimacy of Kader's claims, his words were lost in the successive waves of suicide attackers, which in turn led to targeted assassinations by the Israeli Defense Force.

Israeli politicians also lost little time in claiming a connection between the September 11 attacks and the inflammatory language of the Palestinian media. This view was expressed on September 12 by former Israeli Prime Minister Ehud Barak, who said the attacks were the result of "continuous incitement by Arafat and his media."[47]

In Palestine itself, the Palestine National Authority (PNA) was greatly concerned at the pictures of Palestinians celebrating the September 11 attacks. Fearing that these images would send the wrong signals to the international community, the police and armed gunmen tried to prevent journalists from covering the celebrations. According to the Associated Press, freelance cameramen were called before PNA officials and told not to air the images of people celebrating in the streets. A group associated with Arafat's Fatah organization also issued warnings that were described by the journalists as threatening. Cabinet secretary Ahmed Abdel Rahman was quoted as saying that the PNA "[could not] guarantee the life" of journalists who showed such images. As a result of these threats and the concerns over the safety of journalists, these images were not aired.[48] During the weeks that followed, the PNA repeatedly tried to prevent the media from reporting on Palestinian expressions of anti-Americanism. On October 8, the authorities stopped journalists from attending a march held in protest of the U.S.-led war in Afghanistan—a decision also adopted by government authorities in China and Indonesia. To avoid embarrassment, the PNA went so far as to ban interviews conducted with Palestinians on the subject of the war.[49] Such actions show that while the claims of the Palestinian people deserve to be heard, the PNA has much to learn about democracy and human rights.

Extending outward from the original attacks, the impact of the events of September 11 and the war on terrorism have deeply influenced press freedom and human rights around the world. The reordering of priorities by the international community, the United States' own violations, and the attempts by other regimes to use these violations as an excuse for their own appalling behavior all undermined the struggle for democracy. Indeed, the situation had changed so drastically that repressive regimes like Egypt felt able to tell the international community that the attacks heralded a new type of "democracy"—one founded on arrest without charge, inhumane treatment or torture, and imprisonment for an indeterminate duration.

These comments showed no comprehension of the fundamental principles underpinning democracy. How quickly would these methods infect the whole of society and corrupt the very institutions that uphold human rights? Would it be possible to have a democracy neatly divided between the macro-world of civil society, where all laws and conventions apply, and a much murkier micro-world where the war on terrorism was fought in darkness and in the absence of the rule of law? Surely one would taint the other. And yet the comments of President Mubarak were not contradicted by the members of the international community; in fact, they seeped into the discussion almost without comment—another depressing sign of how far the debate on these issues had traveled since the September 11 attacks.

With the United States adopting laws and procedures that mimicked the authoritarian behavior of other countries, the ability to point to the world's only superpower and highlight its democratic traditions had been stripped away. Moreover, with each indefinite detention, with each failure to allow lawyers to see their clients, with each appearance of a president from a repressive regime on the front lawn of the White House, the arguments for democracy were being reduced to mere rhetoric. After all, who would listen if human rights were diminished to such an extent that they became little more than an assertion of "do as I say, not as I do"?

What is needed from the international community is a completely different approach to freedom of the press, one that specifically acknowledges the media and their freedom to report on news unhindered by government interference. Those who place the war on terrorism above all else need to be reminded of the importance of the media's role in a free society. For this alternative approach to succeed, it is essential that governments reevaluate their own relationship to freedom of the press. Such an approach will be discussed in the next chapter.

NOTES

1. "In Remarks at Kennedy Library, Kofi Annan Recalls President's Words in Inaugural Address: To UN 'We Renew Our Pledge of Support,'" UN Press Release SG/SM, June 6, 1997.

2. "Zimbabwe Democracy: Our Best Defense," *Washington Post*, November 19, 2001.

3. "Looking Back, Looking Forward," Committee to Protect Journalists, http://www.cpj.org (accessed December 2, 2003).

4. Ibid.

5. John Mintz, "Justice Says It Won't Charge U.S. Citizen Moved from Cuba: Man in Custody as Government Deliberates What to Do," *Washington Post*, April 9, 2002.

6. *Johnson v. Eisentrager*, 339 US 763 (1950).

7. Charles Lane, "In Terror War, Second Track for Suspects: Those Designated 'Combatants' Lose Legal Protections," *Washington Post*, December 1, 2002.

8. Editorial, "Civic Lessons for Prosecutors," *Washington Post*, June 1, 2002.

9. Tom Jackman, "Hamdi's Right to Lawyer Argued to Appeals Court; Brief Filed for American-born Detainee," *Washington Post*, June 21, 2001.

10. *Yasser Essam Hamdi, Frank W. Dunham, Jr., as Next Friend of Yasser Essam Hamdi v. Donald Rumsfeld, Secretary of Defense, Commander W. R. Paulette, Norfolk Naval Brig*, FindLaw, http:www.news.FindLaw.com (accessed December 3, 2003).

11. Editorial, "The I-Said-So Test," *Washington Post*, June 20, 2002.

12. Tom Jackman, "U.S. Defies Judge on Enemy Combatant; Justice Dept. Refuses to Provide Documents," *Washington Post*, August 7, 2002.

13. Ibid.

14. Ibid.

15. Tom Jackman, "Judge Allows Appeal of 'Combatant' Order; Decision Could Speed Case to High Court," *Washington Post*, August 22, 2002.

16. Tom Jackman, "Court: U.S. Can Hold Citizens as Enemy Combatants," *Washington Post*, January 8, 2003.

17. As of December 2003, Hamdi has appealed to the U.S. Supreme Court, which is expected to decide to hear the case. Maxim Kniazkov, "In Reversal, Pentagon Grants Detainee of Saudi Descent Access to Lawyer," Agence France-Presse, December 3, 2003.

18. Musue N. Haddad, "Tortured Journalist Hassan Bility Speaks Out," *Perspective* (Atlanta), February 3, 2003.

19. Ibid.

20. Musue N. Haddad, "An Open Communication to a Detained Journalist," *Perspective* (Atlanta), June 25, 2002.

21. Ibid.

22. Ibid.

23. Ibid.

24. Neil A. Lewis, "Sudden Shift on Detainee," *New York Times*, December 4, 2003. On December 3, 2003, the Pentagon announced it would allow Yaser Esam Hamdi to confer with a lawyer. The decision came one day before the Justice Department was due to file a brief before the U.S. Supreme Court asking the Court to uphold a decision of the appeals court that President Bush was within his wartime powers in detaining Hamdi as an "enemy combatant." In allowing Hamdi's lawyer access, the Pentagon said it was not setting a legal precedent. On January 9, 2004, the U.S. Supreme Court announced it will hear the case of Hamdi (Charles Lane, "High Court to Weigh Detention of Citizens," *Washington Post*, January 10, 2004). At the time of writing, on January 13, 2004, Hamdi had still not been given access to a lawyer.

25. Nicholas Watt, "Mugabe Calls UK Reporters Terrorists," *Guardian* (London), November 24, 2001.

26. Reuters News, "U.S. Says Zimbabwe Harassing Press with Terrorist Tag," November 26, 2001.

27. Breffni O'Rourke, "UN: Human Rights Chief Steps Down, Warning of Post-11 September Rights Crackdown," Radio Free Europe/Radio Liberty, http://www.rferl (accessed October 9, 2003).

28. "September 11, One Year On," Human Rights Watch, September 9, 2001, http://www.hrw.org (accessed December 3, 2003).

29. Musa Hitam, quoted in "Human Rights Must Take Back Seat after Terror Attacks: Musa," National Human Rights Society (HAKAM), October 30, 2001, http://www.hakam.org (accessed December 3, 2003).

30. Reuters News Service, "Malaysia: U.S. Denies Anti-terror Laws Similar to Malaysia's," January 24, 2001.

31. Ibid.

32. "Letter to President Aleksandr Lukashenka," Article 19, February 21, 2002, http://www.article19.org (accessed December 3, 2003).

33. "Editors Guild Concern over POTO," *Hindu* (Madras), October 30, 2001.

34. "Jaitley Blames Media for Cynicism," *Times of India* (Bombay), November 1, 2001.

35. Uganda International Journalists Network, http://www.ijnet.org (accessed December 3, 2003).

36. Johann P. Fritz, letter to President Yoweri Musveni, International Press Institute, March 22, 2002, http://www.freemedia.at (accessed December 3, 2002).

37. "'I Fear to Be Blown Up,' Says Musveni," *Monitor/All Africa Global Media*, November 3, 2001, http://www.Africa.online.com (accessed October 10, 2003).

38. Phil Smucker, "For Egypt, a Feeling of Vindication on Crackdowns as Arab States Consider Joining a U.S. Coalition, They Might Ask for Latitude," *Christian Science Monitor*, September 18, 2001.

39. "Opportunism in the Face of Tragedy," Human Rights Watch, http://www.hrw.org (accessed December 3, 2003).

40. Remarks with Egyptian Minister of Foreign Affairs Ahmed Maher, Washington, DC, September 26, 2001, U.S. Department of State, http://www.state.gov (accessed December 3, 2003).

41. Agence France-Press, "Mubarak Says Egypt's Military Courts Vindicated by U.S., Britain," December 15, 2001.

42. "U.S. State Department Rights Report Critique," Human Rights Watch, March 4, 2002, http://www.hrw.org (accessed December 3, 2003).

43. "U.S. Pussyfoots around Egypt Military Courts," *Middle East Times*, http://www.metimes.com (accessed December 3, 2003).

44. "After a 'Wake-up Call from Hell,' Civilization at Stake: Netanyahu," *Investor's Business Daily*, September 21, 2001.

45. Brian Whitaker, "Name-Calling Sharon Likens Arafat to bin Laden," *Guardian* (London), September 14, 2001.

46. Xinhua News Agency, "Palestinians Call for Distinguishing Terrorism from Just Struggle," October 6, 2001.

47. Aidan White, *Journalism and the War on Terrorism: Final Report on the Aftermath of September 11 and the Implications for Journalism and Civil Liberties*, International Federation of Journalists, September 3, 2002, http://www.ifj.org (accessed December 2, 2003).

48. International Press Institute, *IPI World Press Freedom Review, 2001* (Vienna: IPI, 2001).

49. White, *Journalism and the War on Terrorism.*

Chapter 8

RESPONDING TO THE WAR ON TERRORISM

They that can give up essential liberty to obtain a little temporary safety deserve neither liberty nor safety.

—Benjamin Franklin

THE "THREE WISE MEN" OF PRESS FREEDOM

After a November 2001 meeting at a hotel near Russell Square in London, hosted by the international press freedom organization Article 19, the three special rapporteurs* for free expression issued a joint declaration on the impact of the September 11 attacks. The declaration was to be one of the first attempts to protect press freedom in the new post–September 11 environment, and it provided a clear indication to governments that individual rights and liberties should not be sacrificed in the fight against terrorism. Coming as it

---

*One who is designated to give a report.

did from the three men given the task of defending press freedom around the world, the statement carried considerable weight.

The joint declaration was signed by the three special rapporteurs: Abid Hussein, United Nations special rapporteur on freedom of opinion and expression; Freimut Duve, representative on freedom of the media for the Organization for Security and Cooperation in Europe (OSCE); and Santiago Canton, special rapporteur on freedom of expression for the Organization of American States (OAS).* It declared that the events of September 11, 2001, and their aftermath highlighted the importance of "open public debate based on the free exchange of ideas [which] should serve as a catalyst for states all over the world to bolster guarantees of freedom of expression." Moreover, while the attacks were to be universally condemned, the declaration said, "we must not allow terror to triumph over human rights in general and the right to freedom of expression in particular."

The three rapporteurs noted that rights developed over centuries can easily be rolled back and that, in the months following the attacks, some governments had already started to introduce legislation limiting freedom of expression. To counter this trend, the rapporteurs argued, "an effective strategy . . . must include reaffirming and strengthening democratic values, based on the right to freedom of expression."[1] Issued only months after the attacks occurred, the declaration was a rallying call to those who did not wish to see the dilution of human rights; indeed, it was a particularly important one, given the responsibilities of the three men and the strengths of their respective organizations.

Broadly speaking, the combination of the OAS, OSCE, and the UN represented a unique alliance among intergovernmental organizations (IGOs). Although the UN was the only global organization among the three, with the OAS and OSCE promoting democracy at the regional level, the three rapporteurs carried out similar duties and held similar mandates. For example, Abid Hussein's mandate from the UN asked him to promote and protect the Universal Declaration of Human Rights, gather all information pertaining to press freedom violations, seek the cooperation of all governments in his

---

*All three have since been replaced or have retired.

work, form a dialogue with other professionals in the field, and report on free expression to the United Nations Commission on Human Rights (UNCHR).[2] The duties of Canton and Duve were similar. With the rapporteurs having thrown down the gauntlet, others in the human rights community issued their own statements in support of press freedom.

United on the occasion of World Press Freedom Day on May 3, 2002, Kofi Annan, secretary-general of the UN, Mary Robinson, UN high commissioner for human rights; and Koïchiro Matsuura, director-general of the UN Educational, Scientific, and Cultural Organization (UNESCO) issued a joint message which said,

> [T]errorism may provoke governmental responses that lead to laws, regulations, and forms of surveillance that undermine the very rights and freedoms that an anti-terrorism campaign is supposed to defend. Indeed, in the name of anti-terrorism, principles and values that were decades, even centuries, in the making may be put at risk. . . . [W]e reaffirm that press freedom is an indispensable dimension of that wider freedom of expression that is each person's birthright and one of the foundations for human progress.[3]

Distributed on the same day as the press release by Annan, Robinson, and Matsuura, the Manila resolution on terrorism and media provided a joint statement from IGOs and nongovernmental organizations (NGOs). Issued after a UNESCO conference on media and terrorism in the Philippines, it was the clearest sign yet that the IGOs and NGOs were unified in their defense of press freedom against the possible predations of the war against terrorism following September 11. The Manila resolution said that "open public debate and the free flow of information are essential to any long-term solutions to the problems of terrorism." Concerning the media, the resolution said that they have "both a right and a duty to report fully on terrorism in the interest of the public's right to know and to promote open, informed debate about terrorism." The resolution identified areas that could be under specific threat from the war on terrorism, namely, editorial independence, the right to protect confidential sources of information, access to information held by public bodies, freedom of movement, and privacy of communications.[4]

Therefore, from London in the United Kingdom to Manila in the Philippines, the first eighteen months after September 11 saw not only the special rapporteurs on press freedom but also the heads of human rights organizations and international press freedom organizations all articulating the same message: the war on terrorism should not become a vehicle for destroying existing human rights. Less explicit was the notion that it was the duty of governments around the world to uphold this fundamental principle. The only problem was whether the governments were listening or not.

If the declarations and statements of IGOs and NGOs were marshaled in the defense of press freedom, how should governments meet their own implied duty to defend press freedom? The first step would be to challenge the notion that increased security meant an equal and opposite reduction of all individual liberties. Inherent within this logic is the belief that liberty and security are intimately tied together; yet, while it was possible to make explicit connections between, say, the right to privacy and increased baggage searches at airports, the relationship between the media's right to report freely and the antiterrorism laws is not always so easily framed.

Significantly, many governments appear not to have tried to outline the relationship between liberties and security. Instead, they relied on the juggernaut that was September 11 and the war on terrorism to remove any obstacles in their path whether reasonable or not. As a result, the emphasis on security was often self-justifying at best and hollow at worst. For this reason, rather than arguing that protection of individual citizens necessitated a reduction of liberties, governments should have remained true to their democratic ideals and found a balance between the two. Where liberties were diminished, governments needed to create adequate judicial oversight to ensure that the changes were within the law. Moreover, the protection of individual rights should have been made a priority alongside individual security. Positing the two as being mutually exclusive is the final argument of countries bent on seeing the dilution of individual rights and freedoms, not their affirmation.

Regarding the war on terrorism, governments were often prepared to ignore the fact that the civil liberties in their countries provided real proof of the democratic divide between the terrorists and those who fought them. Despite the fact that many governments paid lip service to the idea that the war was founded on the protection of freedoms, few politicians were alert to the irony that, even as they spoke of these principles, governments of varying shades of democracy were working hard to reduce these rights all around the world. Whether France or Liberia, Australia or Malaysia, all adjusted the cut of the war to suit their own purposes.

In the headlong rush to commit new laws to the statute books, few governments stopped to consider whether they had sufficient security already. While President Bush spoke of a war that the present generation might not see the end of, other leaders introduced emergency legislation with the implication that it might remain in effect for the foreseeable future. Surrounded by the uncertainty that lingered after the attacks, the voices questioning these decisions were largely ignored. Security had become the overriding concern to the detriment of many societies that had long encouraged human rights.[5]

Rather than passing repressive new laws, how should governments have responded to September 11? While it would be wrong to argue that no revision of security should have been undertaken or that essential human rights outranked the safety of citizens, governments failed to ask such essential questions as whether the legislation or infringement was legitimate and whether it was necessary and proportionate.

By attempting to define not only the arguments for press freedom but also those principles that were under greatest threat, the Manila resolution gave one of the best statements in support of press freedom in the new environment after the attacks. The resolution argued for a media landscape that placed the onus on governments to allow journalists to report independently, free of harassment and intimidation. Moreover, governments needed to ensure a constant flow of information and provide equal access to that information. Combining these different elements into a cohesive whole would allow for a comprehensive and detailed response to the significant changes that had occurred since the September 11 attacks and redress the balance that had shifted away from liberty and toward security.

THE ROLE OF GOVERNMENTS IN RELEASING THE FREE FLOW OF INFORMATION

One of the biggest challenges for any government is to allow individual citizens, the media, and civil society groups access to the information it holds.

Unblocking the Information Dam

In any democratic society, transparency and access to information are key elements because they allow for a critical examination of governments, enable citizens to review their own information under data protection laws, and provide a right to information on such issues as health and the environment. One of the most important mechanisms for achieving such access is the enactment of a freedom of information act (FOIA).

First enacted in 1766 when Sweden passed its Freedom of the Press Act, FOIAs now exist in over forty countries, and thirty more countries have expressed a clear intention to enact such a law.[6] According to a report by David Banisar of the human rights group Privacy International, the reason for this trend is the breakdown of many of the authoritarian regimes, particularly Communist governments, in the 1980s, and the formation of democracies willing to introduce FOIAs as part of their new legislative initiatives. Elsewhere, Banisar points to the older democracies that are now accepting the need for information laws and to the work of larger IGOs such as the Council of Europe and the Commonwealth, which are keen to see their member states implement such laws. In other parts of the world, international lending banks, such as the World Bank and the International Monetary Fund (IMF), are signaling to donor countries that information laws are fundamental weapons in the battle against corruption.

For these reasons, the trend toward FOIAs has radiated outward from Western Europe and North America, spreading through the countries of the former Soviet Union in Eastern Europe and out toward Asia, where twelve countries were discussing their implementation in 2002. It has also spread southward to Africa, where the decision of South Africa to include an FOIA on its statute books encouraged other countries to tread the same path. In addition, countries with thriving FOIA laws such as Canada, Sweden, and the United States have acted as role models leading to the introduction of FOIAs in other countries.[7]

Unfortunately, this trend was reversed to a certain extent by the events of September 11. In the aftermath of the attacks, both the United States and Canada introduced proposals to limit access to information, while Tony Blair's government in the United Kingdom opted to delay the implementation of its freedom of information law until 2005, a decision that, at the time, prompted little criticism in the media. The attacks encouraged secrecy and applied further pressure on Eastern European countries wishing to join Western institutions to follow suit. As an example, countries applying for NATO membership found themselves being urged to adopt secrecy legislation to protect classified military information. This decision must have confounded certain former members of the Warsaw Pact, which, after facing a yearly diet of lectures on democracy and openness from Western democracies, suddenly found themselves being taught new ways to be secretive by the very same countries.

Whether the September 11 attacks have completely reversed the trend is not yet clear. At present, the war on terrorism appears to have taken precedence over the drive to make governments more accountable. The actions of the United States and Canada and the decision of the United Kingdom regarding their FOIAs were unhelpful in this matter because they gave other countries additional reasons to set aside their own freedom of information programs.

Once again, security has been placed at the top of the agenda, while the rights of the individual have been largely ignored. Much of the work on creating more open forms of government is now in mothballs, awaiting a time when countries are ready to restart their initiatives. This retreat in the face of the crisis has revealed an unwillingness on the part of governments to acknowledge the importance of the free flow of information in all societies, particularly in times of crisis. As the Manila resolution stated, "[O]pen public debate and the free flow of information are essential to any long-term solutions to the problems of terrorism."[8]

While the importance of FOIAs cannot be underestimated, they do not always instantly create open government. Departments and officials can place considerable obstacles in the path of those seeking information, and responses to requests may be unreasonably delayed. Nonetheless, examples of their successful application in the United States reveal how these programs may be beneficial to any society.

Civil society groups in the United States have used the FOIA to expose corruption on various levels, from how defense expenditure has been used to make navy admirals more comfortable or how a security adviser in the Reagan government had engaged in questionable investment practices to how a meatpacking company broke health laws. As a result of these exposures, new criteria were introduced for the furnishings of navy admirals, the Reagan adviser was forced to resign, and the meatpacking company was prevented from tendering for meal-time contracts with schools.[9]

The media in the United States have also used the laws in a similar manner. The *Washington Post* used access to information laws to reveal the startling information that despite Washington, DC's, rising homicide rate, no one had been held accountable for 75 percent of the murders committed between 1988 and 1990; the *Dayton* (Ohio) *Daily News* exposed the fact that military prisoners who had committed appalling crimes were still receiving payment while their victims and relatives struggled to obtain compensation; and the *Orange County* (California) *Register* used FOIA laws to show that military personnel had been injured or killed as a direct result of their faulty night vision goggles, although the military claimed that this was due to "pilot error."[10] Reaching into every aspect of society, these examples show the depth and range of applications under the FOIA. The examples also support the argument that, far from limiting access to information after September 11, the government should have increased it.

As previously mentioned, oversight of the government's actions is an important mechanism when governments are seeking to limit rights in the name of security. However, such oversight need not exist only in the form of the judiciary or the legislative branches of government; it can also come in the form of the media or civil society groups using the FOIA to examine the veracity of government actions and statements. In times of war, governments are prone to say that drastic methods are necessary to protect society and the safety of individuals. The FOIA is a means of holding these statements up to the light to see whether they can be substantiated, particularly when the war on terrorism appears to be without end. In such an environment, without oversight, a society could be held to indefinite ransom as governments increase their hold on the reins of power to guard against a threat, whether substantiated or not. Use of FOI laws by civil society groups or the media can apply a brake on governments. While this strategy may not work indefinitely, it can gain the much-needed time for a dialogue to take place.

The two impulses of government—to provide information or not to provide information—are inherently opposed. Democracy works best when there are extended periods of discussion, but during times of war, governments must make decisions on a far shorter timescale. This inevitable conflict can have both long-lasting and damaging implications. An example of the use of the FOIA in the war against terrorism may be seen in the fight to obtain the names of U.S. citizens detained after September 11. In August 2002, a judge ordered the Department of Justice to release the names of the more than one thousand persons detained. However, behaving in a similar fashion to Judge Doumar in the Hamdi case, the judge stayed her order so that the government could appeal. Later in the year, the Department of Justice disclosed the names of 93 people facing charges and stated that 104 people were arrested on federal charges.[11] The government said disclosures were discriminatory and not the result of the FOIA.

Nevertheless, it was the FOIA application that forced the government to provide the information. As the Reporters Committee for Freedom of the Press pointed out in its detailed report *Homefront Confidential*, this disclosure did not solve the mystery of the number of people held as material witnesses, nor did it reveal any other information on the detainees' arrest: times, dates, charges, among others. Confronted by the government's intransigence, twenty-seven civil rights and public interest groups filed an FOI request for more information, and they later initiated a lawsuit in order to force a hearing before the courts in order to compel the Department of Justice to provide further details on the detainees.[12]

In response to the lawsuit, the Department of Justice released further information toward the end of January 2003. Significantly, in its own submissions, the government's legal department argued that the request should be rejected because it fell under one of the exemptions for law enforcement. While the FOI request was not entirely successful in the face of a determined government's rear-guard action, it served its purpose of ensuring that the U.S. government was well aware of the group's intentions and its desire to compel the government to hand over the detainees' details. The FOIA is, therefore, a powerful tool in the hands of groups intent on disclosing government-held information. When combined with a lawsuit, it can have a powerful and coercive effect, forcing governments to do what they would rather not do—justify themselves before a court of law. For this reason, it is imperative that countries should continue with their FOIA programs, while those that have instituted no such program should start to do so now. After September 11, it would be unfortunate if information were to be held hostage by the war against terrorism.

Reclaiming the Moral High Ground

While many governments appreciate the impact of globalization and the idea that, because of this underlying trend, economic slumps and depressions in one region of the world can directly affect the countries of another, they have not been so willing to accept this principle in the field of human rights in general and press freedom in particular. Just as labeled goods end up in many different parts of the world, press freedom violations are copied, enhanced, and improved upon by one regime after another. Each new development in suppression is watched by other regimes eager to try the violation out for its size and fit.

The relationship between tax inspections on media outlets in Russia, Belarus, and Georgia is one such example of this trend. On May 11, 2000, during a concerted campaign against the remaining independent media in Russia, masked and armed tax police stormed the offices of two media outlets owned by Media-Most. As a justification for the act, authorities cited a pretrial investigation into the security services of Media-Most. The investigation led to the arrest of the organization's owner, Vladimir Gusinsky, who was held in jail on charges that were subsequently dropped by the prosecutor. Afterward, Gusinsky was allowed to leave the country for Spain. It later transpired that the media tycoon had brokered a deal in which he agreed to transfer the ownership of the media company Media-Most to its biggest creditor, the partially state-owned gas company, Gazprom.[13] The raid was to have a considerable impact on other media in the region as, in the following year, copycat tax inspections were used to subdue the media in one of Russia's neighbors, Belarus.

Belarus is another country that has scant regard for the freedom of the media and the right of journalists to report free of harassment and intimidation. On August 21, 2001, the Belarussian newspapers *Narodnaya Volya* and *Nasha Svaboda* were informed by the authorities that a tax inspection would be initiated against them. Within twenty-four hours, police entered the offices of *Narodnaya Volya* and seized ten computers. Two days later, police also confiscated a computer from *Nasha Svaboda*. Press freedom organizations accused the government of attempting to silence the newspapers by fabricating charges against them in the lead-up to the presidential elections.[14]

The media in Georgia also faced a tax inspection in October 2001. In mid-October 2001, an intensive tax investigation was carried out against *Rustavi-2*, an independent television station based in Tibilisi, the capital of Georgia. Although no tax irregularities were discovered, the raid was only the first in a series of violations against the station, which saw it besieged by security forces on October 30, 2001. Only the courage of the station's staff and members of the public who blocked the invading security forces managed to stave off an attempt to close it down. The staff members believed that the violations were carried out as the result of *Rustavi-2*'s reporting of events in the contentious Pankisi Gorge, where it is alleged that Chechen rebels are hiding from Russian soldiers operating across the border.

Obviously, it is impossible to trace exact connections among these events, and it should be acknowledged that tax inspections of media organizations are not new in Belarus, as they had been used to suppress the media as far back as 1996. However, following as they did the Russian raid on Media-Most's outlets, it would seem that the Russian method found favor in the other two countries and allowed government officials to claim that the actions were being undertaken by the police at the behest of independent prosecutors and were, therefore, separate and distinct from the government. Indeed, a Georgian official said of the raids on *Rustavi-2* that "what happened . . . has no political background and is linked to the economic side of the TV company's activities."[15] Given the lack of independence of both the judiciary and the police in all three countries, it is difficult to accept this statement.

The copying of one repressive regime's methods by another shows the willingness of countries around the world to adopt new methods of suppressing the media, and, perhaps more important, reveals the disturbing link between the actions of one country and those of another. If it is possible to establish links between trends in violating press freedom and repressive regimes, then it is also possible to highlight the interrelationships among countries that uphold human rights and the repressive regimes. Once again, a close examination reveals some worrying factors that have a disturbing impact on the attempt to encourage countries around the world to loosen their grip on the media after September 11.

One of the primary difficulties for advocates of press freedom is finding new methods of applying pressure on countries lacking such freedom. While different organizations use a variety of methods, a powerful argument is to compare one country's level of press freedom with that of another, say, for example the United States or countries in the European Union (EU). Unfortunately, if violations are committed in these democratic countries, the press freedom community is denied one of its most powerful motivating tools.

Because of the need to provide examples of democratic countries with an open media environment, many NGOs spend much of their time trying to look in two directions at the same time: first, at those regimes with a history of suppression, and second, at the established democracies to ensure that a high level of press freedom is maintained. However, if other regimes see democratic countries limiting their own media, this knowledge provides the regimes with the opportunity to deride the democratic countries for hypocrisy. This is particularly true when the United States, the United Kingdom, and other countries of the EU have been involved.

Criminal defamation is one international standard for freedom of expression that can be examined in this way. It has long been argued that journalists should not suffer criminal penalties and the stigma of a conviction for defaming individuals, including the heads of governments. Press freedom organizations such as IPI argue that the most suitable forums for defamation are the civil courts and that any remedy should redress the harm caused to the person defamed and not punish the journalists for their writing. Such punishment, press freedom organizations argue, would only have a chilling effect on the media and perhaps encourage self-censorship among journalists. Criminal defamation and insult laws* exist in various forms all over the world, from South America, where they are known as *desacato* laws, to some parts of Africa and in many countries in Eastern Europe. The little known fact about these laws is that they also exist in countries where press freedom is supposedly an essential element of democracy.

In the United Kingdom, for instance, a criminal defamation law remains on the statute books. Though seldom used, the law might still be applied to journalists. The law is in need of a rapid overhaul,

---

*Laws that make it an offense to "insult" the honor or dignity of public officials.

particularly because, while there is no civil libel of the dead under the law of England, Wales, and Northern Ireland, criminal law would apply if the words spoken of a dead person can be shown to have intentionally provoked living relatives into committing a breach of the peace, or that they had a tendency to do so. If found guilty, a defendant faces imprisonment of up to one year and a fine, or both. Where it can be proven that the defendant knew the libel to be untrue, the period of imprisonment may be doubled.[16]

Despite continual attempts to remove this antiquated law from the statute books, successive British governments have refused to do so.[17] Those who defend the criminal defamation law point out that it has not been used since the 1980s and that only a High Court judge can determine whether there is a prima facie case. Whether this safeguard will protect journalists in the future is a moot point.

In the United States, however, there is no such reluctance to act; journalists continue to be prosecuted under state criminal defamation laws. On November 27, 2002, David W. Carson and Edward H. Powers Jr., publisher and editor of the *New Observer* (Kansas City), were given fines and probation by a Kansas trial court judge after being found guilty of criminal libel earlier in the year. The crime of Carson and Powers was to report that Wyandotte County Unified Government Mayor Carol Marinovich and her husband, Wyandotte County District Judge Ernest Johnson, lived outside Wyandotte county, and, as a consequence, were in breach of the election laws governing both positions, a claim described by the prosecutor as "false and malicious."

Although this case provides a clear test in which the Kansas Supreme Court must eventually decide on the constitutionality of the state law, the trial not only limits press freedom in the United States, where the Supreme Court has said speech concerning public affairs is the essence of self-government, but also sets an appalling example for other countries where press freedom is at a premium.[18] At a time when leaders throughout Africa and Latin America are attempting to prevent journalists from commenting on the political process in their countries, a move in the other direction by the United States, even at the state level, serves only to reassure these leaders.

Rather than invoking antiquated laws, courts in the United States should be issuing clear-sighted and well-defined judgments that uphold press freedom and the media's right to engage in political comment, including what one judge called "vehement, caustic, and sometimes unpleasantly sharp attacks on government and public officials."[19] Politicians willingly enter the political arena, and for this reason they should expect criticism from the media. Moreover, because of the media's interest in them, politicians have ample opportunity to address the criticism and refute it if need be. For the courts to protect politicians to the extent that the media are fearful of the repercussions of their own words is not only to wrap politicians in protective cotton wool but also to undermine the entire political process.

While Kansas was busy setting an example for dictators, the Utah Supreme Court was slowly moving in the opposite direction. In a unanimous ruling on November 15, 2002, the Supreme Court of Utah removed a criminal libel law that had been on the state statute books since 1876 because it was "overbroad and unconstitutional" and "infringe[d] upon a substantial amount of constitutionally protected speech." The case involved a sixteen-year-old boy who was arrested after using his Web site to criticize administrators and students at his high school.[20] Speaking after the case had been settled, the legal director for the American Civil Liberties Union of Utah, Janelle Eurick, said, "While perhaps offensive, Ian's statements are not criminal, and the overzealous prosecution of this young man reflects precisely the kind of heavy-handed censorship the First Amendment forbids."[21]

Declaring the 1876 law unconstitutional did not end the prosecution, however, as a 1973 state law also contains penalties for criminal defamation. Unlike the 1876 statute, the later law contains a "malice component," meaning that the state will have to prove the actual malice of the sixteen-year-old defendant. Despite this element, the situation in Utah remains unsatisfactory because it should be left to the civil courts to decide on the case. Therefore, this small step in the right direction has not resolved the problem in Utah or elsewhere in the United States.

Questions over the existence of criminal defamation statutes in member states have also left the EU largely unmoved. Taking advantage of a European Council (EC) meeting in Gothenburg, Sweden, on June 15–16, 2001, IPI and other press freedom organizations wrote to Swedish Prime Minister Göran Persson regarding press freedom. The letter to Persson, who was steering the meeting, expressed concern that defamation and insult laws in member states set a negative example for applicant countries whose leaders wish to stifle criticism and limit the free flow of information. After outlining the reasons for removing these laws, the letter ended with an entreaty that the EC adopt a resolution calling on member states to repeal these laws, a move that would provide countries aspiring to join the EU with clear guidance on this subject. The letter also stated that such an initiative would "echo positively well beyond the EU and its applicants."[22] The EU did not respond.

Ironically, in regions where press freedom is considered to be less advanced than in the West, distinct advances have been made that should be deeply shaming to both the United States and the EU. On February 15, 2001, in his maiden speech to Parliament, Ghanaian President John Agyekum Kufor announced that the country's defamation laws would be repealed. Kufor said the decision had been made as a sign of his confidence in Ghana's media. He added that repealing the law would expand the boundaries of freedom, enabling the Ghanaian media to serve as watchdogs over their government.

In Sri Lanka, after winning a hard-fought election, Prime Minister Ranil Wickremesinghe kept his promise to the media and passed a bill through the Sri Lankan Parliament repealing the country's criminal defamation laws. The decision was seen as a considerable improvement over conditions in previous years when the media had been constantly censored and suppressed under emergency laws passed as the result of the government's bloody conflict with the separatist Liberation Tigers of Tamil Ealam (LTTE or Tamil Tigers).

The question of the commitment of former colonial powers to their former colonial territories is also an extremely difficult one for democratic countries. Perhaps the most vexing aspect of this issue is the question of responsibility for the repressive laws that remain on the statute books long after the former colonizer has handed over sovereignty. While many former colonial powers are now heavily involved in development and creating democratic institutions, few attempts have been made by Western governments, especially in African countries, to apply pressure for the removal of such laws.

Unpalatable as it may seem to those in the West, many regimes that are actively engaged in the repression of the media first learned their methods from their former colonial rulers. Moreover, the laws that cloak these acts in their superficial legitimacy are colonial baggage that became too tempting for the new regimes that readily applied them to suppress their own people. Like the security organizations and the military and police structures left behind by the Western countries, repressive laws, meant for a different time and for a different place, continue to bring misery and suffering to many people.

In Malaysia, a former colony of the United Kingdom, the notorious Internal Security Act (ISA) is a product of the emergency in Malaysia that began in 1948 when communists attempted to overthrow the British colonial government. Despite the end of emergency in 1960, the ISA was kept on the statute books, and a series of amendments have strengthened it. Since it first came into operation, thousands of Malaysians have been arrested without proof of a crime and detained indefinitely—many of them journalists or political rivals. Throughout its application, no evidence has been produced in court to justify the detainees' guilt, nor are those arrested given the opportunity to prove their innocence in court.

Sri Lanka is another country in which the old laws of the United Kingdom have played a new role in stifling dissent. Faced with a stunning defeat at the hands of the Tamil Tigers in 2000, when the army was forced to retreat from the Elephant Pass near Jaffna, the Sri Lankan government introduced chapter 40 of the Public Security Ordinance, which introduced a raft of new powers designed to silence the media. The law was an exact replica of the United Kingdom's colonial law used to prevent acts by Sri Lankans considered to be subversive or dangerous to the government at the time.

The tendrils of the United Kingdom's old colonial laws have

even reached into the horrendous conflict in Israel and Palestine. On December 22, 2002, the Israeli government closed the radical Islamic weekly *Sawt al-Haq wa Al-Hurriya* because it perceived the newspaper as a threat to national security. Apparently, the order for the closure came from the secretive Shin Beth security service, which called the newspaper a mouthpiece for the Islamic resistance group Hamas. The order was formulated under the 1933 Press Ordinance, a law dating back to the United Kingdom's Mandate in Palestine before the founding of Israel. The law was last used in 1953, when its application was unsuccessful.[23]

To a degree, Western governments are complicit in some of the acts of repressive regimes around the world. The laws that the Western countries left behind in former colonies continue to be used against the media. While it would be unfair to blame Western governments for the use of such laws, they have a duty to encourage former colonies to repeal these laws. Western countries must work harder to achieve this goal, whether through economic aid packages or through other forms of persuasion. An important first step would be for Western governments to lead by example and repeal their own repressive laws, an act that would return them to the moral high ground on this issue.

Another possible motivation for impoverished regimes that refuse to improve their media environments is a greater understanding of the relationship between the media and poverty.

TUGGING AT THE STRINGS OF POWER: HOW CHAIRMAN MAO CAME TO BELIEVE IN DEMOCRACY

In his keynote speech on January 29, 2001, at the IPI's World Congress and Fiftieth General Assembly in New Delhi, India, economist and Nobel Laureate Professor Amartya Sen outlined one of the most powerful and convincing reasons why governments around the globe should uphold the principles of press freedom. Expanding on his thesis that no "substantial famine has ever occurred in any independent country with a democratic form of government and a relatively free press," Sen invited his audience to consider the Chinese famine of 1958–1961.[24]

According to Sen, despite a strong commitment to rid the country of starvation, the Chinese central government grossly overestimated the amount of grain that it had in stock during those three years. When it finally recognized the huge discrepancy, it was far too late to act. As a result, between 23 and 30 million people starved to death. The inflated estimates were the fault of local officials who knew that they had failed to meet their own grain quotas but believed that other regions had done better. For this reason, they misreported their own agricultural yields, leading the Chinese central government to overestimate the total amount of grain in the country. Sen argues that some of the blame for the famine lies in the absence of a free press in China. The famine occurred not only because the government had wrong information but also because "people were kept in the dark about the crisis and the mortality, and [because] no newspaper was allowed [to report the truth]."[25] Censorship, in other words, played an important role in preventing the exposure of the fraudulent misreporting.

Sen's excellent book *Development as Freedom*, which asserts that rights are an essential element of development, also deals with the Chinese famine. Sen quotes Chairman Mao as saying, "Without democracy, you have no understanding of what is happening down below; the situation will be unclear. . . ."[26] Mao's statement is a begrudging acceptance that democracy would have been better able than his repressive regime to handle the famine—investigative journalists would have exposed the false accounting and the central government would have been alerted far earlier, averting the famine and perhaps saving the lives of millions of people.[27]

As Sen's example illustrates, the media, together with free and fair elections, can act as an early warning system. Stories of ministerial corruption, government mismanagement, and mistakes in handling the economy all undermine a government in the eyes of the electorate. Through their comments on these subjects and their willingness to confront the government, the media can bring about change.

As a result, the fear that the electorate will cast its vote differently in a future election can motivate governments to resolve these problems with the media. Obviously, this is an uncomfortable truth, and some governments are afraid of the role played by the media, but they must take the rough with the smooth. There is much at stake. In many impoverished countries around the world, a free press is not only a matter of principle but a matter of life and death.

This necessity has never been more evident than in Ethiopia, where a myopic government, facing cyclical famines, refuses to tolerate the activities of the media. Once described as the jailhouse of Africa, Ethiopia is governed by officials who have used repressive laws, police harassment, and imprisonment to punish and harass journalists. After initially being encouraged, the media in the country are virtually on their knees, suppressed by a government with an appalling human rights record. A short report by the London-based freedom of expression organization Article 19, which visited the country in December 2000, outlines a direct connection between the lack of freedom of expression and the famines that have regularly visited the country. According to the report, famines from 1982 to 1985 and from 1999 to 2000 destroyed the lives of thousands and obliterated Ethiopia's economic infrastructure.[28]

Against this background, the government of the Ethiopian People's Revolutionary Democratic Front (EPRDF) rose to power on the twin promises that it would end the cycle of famines and continue with a program of democratic change that started in 1991. To achieve these goals they placed great emphasis on the creation of an independent media. However, the desire to fulfill these promises was short lived. By 2001 over two million people were still reliant on relief aid, and the independent media that had emerged were under constant pressure from the government. Noting that very little had changed for the people of Ethiopia, Article 19's report questioned the success of the democratic program and pondered "how far censorship remained a contributing factor" in the series of rolling famines.[29]

Taking into account the horror of the famines and the intransigence of the government, the report reached three conclusions with regard to the media landscape in Ethiopia. First, there should be "free and inclusive participation by ordinary Ethiopians in debates and decisions about government policy; second, greater access to the information of the government and other official bodies and the introduction of genuine accountability on the [record] of the government; and, third, the increased liberalization of the media." Commenting on the significance of these conclusions, the report said, "[It] reflects the elements of accountability . . . that we [in Article 19] have identified as vital if freedom and development are to go hand-in-hand in the years ahead."[30]

Significantly, Article 19's report provides a direct connection between famine and the free flow of information in an impoverished country. If it is true that the media, particularly foreign media outlets, can bring the plight of starving people to the attention of the world, it is also true that the very principles underlying the media can help to avert the famine in the first place. As Sen argued with relation to China, the early warning role of the media is crucial in countries that have such a fragile infrastructure that the slightest change can bring about disaster. Repressive governments should perhaps consider this vital role the next time their security forces arrest or imprison an independent journalist or close down a newspaper.

Increasingly, the media's involvement in issues concerning sustainable development is being recognized by press freedom organizations. On the occasion of the World Summit on Sustainable Development, held from August 26 to September 4, 2002, the International Federation of Journalists (IFJ) reminded the thousands of delegates attending the conference that "human rights, democracy, and freedom of expression are not on the margins of the struggle for sustainable development. People must be free to speak their minds. They must have access to the information they need to make decisions about the future."[31] The statement appeared to argue that any approach to bringing about sustainable development needs to take into account civil and political rights as well as economic and social rights. This viewpoint was also acknowledged by Amnesty International and Human Rights Watch, both of which have come to accept that the two sets of rights are not mutually exclusive and that the relationship between the two needs to be better understood.

According to enlightened thinkers like Sen, press freedom is at the very intersection between these various rights. Press freedom affects not only the individual citizen who needs information to make decisions on his or her personal life but also the government, where information is needed on food distribution, pollution levels, and numerous other concerns. This recognition of the interconnection between different sorts of human rights is a tremendous advance over the previous position of NGOs working on different sides of the fence and rarely having any contact. Today, NGOs are much more likely than in the past to share information. The press release by IFJ is important, appearing as it did at a conference traditionally set aside for NGOs and IGOs involved in social and economic rights as opposed to civil and political rights.

These relationships are also being explored by the World Bank and the International Monetary Fund. Writing in the *International Herald Tribune* on the subject of the relationship between the media and poverty, Nobel Laureate, former senior vice president of the World Bank, and now professor of economics and finance at Columbia University, Joseph Stiglitz, and Roumeen Islam, a manager at the World Bank Institute, said that in order to "reduce global poverty we must liberate access to information and improve its quality." The article also said that "free speech and a free press not only make abuses of government powers less likely, they also enhance the likelihood that people's basic social needs would be met."[32]

Fostering the free flow of information and allowing citizens access to information are absolutely essential in many countries around the globe. Although NGOs and IGOs from both sides of the human rights divide are now starting to accept the fundamental role of the media, governments often seem unable to follow in their footsteps. On too many occasions, governments seem hamstrung by their fear that a free press might also mean criticism of their policies and a consequent reduction in their popularity. Such ignorance endangers the lives of their people and ensures that their country remains entirely dependent on financial aid from the international community.

Where governments are hesitant, the international community should lead the way. The various international banks can help by making a free press one of the conditions for receiving aid. Media assistance programs funded by these banks can (and do) assist in the development of an independent media and an environment which allows for the free flow of information, but there needs to be a greater number of those programs.

TIPPING GOVERNMENTS IN THE RIGHT(S) DIRECTION

Faced with the challenges of the war on terrorism and the consequences of their initial response, what can governments around the globe do to repair the damage? As previously mentioned, it is clear that an approach needs to be found that upholds the principles of a free press. To ignore this fundamental human right or to weaken it in any way risks losing one of the essential features of a democracy. Moreover, damaging one facet of democracy risks damaging or losing the others.

The September 11 attacks and the war on terrorism have opened up a second front, one that is far closer to home. On this second battlefield, a war of words is being fought over how many basic freedoms citizens are prepared to forgo in order to feel secure against the threat of terrorist attack. This argument has raged back and forth between those who see a reduction in liberties as necessary and those who believe that these freedoms must be safeguarded.

Those who support reduced freedoms see the need for a fine balance between human rights and the need of governments to keep their citizens safe. According to supporters of this view, rights and security are intimately connected and can be altered to address certain situations such as September 11 and the war on terrorism. In their view it is possible and even necessary to reduce one side of the equation while increasing the other side—we give up liberties so that our lives can be made safer. Although this argument has a resonance with many people, it carries within it a fundamental misunderstanding of the nature of human rights.

Many of the rights within, say, the United States or the member states of the EU are the result of slow growth over many centuries. These rights have been constructed and redefined in legislatures and before courts, and they have often been defended at great sacrifice. Human rights have been finely woven into our society, and any attempt to remove them risks damaging not only those rights but also the very fabric of society. Rather than being a society with rights, our society is the sum of those rights. The standard arguments for giving up those rights fall away because they fail on the basis of an error: Certain freedoms cannot be given up for our own protection because they are a part of our very makeup, both as individuals and as the members of a society.

These arguments are particularly relevant to press freedom, which is both a primary human right and a fundamental feature of democratic society. Without the free flow of information, it is impossible for individuals or governments to assess the dangers of the war on terrorism. As a result, press freedom is perhaps the finest example of a human right that is so closely bound to society that it is virtually indistinguishable from the society itself.

With this in mind, a freedom of information act is pivotal to the success of any modern society. Requests for information under such a law hold governments to account and provide for oversight by concerned groups and the media. In the United States, for instance, courts are traditionally fearful of interfering with or hindering administrations in their prosecution of war. For this reason, they have traditionally deferred to the executive branch. However, freedom of information requests allow the media and other groups to continue pressing the government, ensuring that it is not given a completely free rein in meeting the challenges of war.

Aside from the debate over the loss of individual freedoms and security, another difficult question needs to be addressed, one that goes directly to the heart of the attacks on September 11 and that needs to be acknowledged by all of the countries currently engaged in the war against terrorism: What are the root causes of terrorism? While it is difficult to provide an all-embracing answer to this question, it must be asked because it has a direct bearing on the policies and actions of the alliance fighting terrorism. Furthermore, the roots of terrorism are intimately connected to poverty and the absence of human rights.

The relationship between the September 11 attacks and poverty was outlined by the president of the World Bank Group, James Wolfensohn, in an interview with the Italian newspaper *La Stampa*. Interviewed on December 7, 2001, Wolfensohn said,

> The war [in Afghanistan] will not be won until we have come to grips with the problem of poverty and thus the sources of discontent. Not just in Afghanistan, but also in the neighboring regions, in many other countries. . . . Winning the war means tackling the roots of this protest. What are they? Poverty and inequality. Failure to understand this means closing our eyes to the origin of the resentment of the poor against the North.

Following from this idea, Wolfensohn has argued that the war on terrorism is merely one element of the war on poverty, a position that has won him plaudits from many people.[33] The comments of the World Bank president came one month after President Bush presented a similar argument. Addressing the United States on radio, President Bush said, "In our struggle against hateful groups that exploit poverty and despair, we must offer an alternative of opportunity and hope."[34]

Both men appeared to accept the principle that poverty and inequality in the world can be a powerful source of resentment. In addition, the United States, as the lone superpower, the strongest economic power, and the richest country in the world, is the target of envy, which has in turn bred hatred, leading various groups, including al-Qaeda, to plot to attack the country. Although this view overlooks the political situation in the Middle East, it is an argument that carries a certain amount of force. Furthermore, while the United States' foreign policy is clearly a motivating factor, the existence of poverty in certain countries can lead to individuals joining terrorist groups.

The link between poverty and terrorism is also specifically accepted by the United Nations. Attending a development summit in Mexico in early 2002, the president of the UN Assembly, Han Seung-Soo, argued that the world's poorest countries are "the breeding ground for violence and despair."[35] Despite the possibility that Han was grandstanding to ensure that the focus on development was not lost, he, too, recognizes a connection between poverty and terrorism. In an apparent acceptance of this view, the Bush administration announced plans in March 2002 to increase foreign aid by 50 percent over three years from 2004 to 2007.

The notion of poverty as a "breeding ground" for terrorism must also take into account the glaring lack of democracy in many parts of the world. One reason why terrorists choose to bear arms and kill innocent people may be the belief that they have no other viable methods of expression. Distasteful as this notion is, it is no coincidence that groups such as al-Qaeda have sprung from a region where democracy is little more than an expressed hope for millions of people who feel themselves to be both disenfranchised and voiceless. Alienated from the methods of traditional democratic expression that allow for their voices to be heard and legitimized, dissident groups have managed to use the lack of free expression to attract disenchanted people to their various causes. Western governments have a duty to challenge this overwhelming silence and pressure governments in various regions for democratic change. If such change was important before the terrorist outrages of September 11, it is now as essential as the search for the terrorists themselves.

Western governments must realize that addressing this problem is a matter not only of duty but also of necessity because the failure to do so will inevitably lead to the creation of more terrorist groups, more terrorist outrages, more deaths. After September 11, the place where a terrorist outrage takes place is of little significance; terrorism has been globalized and must be confronted by every country. Against this swirling nimbus of terrorism, an independent media and free expression are vital.

For almost every person, access to information is pure empowerment. Access to information allows the members of a society to make decisions not only about their own lives but also about the activities of their governments. The greater the access to information, the greater the sense of belonging to a particular society. Information is not merely one element of society, it is part of the actual fabric of everyday life, and the media have an integral role in its communication and supply. Without information, individuals are totally incapable of taking part in the society they see around them—they are voiceless. It is exactly at this point that feelings of disenchantment and powerlessness arise.

Although he feels that the connection between terrorism and lack of access to information is imprecise and that the correlation is not true in every particular case, Deputy Director of the Committee to Protect Journalists Joel Simon states: "I think that when people don't have information they feel powerless and they believe the decisions that affect their lives are part of conspiracies, and they believe in conspiracies, and when they feel powerless they feel angry." He also thinks that "those attitudes are more likely to develop in countries that are deprived of information and don't understand decisions, processes, how governments work!"[36]

The role of governments should be to provide their citizens with this empowerment, to return to them the right to speak out. While this right exists in Western countries, the threat of terrorism must compel these governments to pressure more repressive governments to create an independent media and allow for the free flow of information. Such governments should be encouraged to create FOIAs to allow for that movement. Western governments should also help the various IGOs around the world to use their own knowledge and expertise to bring about democratic changes. Governments should also place greater emphasis on freedom of expression when trying to argue for democratic change. On the question of poverty, this also entails convincing some governments that press freedom can be beneficial to society.

Moreover, as a means of supporting their own arguments, Western governments must make the necessary alterations to their own media landscapes. Laws that inhibit the free flow of information, such as criminal defamation, should be repealed, and governments with a colonial past must do more to try to convince their former colonies to remove existing colonial laws that have no role in nascent democracies.

Previous discussions have centered on the question of press freedom as an integral element of society that should not be compromised after the September 11 attacks. This view is largely the one that has engaged Western governments. But it is too simplistic because it fails to take into account that the media and their derivative, information, are actually a fundamental part of the war on terrorism. Western governments need to first acknowledge this fact and then place media development at the heart of their formal policies on terrorism. Only by implementing such policies can the free flow of information play a role in helping to defeat terrorism.

NOTES

1. Article 19, "Right to Freedom of Opinion and Expression," Joint Declaration from OSCE, UN and OAS Representatives on Freedom of Expression, Article 19 press release, November 22, 2001, http://www.article19.org (accessed December 3, 2003).

2. Commission on Human Rights, Resolution 1993/45, http://www.unhchr.org (accessed December 3, 2003).

3. UNESCO, "Joint Message for World Press Freedom Day 3 May 2002."

4. Article 19, "Ten IFEX Members Sign On to UNESCO Conference Resolution on Terrorism and Media," Article 19 press release, May 3, 2001, http://www.article19.org (accessed December 3, 2003).

5. An example of this concern for security can be seen in the United Kingdom, which declared a state of national emergency so that it could derogate from Article 5 of the European Convention on Human Rights (ECHR).

6. David Banisar, "Freedom of Information and Access to Government Records around the World," Freedominfo.org, July 2, 2002, http://www.freedominfo.org (accessed December 3, 2003).

7. Ibid.

8. Article 19, "Ten IFEX Members Sign On to UNESCO Conference Resolution."

9. Ralph Nader, "Knowledge Helps Citizens, Secrecy Helps Bureaucrats: The Freedom of Information Act (FOIA)," excerpted from the book The Ralph Nader Reader (New York: Seven Stories Press, 2000), http://www.thirdworldtraveller.com (accessed December 3, 2003).

10. "Examples of Stories Printed Because of FOIA," Your Right to Know, June 9, 1997, http://www.asne.org.

11. Homefront Confidential, Reporters Committee for Freedom of the Press, September 2003, http://www.rcfp.org (accessed December 3, 2003).

12. Ibid.

13. Karl Ömer Oguz, "Russia Report," *IPI World Press Freedom Review, 2000* (Vienna: International Press Institute, 2000).

14. Letter to Aleksandr Lukashenka, Article 19, August 24, 2001, http://www.article19.org (accessed December 3, 2003).

15. See also Johann P. Fritz, letter to Eduard Shevardnadze, International Press Institute, October 31, 2001, http://www.freemedia.at (accessed December 3, 2003).

16. Tom Welsh and Walter Greenwood, eds., *McNae's Essential Law for Journalists*, 15th ed. (London: Butterworths, 1999), pp. 201–203.

17. In 1994, a British Law Commission recommended the abolition of criminal libel, but Prime Minister John Major's Conservative government did not act on the recommendation.

18. *Garrison v. Louisiana*, 379 US 64 (1964).

19. *New York Times v. Sullivan*, 376 US 254 (1964).

20. *State of Utah v. Ian Michael Lake*, American Civil Liberties Union Protecting Constitutional Freedoms in Utah, http://www.acluutah.org (December 3, 2003).

21. "Supreme Court Throws Out 1876 Criminal Libel Statute," Reporters Committee for Freedom of the Press, November 19, 2002, http://www.rcfp.org.

22. Coordinating Committee of Press Freedom Organizations, letter to Göran Persson, International Press Institute, June 13, 2001, http://www.freemedia.at (December 3, 2003).

23. Anthony Löwstedt, "Israel Report," *IPI World Press Freedom Review, 2002* (Vienna: International Press Institute, 2003).

24. Michael Kudlak, ed., *IPI Congress Report: New Delhi 2001* (Vienna: International Press Institute, 2001), p. 80.

25. Ibid.

26. Amartya Sen, *Development as Freedom* (London: Oxford University Press, 1999), p. 182. See also Stuart R. Schram, ed., *Mao Tse Tung Unrehearsed: Talks and Letters, 1956–1971* (Hammondsworth, UK: Penguin Books, 1976).

27. Although not on the same scale as the famine, the Severe Acute Respiratory Syndrome (SARS) epidemic in China and elsewhere during 2003 reinforced the important role played by the media in a crisis. Commenting on this in an April 22, 2003, letter to the Chinese government, the International Press Institute (IPI) said the repressive media environment in the country had assisted the Chinese government in its initial attempts to

downplay the seriousness of the disease. The IPI noted, "The decision to view information itself as dangerous had had a divisive effect on Chinese society and represents a serious impediment to any concerted response to a crisis such as SARS." Letter to His Excellency Hu Jintao, president, People's Republic of China, from Johann P. Fritz, director, International Press Institute, April 22, 2003, http://www.freemedia.at (accessed December 3, 2003).

28. Article 19, "Ethiopia: Still Starving in Silence? Famine and Censorship Revisited," *Censorship News* 57 (May 2002).

29. Ibid.

30. Ibid.

31. International Federation of Journalists, "Journalists Say Johannesburg Summit on Sustainable Development Must Boost Democracy and Press Freedom," press release, August 19, 2001.

32. Joseph Stiglitz and Roumeen Islam, "A Free Press Is Crucial in Overcoming Global Poverty," *International Herald Tribune*, November 14, 2002.

33. James Wolfensohn, "The War Against Terrorism Will Be Won by Eliminating Poverty," *La Stampa*, December 7, 2001, http://www.world bank.org.

34. Office of the Press Secretary, "Radio Address by the President to the Nation," press release, The White House, November 10, 2001, http://www.Whitehouse.gov.

35. "Poverty Fueling Terrorism," BBC News, March 22, 2002, http://www.news.bbc.co.

36. Joel Simon, telephone interview, March 18, 2003.

CONCLUSION

In the period since the September 11 attacks, the impact of the Bush administration on press freedom has been threefold: It has sought to influence the media in order to win the propaganda battle over its war in Afghanistan; it has encouraged a censorious and self-censorious environment in the United States, which has allowed the administration to alter the fine balance between security and liberty virtually unchallenged; and, owing to the wider war on terrorism, it has deeply harmed the cause of press freedom around the world.

One of the Bush administration's first aims was to prevent the airing of the views of al-Qaeda leader Osama bin Laden, the spread of anti-American sentiment, and the incitement of Muslims. Evidence for this strategy can be found in the Voice of America (VOA) and Al-Jazeera incidents.

During late September of 2001, members of the State Department sought to stop journalists in the Voice of America newsroom from interviewing Taliban leader Mullah Omar and then broadcasting a news report containing parts of the interview. Under pressure from the State Department, the Broadcasting Board of Governors (BBG), which had been designed as a protective firewall for the VOA by the Clinton administration, failed to uphold the principle that the journalists themselves were entitled to make the decisions concerning the Omar interview. With their independence threatened, the newscasters, with the support of the acting director of the VOA, chose to ignore the comments of U.S. State Department officials and aired the report. Although this broadcast was a victory for the journalists in the face of considerable outside pressure, the incident highlighted a number of problems for a free press in the period after September 11.

The incident showed that, after the attacks, questions about which persons were suitable for VOA interviews and who was allowed to express an opinion on the network were no longer considered to be the sole preserve of the newsroom staff. Instead, they were now part of a wider attempt at public diplomacy and the perceived need to express the foreign policy objectives of the United States, particularly the justification for the war in Afghanistan and the wider war on terrorism. For this reason, the Bush administration, through the offices of the State Department, sought to exercise control over the decision-making process; however, this desire had unforeseen consequences for the Bush administration and the VOA.

Overall, the effect of this new policy was to undermine the way in which the United States was viewed in the Middle East. The attempted censorship was reported in the region, and it appeared to confirm Arab prejudices that the U.S. media were not prepared to listen to opinions that contradicted the official viewpoint of the U.S. government. In essence, the VOA incident lent credence to the belief that Arab perspectives on numerous problems in the Middle East were to be excluded from news reporting on the region. Indeed, for many in the Middle East, it served only to heighten the view that both the media and the government in the United States were biased. The accusations of bias in the VOA case were exacerbated by the incident involving Al-Jazeera.

The clumsy attempt by the U.S. State Department to influence the independent news values of Qatar-based broadcaster Al-Jazeera not only cheapened U.S. diplomacy but reduced press freedom to a contradictory twin track on which this fundamental right was to be upheld and affirmed within the United States but ignored and over-ridden elsewhere. For all intents and purposes, the incident served notice that the Bush administration cared little for this basic right if it prevented the administration from winning over hearts and minds in the Middle East.

By contacting the emir of Qatar and asking him to soften the reporting stance of Al-Jazeera, the Bush administration not only alienated much of the Arab world but also revealed a deep-seated prejudice in the way it viewed the Middle East media. Crucially, at this time, the State Department overlooked the perceived bias of news reports in the United States in order to challenge the reporting standards of a Middle Eastern television network. In reality, the dif-ference between the patriotic reporting of Fox News and the Arab perspectives of Al-Jazeera was only a difference in viewpoint: one reported from the perspective of the U.S. government and the other did not.

Moreover, in accusing Al-Jazeera of bias, the Bush administra-tion overlooked some of the more extreme reporting emanating from certain U.S. journalists who allowed emotion to preclude objectivity. Their calls for revenge, breaches of the Geneva Conven-tion, bloody deaths, and carpet bombing escaped the censure of the Bush administration, but Al-Jazeera's attempts to provide a context for the September 11 attacks by interviewing Islamic fundamental-ists and questioning U.S. policy in the region were vilified. The con-tradiction was extreme, and it resonated among the Arab people—the very people to whom the Bush administration was attempting to explain and justify its actions.

Why, though, was the State Department prepared to risk so much and go to such extreme lengths to pressure a foreign news net-work? The answer lay in the propaganda war that attended the con-flict in Afghanistan. From the outset, statements from American offi-cials indicated that the U.S. government was failing to convince the so-called Arab street that it was going to war because it had been unjustly attacked. Speaking on CNN, a U.S. official said that "we are getting hammered in the Arab world," while another official commented, "This is a battle for public opinion. We're doing everything we can to win it." There can be little doubt that these views represented the Bush administration's thinking at the time. Faced with an independent network outside its sphere of influence, the Bush administration believed that it was losing the propaganda battle. The criticism of Al-Jazeera and the attempt by the State Department to influence its reporting were indicative of this belief.

Additional evidence for these assertions may be seen in the Bush administration's handling of the bin Laden tapes. The airing of the tapes on Al-Jazeera outraged government officials and, when excerpts from the tapes started appearing on U.S. networks, the Bush administration sought to weaken their impact by convincing media executives that the tapes should not be shown in their entirety. To achieve this end, National Security Advisor Condoleeza Rice conducted a conference call with the heads of the leading U.S. networks in which she alleged that bin Laden might be using the tapes to pass coded messages to his followers. Accepting the national security argument at face value, the media executives agreed to alter the way in which they aired the tapes.

The assertion that the tapes might carry hidden messages lacked supporting evidence, however. As a number of journalists have said, the idea that bin Laden could transmit a coded message when he was unsure of the exact segment of a twenty-minute speech that was to be translated and broadcast defies belief, yet it was successfully argued to the U.S. media by a convincing and articulate Rice. Moreover, the fact that the tapes had already been broadcast by Al-Jazeera negated the attempts to stop them from reaching the public domain. Once again, the true reason for the conference call is much more likely to have been bin Laden's exhortations for a jihad against the United States, which was endangering U.S. attempts to influence popular Arab opinion. Rice herself appeared to acknowledge this point when she stated that the messages could be used to incite Muslims. Her statement on incitement was made without offering any proof, yet it had an impact on media executives who should have been more skeptical.

Castigated for these attempts to infringe press freedom by the media and press freedom organizations, the Bush administration later altered its approach to the question of public diplomacy and the sophisticated propaganda coups of bin Laden and the al-Qaeda terrorist organization. Bush administration officials such as Condoleeza Rice, Donald H. Rumsfeld, and Colin Powell, as well as British Prime Minister Tony Blair, began to appear regularly on Al-Jazeera television to justify the actions of the allied forces in Afghanistan. In the public diplomacy arena, Blair's Director of Communications Alasdair Campbell and his counterpart in the Bush administration, advisor to the president Karen Hughes, developed a joint communications body called the Coalition Information Center (CIC). According to staff members, the aim of the CIC was to "beat down misconceptions about our motives. . . ." In an attempt to turn the tide of Arab skepticism about allied motives for the war in Afghanistan, President Bush also appointed advertising specialist Charlotte Beers as Under-Secretary of State for Diplomacy.

All of these actions not only emphasized the importance of swaying public opinion in the Middle East but also tacitly acknowledged that the previous infringements of the media had weakened the United States' justification for the war in Afghanistan. As such, they were yet further proof that the initial policy sought to prevent opposing views from appearing in the media.

On the domestic front, various members of the Bush administration actively encouraged an environment that stifled debate in the United States. Reacting to the comments of comedian and social critic Bill Maher in late September 2001, presidential spokesperson Ari Fleischer said, "[Maher's comments are] reminders to all Americans that they need to watch what they say, watch what they do. This is not a time for remarks like that; there never is. . . ." The pressure on journalists increased in December when, appearing before the Senate Judiciary Committee, Attorney General John Ashcroft baldly stated:

> We need honest, reasoned debate, not fear mongering. To those who
> pit Americans against immigrants, and citizens against noncitizens;
> to those who scare peace-loving people with phantoms of lost lib-
> erty, my message is this: Your tactics only aid terrorists—for they

erode our national unity and diminish our resolve. They give ammunition to America's enemies, and pause to America's friends. They
encourage people of good will to remain silent in the face of evil.[1]

Widely reported, these two statements served notice to the
media and various civil society organizations that the Bush administration was not prepared to tolerate dissent.

Instead of taking advantage of the huge wave of support for President Bush in the days and weeks after the attacks to change the relationship between security and basic freedoms, Bush administration
officials such as Fleischer and Ashcroft should have worked to break
the cycle of patriotic correctness that existed at the time. Throughout
this period, reporters who criticized or questioned the government
found themselves stranded in a journalistic no-man's land where
the public's sense of patriotism was further inflamed by conservative
talk show hosts and then reflected back on the journalists. Rather
than claiming that dissent "aided terrorists" (Ashcroft) or that Americans "need[ed] to watch what they say, watch what they do" (Fleischer), the Bush administration should have upheld the tradition of
informed debate and dissent in American society.

By ignoring this opportunity, they impugned the legitimate right
of citizens from every walk of American life to say and discuss any
issue they wish. The outcome was particularly hard on the journalists who lost their jobs, found their words grossly distorted, or were
forced because of the "censorious environment" to lapse into
silence. Commenting on McCarthyism in the 1950s, broadcaster
Edward R. Murrow once said, "We should not confuse dissent with
disloyalty." Based on the spoken words of officials, the Bush administration appeared to have done precisely that after September 11.

The pressures to conform were also acknowledged by journalists
and media executives. At a dinner in November 2001, Chairman of
CNN Walter Isaacson commented, "In this environment it feels
slightly different. . . . If you get on the wrong side of public opinion,
you are going to get into trouble."[2] Instead of tempering and
calming the overheated situation, the government became a part of
this cycle, serving only to encourage the silence. This calculated act
was to pay an immediate dividend for the Bush administration.

Directly after the September 11 attacks, the government announced a full-scale review of the country's security measures to combat future terrorist threats. The decision led to an adjustment in the delicate balance between security and civil liberties. One of the first signs of this change came with the passage of the USA Patriot Act, which passed through the legislature without the benefit of a committee report within one month of the attacks. Indeed, such was the haste with which it was pushed through the legislature that it is doubtful whether all the members of both houses had time to read and reflect on its provisions. Following the passage of this law, the Bush administration quietly shut off elements of the information flow within the country by attempting to restrict Congressional access to secret information, altering the government's policy on freedom of information laws, and ordering agencies to withdraw sensitive information from Web sites. State legislatures followed suit by passing similar laws limiting access to information.

Shielded by blanket public support and with Bush officials seeming to encourage the public in its criticism of the media, the government tried to introduce its contentious Total Information Awareness (TIA) system* free of Congressional oversight. The absence of true debate had strengthened the government's hand, allowing it to alter the civil liberties landscape without substantial opposition. A demonstration of the Bush administration's confidence at this time can be seen in its proposal for an Office of Strategic Influence (OSI), a body apparently designed to spread disinformation among the media. This proposal had broad implications for the future relationship between the government and journalists as it would have destroyed the credibility of the media.

Outside the United States, the war on terrorism was also to have far-reaching implications for press freedom. On September 20, 2001, President Bush said, "From this day forward any nation that continues to harbor terrorists will be regarded by the United States as a hostile regime."[3] If the words carried a threat, they also implied that nations that supported the war on terrorism would be deemed friends of the United States—irrespective of their human rights

---

*Subsequently changed to Terrorism Information Awareness

records. Unfortunately for democracy, countries with appalling human rights records lined up to join the coalition against terrorism. As a result, the United States and Western governments found themselves allied with such stalwart opponents of human rights as China, Pakistan, Russia, Turkmenistan, and Uzbekistan.

In joining the coalition against terrorism, many of these countries brought to the bargaining table somewhat dubious tales of their own problems with terrorism. Many government leaders tried to link their own internal terrorism with the events of September 11 by claiming that their own groups had links with bin Laden and al-Qaeda. Although most such relationships were tenuous in the extreme, the Bush administration, and in particular the State Department, was in such need of assistance in fighting terrorists that it listened to these claims and altered some of its own policies accordingly. The consequence of the post–September 11 coalition against terrorism was therefore an unseemly trade-off between human rights and security in which the West relaxed its call for increased democratic rights in these countries.

The flawed election in Pakistan in which dictator Pervez Musharraf maintained his position is one of the most shameful examples of the Bush administration's political and moral elasticity during this period. Aside from the outcry among human rights and civil society organizations, the election was largely accepted by the West, demonstrating to other countries around the world that support for the war on terrorism could have beneficial results. Another example of this new environment was the visit paid by authoritarian President Islam Karimov of Uzbekistan to Washington, DC. During his visit, Karimov met President Bush at the White House and received a generous aid package for his country. He then returned home to continue with his program of stifling human rights in Uzbekistan. Once again, a lack of democracy and the repression of citizens proved to be no bar to appearing on the international stage with the president of the United States.

While the Bush administration can truthfully claim that during this period it continued to criticize these countries in its Human Rights Reports and through the comments of various officials, the mere fact of allowing such people to tread the White House lawn diminished the value of such comments. Such visits implied that support for the Bush administration in its war against terrorism paid a healthy dividend and, for many countries, that dividend meant that they were spared the need to continue with their own democratization programs.

Outside the circle of the alliance against terrorism, the situation was perhaps even worse. Despite discussion in the United States about the long-term impact of the changes to civil rights on the domestic front, there has been little comment on the wider effects of these changes outside the country. Since the terrorist attacks, the abuses in the United States have rippled outward and actively encouraged countries around the world to follow with their own acts of repression. Countries from Benin to Zimbabwe and from Egypt to Uganda have used the war on terrorism to attack their own media. In some incidents, like the Bility case in Liberia, which followed the Hamdi case in the United States, the actual methods used in U.S. court cases have been adopted, while in other countries, the acts of the United States have been seen as a justification for repressive behavior. One of the most worrying developments was the admission by the Bush administration that it could learn lessons in the fight against terrorism from a country such as Egypt, which suppresses and smothers all forms of dissent. Such recognition appeared to sanction repression as a legitimate act by a sovereign state, leading to the extraordinary comment from Egypt's President Hosni Mubarak that a new "concept of democracy" was needed, one that differed substantially from the concept that Western states had previously defended by using repressive methods to uphold democracy. The fact that this statement was received in the post–September 11 world without undue criticism was an indicator of the new way in which the question of human rights was viewed after the attacks.

Sadly, in the months since the attacks, the view of President Mubarak toward press freedom and human rights in general has become the prevalent one of governments around the world. Of course, democracy still exists, as do the rights that were cherished before the fateful day when the airplanes struck the World Trade

Center. However, there is a new pragmatism that seems willing to diminish civil rights to increase security, irrespective of whether it is necessary to do so. Moreover, in seeking to create this new security, the Bush administration has overlooked the importance of the United States' support for democracy and human rights.

As this book is being written, a vacuum is slowly forming in the human rights and press freedom fields, encouraged by the willingness of the Bush administration to forge alliances with countries that are deeply prejudicial to these rights and fed by the actions of the Bush administration within the United States. "Things fall apart; the center cannot hold," wrote the Irish poet William Butler Yeats, and this line aptly describes the real danger for the future. With its economic strength, democratic institutions, and public support for human rights, the United States is at the very center of the human rights tradition. If it is to alter this position, if it is to turn its back on the calls for aid and assistance from other parts of the world, then the dangers described in Yeats's poem may become a reality— press freedom and human rights in general will have become irreparably damaged, and things will have fallen apart. The Bush administration and future American administrations need to recognize this situation, and the chain of events that has been set in motion, and take corrective action.

This book opened with a reflection on the power of the television images drawn from September 11, and it closes with a plea for broadcasters and the print media to be allowed to continue their work unmolested by governments. A constant theme in the media sphere since September 11 has been the attacks on individual journalists and media outlets for their willingness to provide opposing views. Critics have labeled media outlets expressing such views as the "Voice of bin Laden" or the "Voice of the Taliban," while the media have replied that airing opposing views is an expression of good reporting. In addition, by exploring a variety of opinions, the media argue that they are expressing the need of the American public to understand and appreciate the acts that were perpetrated against them on September 11.

For governments to exclude views that oppose their own undermines the very arguments that these governments wish their own publics to understand: in essence they are the sound of one hand clapping. All of us need to accept the principle that we are not just what we say, we are also what we allow to be said, and we must measure ourselves by our openness to the thoughts of others, no matter how unpalatable. In the overwhelming desire to bring the perpetrators of the September 11 attacks to justice, the need to hear opposing views has been forgotten, and the media have borne the brunt of this act of forgetting. Indeed, the media have been attacked for reminding everyone that there is more than one side to the argument. To exclude those opposing voices risks a society in which the media are merely the echo of the government and citizens fear to dissent from the accepted viewpoint. If this were to happen in the United States, it would ensure victory to those who sought to destroy democracy on September 11.

NOTES

1. John Ashcroft, testimony before the Senate Judiciary Committee, December 6, 2001.

2. Alessandra Stanley, "Opponents of the War Are Scarce on Television," *New York Times*, November 9, 2001.

3. George W. Bush, "Address to a Joint Session of Congress and the American People," The White House, September 20, 2001, http://www.whitehouse.gov (accessed December 3, 2003).

BIBLIOGRAPHY

"ABC Anchor Never Insulted Bush During Crisis Coverage, Did Label His Trip 'A Little Strange.'" Media Research Center, September 19, 2001, http://www.mediasearch.org (accessed November 18, 2002).

Abunimah, Ali. "No to U.S.-Demanded Crackdown on Free Media," October 4, 2001, http://www.globalissues.org (accessed August 26, 2002).

"Address to a Joint Session of Congress and the American People." Transcript, September 20, 2001, The White House, http://www.whitehouse.gov (accessed January 7, 2004).

"After a 'Wake-Up Call from Hell,' Civilization at Stake—Netanyahu." *Investor's Business Daily*, September 21, 2001.

Africa News Service. "Government Release a Black List of Foreign Journalists Accused of 'Aiding Terrorism.'" November 26, 2001.

Agence France-Presse. "Chechens Would Have 'Massacred All Hostages' If Not for Deadly Gas." November 1, 2002.

Ahari, Ehsan. "Al-Jazeera's Unwitting Role in the 'Unrestricted' Afghan War." Center For Defense Information, October 25, 2001, http://www.cdi.org (accessed August 21, 2002).

Ahrens, Frank. "Cracking Signals—Voice of America Is Pulled Between Journalism and Propaganda." *Washington Post*, November 10, 2001.

———. "Radio Station Can't Shake Marionette Image." *Washington Post*, November 25, 2001.

"Airwaves Battle—Access to Info Is Basic Right in Democracy" (editorial). *South China Morning Post* (China), October 12, 2001.

"Al-Assad Discusses Impact of September 11 Events with U.S. Congressman." Text of Report by Syrian News Agency SANA Website (accessed September 5, 2002).

"Al Jazeera TV Chief Editor Comments on New al-Qa'idah Tape." *Al-Watan*, April 17, 2002.

"Al Jazeera Wins Court Victory." *Arabian Internet News*, December 6, 2001.

"Al-Jazeera Correspondent Released." *Jordan Times* (Jordan), December 17, 2001.

"Al-Jazeera Office Closed." Committee to Protect Journalists, August 8, 2002, http://www.ifex.org (accessed August 28, 2002).

"Al-Jazeera Reporter Defends Not Airing Bin Laden Tape." FWN Select, Distributed Via Comtex News, February 4, 2002.

"Al-Jazeera TV—Inside the Afghan Crisis." BBC Monitoring Unit, October 4, 2001.

"Al-Jazeera's Office Resumes Work after Suspension Is Reversed." BBC Monitoring Unit, July 25, 2002.

"Al-Jazeera's Riot Coverage Hurts Delhi—So Reporter Goes." Asia/Africa Intelligence Wire, July 12, 2002.

Albright, Madeleine K. Comment: "Clear on Chechnya." *Washington Post*, March 8, 2000.

Allen, Mike. "Bush Defends Putin on Moscow Theater Siege." November 18, 2002.

Alter, Jonathan. "The Best Propaganda-Disinformation Has Its Uses, But It's Not the Way to Win the Muslim World." *Newsweek*, March 4, 2002.

"America Aiming to Win Battle of the Airwaves" (editorial). *Birmingham Post* (United Kingdom), October 18, 2001.

"America's War Reports Bomb the Taste Barrier." *Business*, October 28, 2001.

Amnesty International. "Central Asia: No Excuse for Escalating Human Rights Violations." Amnesty International Report, AI Index: EUR 4/003/2001, October 11, 2001.

———. "China Fight Against Terrorism Is No Excuse for Repression." October 11, 2001, http://www.amnesty.org (accessed January 7, 2003).

———. "Rights at Risk: Amnesty International's Concerns Regarding Security Legislation and Law Enforcement Measures." Amnesty International Report, January 21, 2002.

"Arab TV Reporter Says He Was Beaten by Afghans." *Washington Post*, November 15, 2001.

"Arab Writer Says Al Jazeera TV's Coverage of Saudi Policy Lacks 'Professionalism and Objectivity.'" *Al-Hayat* (London), July 21, 2002.

"Arabic News Channel Al-Jazeera 'Unbalanced.'" Interspace, Reuters News Service, October 10, 2001.

"Article 19 Expresses Concern over the Recent Adoption in Parliament of the Law on the Fight Against Terrorism." Press release, Article 19, February 22, 2002, http://www.ifex.org (accessed September 9, 2002).

"Ashcroft Smear, The" (editorial). *Washington Post*, December 7, 2001.

Associated Press. "Lawmakers Decry TV Station's Ban on Flag-Wearing Newscasters." September 28, 2001.

———. "Should TV Journalists Wear U.S. Flag Symbols?" September 21, 2001.

Atkins, Ralph, and Stephen Fidler. "Israel Truce Clears Way for Fight Against Terror." Financial Times (FT.Com), http://www.ft.com (accessed February 26, 2003).

Ayuso, Rocio. "Media Find Objectivity Difficult in Times of Patriotic Fervor." Agencia EFE S.A., October 2, 2001.

"Baby Killing Lies and the 1991 Gulf War." San Francisco Bay Area Independent Media Center, March 1, 2002, http://www.sf.indymedia.org (accessed December 9, 2002).

Banisar, David. "Freedom of Information and Access to Government Records Around the World." *Privacy International*, July 2, 2002.

Barber, Ben. "Bush Opposes Legislation to Restructure VOA." *Washington Times*, March 26, 2002.

Baroud, Ramzy. "About Bias in the Media." *Milli Gazette* (India), September 6, 2002.

Barton, Teresa. "Dissent Healthy for Nation." *South Bend Tribune*, November 7, 2001.

Bauder, David. "ABC Replacing 'Politically Correct' with Comedy Show Starring Jimmy Kimmel." Associated Press, undated.

Bayley, Anita C. "Advertisers Exercise Freedom of Speech." *Times Union*, October 7, 2001.

BBC Correspondents (Various). *The BBC Reports on America, Its Allies and Enemies, and the Counterattack on Terrorism*. Woodstock, NY: Overlook Press, 2002.

"Be Careful What Gets Stiffed." *Los Angeles Times*, October 2, 2001.

Beatty, Sally. "CNN Ends Ties with al Jazeera Network." *Asian Wall Street Journal*, February 4, 2002.

————, and Jeanne Cummings. "Networks Hear from Bush on Use of al Qaeda Footage." *Wall Street Journal*, October 11, 2001.

Beck, Simon. "Storm over Block on Wei TV Broadcast—White House Red-Faced after Censorship Admission." *South China Morning Post* (China), December 19, 1997.

Becker, Elizabeth. "Administration Capitalizing on Tape." *Milwaukee Journal Sentinel*, December 15, 2001.

"Belarus Prepared to Fight International Terrorism-Security Offical." Excerpt from Report by Belarusian Radio, October 30, 2001.

Bell, Graham Boyd. "How We Learned to Stop Worrying and Love the War." Eye Weekly, October 18, 2001, http://www.eye.net (accessed September 2, 2002).

Bell, Steve. "On Being an American Journalist." *USA Today*, July 1, 2002.

Berringer, Felicity. "Federal Worker Sentenced for Passing on Information." *New York Times*, January 16, 2003.

————. "Voice of America Under Pressure to Toe U.S. Line." *New York Times*, October 8, 2001.

Berringer, Felicity, and Bill Carter. "At U.S. Request, Networks Agree to Edit Future bin Laden Tapes." *New York Times*, October 11, 2001.

Berkowitz, Bill. "Freedom of Information Act on the Ropes." Working for Change, November 10, 2002, http://www.workingforchange.com (accessed December 12, 2002).

Bernstein, Richard, and the staff of the *New York Times*. *Out of the Blue: The Story of September 11, 2001*. New York: Times Books, 2002.

"Big Media's FCC Friends and Foes." Index on Censorship, http://www.indexonline.org (accessed November 7, 2002).

Billhartz, Cynthia. "Maher's Comments Lead to Show's Supension." *St. Louis Post-Dispatch*, September 22, 2001.

"Bin Laden Interviewer Was Under Duress, TV Station Says." *Los Angeles Times*, February 3, 2002.

"Bin Laden Video Poses Threat" (editorial). *Electronic Media*, October 22, 2001.

"Biography." Wei Jingsheng, http://www.weijingsheng.org (accessed March 21, 2003).

"Biography of FCC Chairman Powell." Federal Communications Commission, http://www.fcc.gov (accessed November 7, 2002).

Birnbaum, Norman. "Americans Able to Think for Themselves." *Financial Times* (London), October 16, 2001.

Bivens, Matt. "U.S. Closing Eyes to Uzbek Rights Record?" *Moscow Times* (Russia), November 1, 2001.

Bloom, Jonah, and Douglas Quenqua. "Fleischer Should Retract Comment" (editorial). *PR Week*, October 8, 2001, p. 10.

Boucher, Richard. "Richard Boucher Holds State Department Briefing." Reuters News Service, June 16, 2000.

Boyle, Jon. "U.S. Rebukes Russia for Bombing Georgia." *Birmingham Post* (United Kingdom), August 26, 2002.

Bozell, L Brent, III. "Deadly Media Game with No Winners." *Washington Times*, September 10, 2002.

Broad, William J. "U.S. Tightening Rules on Keeping Scientific Secrets." *New York Times*, February 17, 2002.

"Broadcasters Clear on the TV News Battle Lines." *Business*, October 21, 2001.

Broder, David. "Losing War for Public Support." *Bergen County Record*, November 5, 2001.

Bryson, Jennifer. "Analysis: Is Rumsfeld's Criticism of Al-Jazeera Justified?" October 30, 2001, http://www.newsmax.com (accessed October 29, 2002).

Bumiller, Elisabeth. "New Slogan in Washington: Watch What You Say." Global Issues, October 7, 2001, http://www.globalissues.org (accessed August 26, 2002).

Burke, David. "A Truthful Voice." *Washington Post*, October 10, 2001.

"Bush Administration Shuts Down the OSI, The." Reporters Sans Frontières, February 27, 2002, http://www.rsf.org (accessed September 3, 2002).

"Bush Appoints Norman Pattiz to Second Term on Broadcasting Board of Governors." PR Newswire, August 13, 2002.

"Bush Restricts Lawmakers Access to Classified Information." Secrecy News, October 10, 2001, http://www.fas.org (accessed December 15, 2002).

"Bush Strikes Common Understanding with China on Fighting Terrorism." *Independent Business Weekly* (New Zealand), October 24, 2001.

Buttry, Stephen. "U.S. Paid Broadcasts Called Pro-Taliban Voice of America." *Omaha World-Herald*, November 5, 2001.

Byrne, Ciar. "Journalists Face Increasing Danger Warns CNN Chief." *Guardian* (London), November 20, 2002.

"Call for Press Freedom During Times of War." http://www.nwu.org (accessed August 21, 2002).

Campagna, Joel. "Between Two Worlds: Qatar's Al-Jazeera Satellite Channel Faces Conflicting Expectations." Committee to Protect Journalists, http://www.cpj.org (accessed August 26, 2002).

Campbell, Duncan. "Patriots Attack Media Amid Cries of Treason." *Guardian* (London), October 3, 2001.

———. "U.S. Buys Up All Satellite War Images." *Guardian* (London), October 17, 2001.

———. "War in Afghanistan—Propaganda—U.S. Plans TV Station to Rival Al-Jazeera." *Guardian* (London), November 23, 2001.

"Can Journalism Be Impartial?" *Columbia Journalism Review*, http://www.cjr.org (accessed September 3, 2002).

Carter, Jimmy. Comment: "The Troubling New Face of America." *Washington Post*, September 5, 2002.

"Censoring the Enemy." http://www.pbs.org (accessed August 29, 2002).

"Censorship in Pashto and Arabic" (editorial). *New York Times*, October 10, 2001.

Chalmers, Patrick. "U.S. Denies Anti-Terror Laws Similar to Malaysia's." Reuters News Service, January 24, 2002.

Chamberlain, Gethin. "West Fast Losing the War of Words." *Scotsman* (United Kingdom), October 15, 2001.

Charter, David, and Joanna Bale. "Blair Office Defends 'Censoring bin Laden.'" *Times* (London), October 15, 2001.

"Chronology of Anthrax Events." Sun-Sentinel.com, http://www.sun-sentinel.com (accessed December 4, 2002).

"Clinton Administration Attempt to Censor Interview of Chinese Dissident Wei Jinsheng Is Resisted by Voice of America." China Reform Monitor, December 22, 1997, http://www.afpc.org (accessed October 3, 2002).

"CNN Defended Taliban Propaganda; CNN Context Policy Condemned; Koppel Mocked Flag Lapel Pins, Ailes Explained Rivera Hiring." Media Research Center, November 5, 2001, http://www.mediaresearch.org (accessed August 30, 2002).

Cohen, Ariel. "Radio Liberty Launches Controversial Chechen Service." March 27, 2002, www.cacianalyst.org (accessed October 1, 2002).

"Colonial-Era Laws Used to Repress Media." Helen Suzman Foundation, http://www.hsf.org (accessed March 5, 2003).

"Column that Got Tom Gutting Fired from His Job at the Texas City Sun, The." Bush Times, September 2, 2002, http://www.bushtimes.com (accessed September 2, 2002).

Comment: "The CNN of the Arab World Deserves Our Respect." *Los Angeles Times*, October 22, 2001.

"Confidentiality of Professional and Personal Communications Under

Threat." Press release, Reporters Sans Frontières, May 24, 2002, http://www.ifex.org (accessed September 5, 2002).

"Controversial POTO Clauses to Be Dropped." Asia/Africa Intelligence Wire, December 6, 2001.

"Controversial U.S. Unit Closed after 'Media Manipulation' Row." BBC Monitoring Unit, February 27, 2002, Dow Jones and Reuters, http://www.factiva.com (accessed January 9, 2004).

Cornwell, Rupert. "Risk to Journalists 'Increased by War on Terrorism.'" *Independent* (London), March 27, 2002.

Coulter, Ann. "This Is War." National Review Online, September 13, 2001, http://www.nationalreview.com (accessed November 18, 2001).

"CPJ Asks Pentagon to Explain Al-Jazeera Bombing." Committee to Protect Journalists, January 31, 2002, http://www.cpj.org (accessed August 28, 2002).

"CPJ Concerned at VOA Interview Policy, 'Harassment of Journalist.'" Committee to Protect Journalists, BBC Monitoring Unit, February 7, 2002.

"CPJ Concerned over Missile 'Attack' on Al-Jazeera TV." Committee to Protect Journalists, BBC Monitoring Unit, November 15, 2001.

"CPJ Dismayed by U.S. Pressure Against Satellite News Channel." Committee to Protect Journalists, October 5, 2001, http://www.ifex.org (accessed August 28, 2002).

"CPJ Protests Closure of Al-Jazeera Television Bureau." Committee to Protect Journalists, March 22, 1999, http://www.ifex.org (accessed August 28, 2002).

"CPJ Protests Closure of Al-Jazeera Television Station." Committee to Protect Journalists, June 23, 1999, http://www.ifex.org (accessed August 28, 2002).

Craner, Lorne W. "Country Reports on Human Rights Practices for 2001." *DISAM Journal of International Security Assistance*, April 2002.

Credit, Sandra Sobieraj. "Media Asked to Downplay bin Laden." *Tulsa World*, October 11, 2001.

Cuprisin, Tim. "Maher Continues His Apology Campaign." *Milwaukee Journal Sentinel*, September 27, 2001.

———. "Request to Pull Tapes Not Necessary." *Milwaukee Journal Sentinel*, October 10, 2001.

Dabbakeh, Saleh. "Winning the Battle for Afghanistan." *Star* (Jordan), October 16, 2001.

Dalglish, Lucy. "War Breeds Conflicting Views of American Journalism." *New Media and the Law*, October 1, 2001.

Dao, James, and Eric Schmitt. "Pentagon Readies Efforts to Sway Sentiment Abroad." *New York Times*, February 19, 2002.

Daugherty, Rebecca. "Ashcroft's FOI Act Memo Prompts Concerns." Reporters Committee for Freedom of the Press, http://www.rcfp.org (accessed November 5, 2002).

———. "Open Government Advocates Continue to Struggle for Information after September 11." The Reporters Committee for Freedom of the Press, http://www.rcfp.org (accessed November 5, 2002).

Day, Julia. "U.S. Steps Up Global PR Drive." *Guardian* (London), July 30, 2002.

Deans, Jason. "UK TV Free to Show Bin Laden Footage." *Guardian* (London), October 11, 2001.

Deen, Thalif. "U.S. Networks Criticized for Patriotic Bias in Journalism." *Asia Times*, December 12, 2001.

Dettmer, Jamie. "What Price Freedom?" *Business A.M.*, March 1, 2002.

DeYoung, Karen. "Bush to Create Formal Office to Shape U.S. Image Abroad." *Washington Post*, July 30, 2002.

Dias, Monica, Phillip Taylor, Heather Palmer, and Kristin Gunderson. "Journalists Face Arrests, Obstacles after Terrorist Attacks." *New Media and the Law*, January, 2002.

"Disinformation Nonsense" (editorial). *Washington Times*, February 25, 2002.

"Disorganized at Defense" (editorial). *Washington Times*, February 27, 2002.

"Dissidents Issue Letter Urging U.S. President to Pressure China on Human Rights," *BBC Monitoring International Reports*, October 21, 2001.

"Domestic Coverage." Reporters Committee for Freedom of the Press, http://www.rcfp.org (accessed November 5, 2002).

"Duma Approves Inquiry about RFE/RL's Status in Russia." IPR Strategic Information Database, May 1, 2002.

Dowd, Maureen. "On the Brink of War, Articles and Comments from the *New York Times*." *New York Times*, October 1, 2001.

———. "We Love the Liberties They Hate." *New York Times*, September 30, 2001.

Downie, Leonard, Jr., and Robert G. Kaiser. *The News about the News*. Borzoi Books, 2002.

Easterbrook, Gregg. "Free Speech Doesn't Come without Cost." *Wall Street Journal*, November 5, 2001.

"Editors Guild Concern over POTO." *Hindu* (India), October 30, 2001.

EFE News Service. "Al Jazeera Broadcasts New Message from Bin Laden." December 27, 2001.

"11 September 2001-11 January 2002: One Hundred and Twenty Days of Abuses to Enduring Freedoms." Press release, Reporters Sans Frontières, January 9, 2002, http://www.ifex.org (accessed September 5, 2002).

Elgood, Charles. "Broadcasters Will Screen bin Laden Video." Reuters News Service, October 11, 2001.

El-Nawawy, Mohammed, and Adel Iskandar. *Al-Jazeera: How the Free Arab News Network Scooped the World and Changed the Middle East.* Cambridge, MA: Westview Press, 2002.

Engel, Matthew. "American Media Cowed by Patriotic Fever, Says Network News Veteran." *Guardian* (London), May 17, 2002.

———. "U.S. Soft-Pedals on Allies 'Human Rights' Records." *Guardian* (London), March 5, 2002.

Entous, Adam. "U.S. Urges Limits on Broadcasts of bin Laden Messages." Reuters News Service, October 10, 2001.

"Examples of Stories Printed Because of FOIA." American Society of Newspaper Editors, http://www.asne.org (accessed March 4, 2003).

"Experts on Freedom of Expression Blast Attacks on Media." Press release, United Nations, December 11, 2002, http://www.193.194.138.190 (accessed March 7, 2003).

Farhi, Paul. "The Networks, Giving Aid to the Enemy?—Unedited Bin Laden Video Sparks Debate." *Washington Post*, October 12, 2001.

———. "WJLA's Correction—Pull Maher." *Washington Post*, September 22, 2001.

"FCC Moves to Intensify Media Consolidation." Fairness and Accuracy in Reporting, April 20, 2001, http://www.fair.org (accessed November 7, 2002).

"FCC Moves to Lift Cross-Ownership Ban." Fairness and Accuracy in Reporting, October 26, 2001, http://www.fair.org (accessed November 7, 2002).

"FedEx and Sears Pull Ads from ABC's 'Politically Incorrect.'" *Dow Jones Business News*, September 20, 2001.

"Feds Open 'Total' Tech Spy System." Wired News, August 7, 2002, http://www.wired.com (accessed December 17, 2002).

Ferreira-Marques, Clara. "Rights Groups Reject Official Chechnya Death Toll." Reuters News Service, March 25, 2002.

Fireman, Ken. "U.S. Asks of Newspapers: No Unedited bin Laden Comments." *Newsday*, October 12, 2001, http://www.newsday.com (accessed November 5, 2001).

Fisk, Robert. "War on Terrorism—the Loose Conjecture Is Unlikely to Cut Much Ice with the Arab Nations." *Independent* (London), October 5, 2001.

Fleischer, Ari. "Ari Fleischer Holds White House Briefing." FDCH Washington Transcript Service, September 28, 2001.

Fletcher, Martin. "Publicity Queen Sells America to the Muslims." *Times* (London), October 16, 2001.

Floyd, Abrams. "Balance Act." *Columbia Journalism Review* (November 2001).

Fones-Wolf, Elizabeth. "The Voice of America and the Domestic Propaganda Battles, 1945–1953." Reuters News Service, July 1, 2001.

"For Whom the Liberty Bell Tolls." *Economist* (London), August 29, 2002, http://www.economist.com (accessed September 5, 2002).

Foreign Staff. "Arab Broadcaster Dismissed as Mouthpiece of Al Qaeda." *Scotsman* (United Kingdom), April 16, 2002.

"Former Voice of America Director Sanford Ungar Is Concerned—Verily" (editorial). *Richmond Times Dispatch*, October 16, 2001.

Frankel, Glenn. "Wanted Egyptian Says He's No Terrorist—Britain Refuses Extradition Requests." *Washington Post*, August 22, 2002.

"Free Pass on Chechnya, A " (editorial). *Washington Post*, July 21, 2001.

Freedom Forum. "State Department Defends Journalistic Interference with VOA." http://www.freedomforum.org (accessed August 28, 2002).

"Freedom of Information." Reporters Committee for Freedom of the Press, http://www.rcfp.org (accessed November 5, 2002).

Fritz, Johann P., director, International Press Institute. Letter to U.S. Attorney General John Ashcroft, August 1, 2001, http://www.freemedia.at (accessed March 5, 2003).

———. Letter to U.S. Attorney General John Ashcroft. September 10, 2001, http://www.freemedia.at (accessed December 16, 2002).

———. Letter to Andre DeNesnera, news director, Voice of America, October 2, 2001, http://www.freemedia.at (accessed October 1, 2002).

———. Letter to Bill Graves, governor of Kansas, April 6, 2001, http://www.freemedia.at (accessed March 5, 2003).

———. Letter to U.S. Secretary of State Colin Powell, October 8, 2001, http://www.freemedia.at (accessed October 31, 2002).

———. Letter to Ranil Wickremasinghe, prime minister of Sri Lanka, July 8, 2002, http://www.freemedia.at (accessed March 13, 2003).

"Full Text of Taleban Leader Mullah Omar Mohammed's Interview with Voice of America." *South China Morning Post* (China), September 28, 2001.

Gaffney, Frank J., Jr. "Disinformation? U.S. Viewpoints Need Promotion in Islamic World." *Investor's Business Daily*, March 12, 2002, p. 16.

"German Chancellor Backs Russia's Fight Against Terrorism." Text of Report by German Deutschlandfunk Radio, November 12, 2002, BBC Monitoring Unit, November 12, 2002.

Gersham, John. "Human Rights: Celebration and Concern." TomPaine.commonsense, http://www.tompaine.com (originally published in *Foreign Policy in Focus*) (accessed January 7, 2003).

Ghattas, Kim. "Mideast Media—Ruffled Feathers Nothing New for Al Jazeera TV." *Global Information Network*, October 8, 2001.

Gibson, Owen. "U.S. Rethinks Media Ownership Rules." *Guardian* (London), June 18, 2002.

Gittings, John. "U.S. Claims China and Russia as Allies." *Guardian* (London), October 22, 2001.

Giuffo, John. "The FOIA Fight." *Columbia Journalism Review*, July/August, 2002, http://www.cjr.org (accessed September 3, 2002).

Glasser, Susan B., and Peter Baker. "Blasts Go Off at Moscow Theater." *Washington Post*, October 26, 2002.

Goldberg, Bernard. *Bias.* New York: Regency Publishing, 2002.

Goldberg, Bernhard. "Terrorist Helper." Claywaters.Com, May 2, 2002, http://www.claywaters.com (accessed September 10, 2002).

Goldberg, Jonah. "Free Speech Fretters Overreact." Townhall.com, October 4, 2001, http://www.townhall.com (accessed September 10, 2002).

———. "L'Affaire Coulter." National Review Online, October 3, 2001, http://www.nationalreview.com (accessed November 18, 2001).

Goldborough, James O. "The Office of Strategic Influence: Is It the Truth or Is It a Lie?" *San Diego Union-Tribune*, February 28, 2002.

Goodman, Walter. "What We Saw, What We Learned." *Columbia Journalism Review*, May/June 1991, http://www.cjr.org (accessed November 6, 2002).

Gorman, Steve. "Maher Sorry for Politically Incorrect Statement." Reuters News Service, September 20, 2001.

"Governments Exploiting Fear to Increase Secrecy" (editorial). *Palm Beach Post*, February 26, 2002.

Graff, Peter. "Russia Roars at Washington over Chechnya." Reuters News Service, February 18, 2002.

Green, Miranda. "Washington Focuses on Propaganda War." *Financial Times* (London), March 13, 2002.

Gridneva, Galina, and Valery Zhukov. "EU Revises Strategy of Cooperation—Central Asia." ITAR-TASS World Service, December 14, 2002.

Grimes, Christopher. "Networks Vow Not to Broadcast al-Qaeda Live." *Financial Times* (London), October 11, 2001.

———. "TV Networks Agree Not to Air Unedited al-Qaeda Tapes." FT.Com (*Financial Times*, London), October 10, 2001.

Grossman, Lawrence K. "Wanted: A New Breed of Media CEOs with Old-Fashioned Values." *Columbia Journalism Review*, July/August 2002, http://www.cjr.org (accessed September 3, 2002).

Gudkov, Lev. "How Are We Any Worse?" *What the Papers Say*, January 14, 2002, http://www.wps.ru (accessed September 9, 2002).

Gumbel, Andrew. "Free Speech Has Become Second Casualty of War." *Independent* (London), September 28, 2001.

Gup, Ted. "The Short Distance Between Secrets and Lies." *Columbia Journalism Review* (May 2002).

Gutting, Tom. "Censoring Dissenting Voices Is a Danger to Us All." Libertad de Prensa, http://www.libertad-prensa.org.

Habib, Randa. "Jordan Rebukes Qatar over 'Defamatory' Al-Jazeera Programme." Agence France-Presse, August 8, 2002.

Haddad, Musue N. "Tortured Journalist Hassan Bility Speaks Out." http://www.theperspective.org (accessed August 19, 2002).

Hall, John. "Network Turns into Bullhorn for Bin Laden." *Richmond Times-Dispatch*, October 14, 2001.

———. "Tired and Demoralized VOA Faces Changes." *Richmond Times Dispatch*, February 28, 2002.

Hannity, Sean, and Alan Colmes. "Interview with Bob Zelnick." Transcript, *Hannity and Colmes*, Fox News Channel, October 23, 2001.

———. "What's Going on Between State Department and Voice of America." Transcript, *Hannity and Colmes*, Fox News Channel, October 18, 2000.

Harba, Farida. "Uzbek Media Campaign Secures Popular Support for Anti-Terrorism Campaign—Or Does It?" Eurasianet.org, November 15, 2001, http://www.eurasianet.org (accessed August 26, 2002).

Harper, Jennifer. "Networks Back Rice's Call for Discretion." *Washington Times*, October 11, 2001.

———. "Study Says Begrudging Media Is Back on Track—September 11 Curbed Critics a Bit." *Washington Times*, August 5, 2002.

———. "U.S. Eyes Al Jazeera as Useful, Dangerous—Arab TV Network's Aim Still Not Clear." *Washington Times*, October 17, 2001.

Hart, Peter, and Seth Ackerman. "Some Journalists Are Silence, While Others Seem Happy to Silence Themselves." Fairness & Accuracy in Reporting, Extra! November/December 2001, http://www.fair.org (accessed August 26, 2002).

Haubold, Natasha. "Where Does the Pentagon's Money Go?" Federal Computer Week, February 17, 2000, http://www.fcw.com (accessed November 7, 2002).

Heintz, Jim. "Chechen Rebels Take Hundreds Hostage in Moscow." *Bergen County Record*, October 24, 2002.

"Helicopter Ban in Wake of Attacks Frustrates Broadcast Journalists." Reporters Committee on Freedom of the Press, September 21, 2001, http://www.rcfp.org (accessed November 5, 2002).

Helle, Dale. "Information Warfare." *Washington Times*, March 13, 2002.

———. "With Friends Like These—New U.S. Allies Get a Decidedly Mixed Report Card." *Washington Times*, January 16, 2002.

Hentoff, Nat. "America, Land of the Free Press?—We Must Show We Do Not Fear Letting Enemy Expose Itself." *Washington Times*, October 22, 2001.

Hewitt, Duncan. "Despatches" (*sic*), December 18, 1997, http://www.news.bbc.co.uk (accessed October 3, 2002).

Hiatt, Fred. "Democracy—Our Best Defense." *Washington Post*, November 19, 2001.

Hickey, Neil. "Perspectives on War: Different Cultures, Different Coverage." http://www.cjr.org (accessed September 3, 2002).

"Higher Media Council Finalizes Draft Press Law." *Jordan Times* (Jordan), January 25, 2002.

Hilden, Julie. "Should Networks Bar Bin Laden from Broadcasts?" *Bergen County Record*, October 24, 2001.

Hillman, Robert G. "U.S., Britain Establish Center to Give Details on War's Goals." *Dallas Morning News*, November 1, 2001."History of Public Diplomacy." http://www.gannettonline.com (accessed October 4, 2002).

Hodgson, Jessica. "West's 'Double Standards' over Bin Laden Tapes." *Guardian* (London), April 26, 2002.

Holtzman, Michael. "Privatize Public Diplomacy." *New York Times*, August 8, 2002.

Howe, Russell Warren. "Al Jazeera, Twisting Everybody's Nose." *Chicago Sun-Times*, April 7, 2002.

Hussain, Zahid, and Stephen Farrel. "Musharraf's TV Plea for Support." *Times* (London), September 20, 2001.

Hutzler, Charles. "China to Step Up Its Campaign against Separatists." Reuters News Service, October 12, 2001.

"Hyde, Lantos Introduce Reform of U.S. Public Diplomacy—Will Improve America's Outreach to International Mass Audiences." U.S. Newswire, March 14, 2002.

Idriss, Jazairy. "Public Diplomacy at Crossroads." *Washington Times*, August 19, 2002.

"IFEX Members Sign on to UNESCO Conference Resolution on Terrorism and Media." May 3, 2002, http://www.ifex.org (accessed March 4, 2003).

"IFJ Condemns Draft Media Law as 'Statement of Failure' on Press Freedom." Press release, International Federation of Journalists, February 10, 2003.

"IFJ Criticizes Government for Linking Journalism to Terrorism." Press release, International Federation of Journalists, November 23, 2001, BBC Monitoring Unit (accessed August, 20, 2002).

"IFJ Urges Government to Withdraw Proposed Criminal Code Amendments." Press release, International Federation of Journalists, February 13, 2002, http://www.ifex.org (accessed September 5, 2002).

"Incorrect Host May Need a Foxhole." *Spokesman Review*, October 1, 2001.

"Independence of U.S. International Broadcasting." Remarks of Senator Joseph R. Biden Jr., Voice of America Headquarters, Washington DC, October 13, 1999, http://www.foreign.senate.gov (accessed October 3, 2002).

"Independent Commission of Inquiry Must Investigate Raid on Moscow Theater." Press release, Human Rights Watch, October 24, 2002, http://www.hrw.org (accessed January 22, 2003).

"Independent Television Station Rustavi—2 Harassed and Intimidated." International Press Institute, October 31, 2002, http://www.ifex.org (accessed March 12, 2003).

"India Expels Al-Jazeera TV Correspondent over Coverage on Kashmir, Gudjarat." *Asian Age* (India), July 7, 2002.

"India May Offer Refuelling and Overflight Facilities to U.S." *Press Trust of India* (India), September 24, 2001.

"India Submits Its Report on Terror Legislation to UN." *Hindustan Times* (India), February 15, 2002.

"Information Ministry to Be Dissolved." *Jordan Times* (Jordan), October 29, 2001.

"Internal Security Act Must Go, The." August 1, 2000, http://www.malaysia .net (accessed September 5, 2002).

"International Broadcasting Bureau, The." http://www.dosfan.lib.uic.edu (accessed October 1, 2002).

International Federation of Journalists. "World Journalists Condemn 'Knee-Jerk Censorship' in Voice of America Taliban Row." http://www.ifj.org. (accessed August 26, 2002).

Jack, Andrew. "Moscow Theatre Assault." *Financial Times* (London), October 28, 2002.

"Jaitley Blames Media for Cynicism." *Times of India* (India), November 1, 2001.

Jamieson, Robert L., Jr. "Don't Give the Terrorists Victory over Truth." *Seattle Post-Intelligencer*, October 11, 2001.

Janardhan, N. "Seeing an Ease-Up in Media Restrictions." Global Information Network, October 15, 2001.

Jardine, Kay. "No. 10 Warns TV Stations Not to Spread bin Laden's Propaganda." SMG Newspapers Ltd., October 15, 2001.

Jensen, Elizabeth. "Bin Laden Interview Raises Questions." *Los Angeles Times*, October 18, 2001.

Jensen, Robert. "Here's the Choice—Journalist or American." *Milwaukee Journal Sentinel*, June 30, 2002.

"Joint Declaration from OSCE, UN, and OAS Representatives on Freedom of Expression." Article 19, November 21, 2001, http://www.ifex.org (accessed March 4, 2003).

"Joint Message for World Press Freedom Day 3 May 2002." UNESCO, http://www.portal.unesco.org (accessed March 4, 2003).

"Jordan Press Association Submits Proposed Amendments to Press Law." *Jordan Times* (Jordan), July 2, 2002.

"Jordan Shuts Down Al Jazeera TV Office, Revokes Accreditation of Correspondents." *Al-Bawaba News*, August 7, 2002.

"Jordan Will Not Retract Decision to Close Al-Jazeera Office, Minister Says." *Al-Dustur* (Jordan), August 11, 2002, translation, BBC Monitoring Unit, August 11, 2002.

"Jordanian Media Launch Strong Attacks on Qatar's Al-Jazeera TV." BBC Monitoring Unit, August 8, 2002.

"Journalists Ask Premier to Repeal Press Law." *Jordan Times* (Jordan), October 19, 2001.

"Journalists Risk Ten-Year Jail Sentences Under New Anti-Terrorist Law." Press release, Reporters Sans Frontières, March 21, 2002, http://www .ifex.org (accessed September 5, 2002).

ufman, Edward. "A Broadcasting Strategy to Win Media Wars." *Washington Quarterly* (Spring 2002): 115–27.

efer, Bryan. "Closing Down Debate: Ashcroft's Attack on Dissent." Spinsanity, December 10, 2001, http://www.spinsanity.org (accessed August 26, 2002).

lly, Kathy. "What about the Incubators?" http://www.emperorsclothes.com, April 14, 2000.

Kennedy, George. "Perspectives on War: British See Things Differently." *Columbia Journalism Review*, July/August 2002, http://www.cjr.org (accessed September 3, 2002).

Kinsley, Michael. "The Rush to Pressure the Press." *Washington Post*, November 9, 2002.

Kirschten, Dick. "Broadcast News." May 1, 1999, http://www.govexec.com (accessed March 21, 2003).

Knightley, Phillip. "The Disinformation Campaign." *Guardian* (London), October 4, 2001.

———. *The First Casualty*, rev. ed. London: Prion, 2000.

"Knowledge Helps Citizens, Secrecy Helps Bureaucrats—The Freedom of Information (FOIA)." Excerpted from the book *The Ralph Nader Reader* (Seven Stories Press), January 10, 2000, Third World Traveler (originally appeared in the *New Statesman* [January 10, 1986]), http://www.thirdworldtraveler.com (accessed January 9, 2004).

Koryashkin, Pavel. "Terrorism Common Enemy for Russia." ITAR-TASS World Service, November 22, 2001.

"Kow-Towing to China: Clinton's Engagement' Policy Means Joining Beijing in Stifling Human Rights in America." Center for Security Policy, No. 97 D-198, December 18, 1997.

Krasnow, Erwin G., and Lawrence D. Longley. *The Politics of Broadcast Regulation*. New York: St. Martin's Press, 1973.

Kristof, Nicholas B. "Security and Freedom." *New York Times*, September 10, 2002.

Krugler, David F. *The Voice of America and the Domestic Propaganda Battles, 1945-1953*. University of Missouri Press, 2000.

Kuchment, Anna. "Selling the U.S.A." *Newsweek International*, November 26, 2001.

Kurtz, Howard. "CNN Chief Orders 'Balance' in War." *Washington Post*, October 31, 2001.

———. "Commentators Are Quick to Beat Their Pens into Swords." *Washington Post*, September 13, 2001.

———. "Media Ethics during the War on Terrorism." Transcript, CNN, October 12, 2001, http://www.asia.cnn.com (accessed November 4, 2002).

———. "ABC News Chief Apologizes." *Washington Post*, November 1, 2001.

———. "Peter Jennings, In the News for What He Didn't Say." *Washington Post*, September 24, 2001.

———. "Tom Brokaw, Putting a Familiar Face on the Anthrax Story." *Washington Post*, October 18, 2001.

Kurtzman, Daniel. "Suddenly a Wisp of '1984' Is in the Air." *Bergen County Record*, July 31, 2002.

Kyodo News (Japan). "China Says bin Laden Gave Xinjiang Separatists Help." January 21, 2002."

L.A. Press Club Southern Californian Awards." PR Newswire, June 20, 2002.

Lake, James V. Plummer. "TV Host Stepped over the Line with Comments." *Times Union*, November 11, 2001.

Lamb, Christina, and Ben Aris. "Chechen Rebels' Link to al-Qaida Probed." *Chicago Sun-Times*, October 27, 2002.

Lane, Charles. "High Court to Weigh Detention of Citizens." *Washington Post*, January 10, 2004.

Lara, Adair. "This Is No Time to Keep Your Mouth Shut." *San Francisco Chronicle*, October 4, 2001.

Last, Jonathan V. "When VOA Becomes Voice of Islam in Nigeria." March 10, 2002, http://www.thisdayonline.com (accessed October 3, 2002).

"Lead But Don't Ignore Law, Patten Tells U.S." *Times* (London), October 4, 2002.

Lee, Mathew. "U.S.: New Weapon in Propaganda War vs bin Laden, Taliban." Agence France-Presse, November 6, 2001.

Leiberman, David. "Media's Big Fish Watch FCC Review Ownership Cap." *USA Today*, July 8, 2001.

Leonard, Tom. "TV Bosses Defend Right to Broadcast bin Laden Videos." *Daily Telegraph* (London), October 16, 2001.

"Letter to Bush Administration and Congressional Leaders Regarding War Coverage." Reporters Committee for Freedom of the Press, October 17, 2001, http://www.rcfp.org (accessed November 5, 2002).

"Light in the Darkness." *Northwest Arkansas Times*, April 4, 1996.

Little, Alison. "TV Chiefs Ready to Resist Calls for Censorship." *Express* (London), October 15, 2001.

Loeb, Vernon. "Bomb Hits Kabul TV Station." *Washington Post*, November 14, 2001.

Lowe, Kinsey. "TV Turns Cold Shoulder to Al Qaeda Videotape." *Los Angeles Times*, October 14, 2001.

Lucas, Scott. "How a Free Press Censors Itself." *New Statesman* (London), November 12, 2001, pp. 14–15.

Lydersen, Kari. "Fighting for Our Freedom of Thought and Expression." Chicago Media Watch, http://www.chicagomediawatch.org (accessed September 2, 2002).

Lynch, Timothy. "Breaking the Vicious Cycle: Preserving Our Liberties While Fighting Terrorism." *Policy Analysis*, no. 443 (June 26, 2002).

MacArthur, John R. "Censorship and the War on Terrorism." Interviewed by Gerti Schoen. http://www.mediachannel.org (accessed August 26, 2002).

———. "Lies the Pentagon Told U.S." *Toronto Globe and Mail* (Canada), March 11, 2002.

———. "Remember Nayira, Witness for Kuwait" (editorial). *New York Times*, January 6, 1992.

———. *Second Front: Censorship and Propaganda in the Gulf War*. Berkeley: University of California Press, 1993.

———. "The Ugly American Mindset." *Globe & Mail*, June 11, 2001.

———. "Unleash the Press." *Nation*, November 19, 2001, http://www.thenation.com (accessed August 26, 2002).

MacDonald, Gayle. "Media Fear Censorship as Bush Requests Caution." Common Dreams News Center, November 4, 2002, http://www.commondreams.org (accessed November 4, 2002).

MacLeod, Catherine. "New Allied Strategy to Fight 'Lies of the Taliban.'" *Herald* (United Kingdom), November 1, 2001.

Madigan, Michael, and Ian McPhedran. "Boatpeople Ignore Navy Orders and Reach Land." *Courier Mail* (Australia), September 14, 2001.

"Marc Nathanson Tells Congress Millions Tune In to U.S. International Broadcasting." October 19, 2001, http://www.voa.gov (accessed August 27, 2002).

Markoff, John. "Pentagon Plans a Computer System that Would Peek at Personal Data of Americans." *New York Times*, November 9, 2002.

Marlatt, Andrew. "Still Open to Winks and Nods." *Washington Post*, March 3, 2002.

McGreary, Johanna, Paul Quinn-Judge, and Yuri Zarakhovich. "Bloody Drama His Back to the Wall, Putin Retakes a Moscow Theater from a Chechen Suicide Squad, But the Cost Is High." *Time*, November 4, 2002.

McGuire, Mark. "Voice of America a Vital Tool." *Times Union,* November 19, 2001.

McMasters, Paul. "Is the Press Guilty of Treason?" Freedom Forum, August 8, 2002, http://www.freedomforum.org (accessed August 26, 2002).

"Media Chronology Post–11 September 2001." BBC Monitoring Research, January 16, 2001.

"Media Faced Government Restrictions and Pressure During Coverage of Hostage Standoff." Press release, Committee to Protect Journalists, October 28, 2002.

"Media March to War." Fairness & Accuracy in Reporting, September 17, 2001, http://www.tvnews3.televisionarchive.org (accessed August 20, 2002).

Memorandum. Members of the Board, IBB Notices, notices@ibb.gov, subject: The "Firewall" (accessed October 4, 2002).

Mendel, Toby. "Consequence for Freedom of Expression of the Terrorist Attacks of September 11." Article 19, May 2002.

Mendis, Ranil. "The Bias of the Western Media." http://www.origin.island .lk (accessed September 6, 2002).

Middle East News Agency. "Egyptian Delegation Offer Condolences on U.S. Attacks." September 20, 2001.

———. "Israel Says Al Jazeera Violated Agreement." March 26, 2002.

———. "Palestinian Press Syndicate Denounces Attack on al-Jazeera Reporter in Gaza." December 23, 2001.

———. "U.S. Presses Qatar to Rein in Al-Jazeera Channel." October 4, 2001.

"Middle East Press Criticize U.S. Pressure on Al-Jazeera TV." BBC Monitoring Unit, October 11, 2001.

Milbank, Dana, and Peter Baker. "Bush Wary of Confronting Putin." *Washington Post,* May 26, 2002.

Miller, Christian T. "U.S. Strikes Back—The Region-Arab Satellite TV Station a Prime Battlefield in Information War." *Los Angeles Times,* October 12, 2001.

Miller, Mark Crispin. "What's Wrong with This Picture." January 7, 2002, www.baltimorechronicle.com (reprinted on the *Baltimore Chronicle* site with permission from the *Nation*) (accessed November 7, 2002).

Mitchell, Steve. "Experts Dispute Russia Gas Label." Center for Defense Information, November 1, 2002, http://www.cdi.org (accessed January 22, 2003).

Mohan, Raja C. "Russia Gains Concessions on Chechnya." *Hindu* (India), September 28, 2001.

Mokhiber, Russell. "Kill, Kill, Kill." http://www.zmag.org (accessed October 31, 2002).

Monaghan, Elaine. "Bush Team Renews U.S. Criticism on Chechnya." Reuters News Service, January 24, 2001.

Monkerud, Don. "A Call for Freedom of the Press." http://www.mothers-alert.org (accessed October 3, 2002).

Moon, Mimi. "States Also Limit Access in Wake of 9/11." Reporters Committee for Freedom of the Press, http://www.rcfp.org (accessed November 5, 2002).

Moor, Bill. "He Is Ready for Another Job after His 15 Minutes of Fame." *South Bend Tribune*, October 5, 2001.

Moran, Michael. "In Defense of Al-Jazeera." MSNBC, October 18, 2001, http://www.msnbc.com (accessed August 28, 2002).

Moreno, Katarzyna. "The Osama Shortfall—Al Jazeera's New Status Cost It Money." March 4, 2002, http://www.forbes.com.

Mufson, Steven. "Foreign Policy's 'Pivotal Movement.'" *Washington Post*, September 27, 2001.

Murphy, Jeremy. "Charlotte, n.c. Cable TV." *Mediaweek*, November 26, 2001.

Murphy, Joe. "Blair Tells BBC to Censor al-Qaeda." *Sunday Telegraph* (London), October 14, 2001.

Nagorski, Andrew, Roy Gutman, and Eve Conant. "America's New Friend." *Newsweek International*, November 19, 2001.

Nakashima, Ellen. "Broadcast with Afghan Leader Halted—State Department Pressure Voice of America Not to Air 'Voice of Taliban.'" *Washington Post*, September 23, 2001.

———. "Bush Choice to Head VOA Pledges Independent Voice—News Will Be Accurate, Objective, Reilly Tells Staff." *Washington Post*, October 9, 2001.

"Name Calling Sharon Likens Arafat to Bin Laden." *Guardian* (London), September 14, 2001.

Nancy Chang. "The USA Patriot Act: What's So Patriotic about Trampling on the Bill of Rights?" Center for Constitutional Rights, http://www.ccr-ny.org (accessed January 1, 2003).

"National Security Advisor Interview with Al-Jazeera TV." Transcript, October 16, 2001, The White House, http://www.whitehouse.gov (accessed January 7, 2004).

Nelson, Bill. "Grave Questions of Invasion of Privacy." Salon.com, November 26, 2002, http://www.archive.salon.com (accessed December 17, 2002).

"Networks Accept Government Guidance." Fairness & Accuracy in Reporting, October 12, 2001, http://www.fair.org (accessed November 4, 2002).

"Neutral Turkmenistan Spurns German Airbase Request." Radio Free Europe/Radio Liberty, January 7, 2002, http://www.rferl.org (accessed January 7, 2004).

"Newspaper Editor, Publisher Gets Fines and Probation for Criminal Libel." Reporters Committee for Freedom of the Press, December 4, 2002, http://www.rcfp.org (accessed March 5, 2003).

Noah, Timothy. "Whopper of the Week: Karl Rove, Ari Fleischer, and Dick Cheney." Slate.com, September 28, 2001, http://www.cooperativeresearch.com (accessed December 10, 2002).

North, Gary. "White House Shoots Down Air Force One Story." Lew Rockwell.com, http://www.lewrockwell.com (accessed December 10, 2002).

"On Capitol Hill, Free Expression Groups Question the USA Patriot Act." Bookselling This Week, April 29, 2002, http://www.news.bookweb.org (accessed December 6, 2002).

"140 Die in Theater Siege Climax." CNN.com, http://www.cnn.com (accessed October 27, 2002).

"Opportunism in the Face of Tragedy: Repression in the Name of Terrorism." Report, Human Rights Watch, http://www.hrw.org (accessed September 5, 2002).

O'Reilly, Bill. "Back of the Book—Bill Maher on the Defensive." *Media Transcripts*, September 20, 2001.

O'Rourke, Breffni. "Human Rights Chief Steps Down, Warning of Post–11 September Rights Crackdown." Radio Free Europe/Radio Liberty, http://www.rferl.org (accessed January 7, 2003).

Oruc, Saadet, and Alparslan Esmer. "VOA Interview with PKK's Ocalan Banned from Airwaves." *Turkish Daily News*, undated.

"Outcome of FCC's Media Ownership Proceeding Will Hurt National Security, Including a Weakened News Media." Center for Digital Democracy, http://www.democraticmedia.org (accessed November 7, 2002).

"PACE moves to Suspend Russia." IPR Strategic Business Information Database, April 10, 2000.

Page, Jeremy. "China Calls for Support against Islamic Separatists." *Asian Wall Street Journal*, October 12, 2001.

"Pakistan: Entire Election Process 'Deeply Flawed.'" Press release, Human Rights Watch, October 9, 2002, http://www.hrw.org (accessed January 9, 2003).

Pan, Phillip P. "Separatist Group in China Added to Terrorist List—U.S. Endorses Fight against Ethnic Uighur." *Washington Post,* August 26, 2002.

Pankin, Alexei. "Flint, Kiselyov—Last Bastions of Free Speech." *Moscow Times* (Russia), December 4, 2001.

———. "Press Freedom under Attack in the U.S.A." *Moscow Times* (Russia), October 16, 2001.

Park, Steve. "Voice of America Raises the Volume—Broadcast Finds New Purpose as U.S. Presses War on Terror." *Washington Times,* January 28, 2002.

"Passing of Anti-Terrorist Law that Impedes Press Freedom Causes Concern." Press release, International Press Institute, March 22, 2002, http://www.freemedia.at (accessed September 5, 2002).

"Payne Awards in Ethics Honor Jay Harris, Voice of America and KOMU-TV." April 16, 2002, http://www.jcomm.uoregon.edu (accessed August 26, 2002).

"Pearl's Killing Sheds Light on Disturbing Trend." *St. Louis-Dispatch,* February 23, 2002.

"Pentagon's Propaganda Plan Is Undemocratic, Possibly Illegal." Fairness & Accuracy in Reporting, February 19, 2002, http://www.fair.org (accessed September 3, 2002).

Perigard, Mark A. "White House to Press—Cancel the Osama Show." *Boston Herald,* October 11, 2001.

Persico, Joseph E. "Deception Is Part of the Art of War." *Wall Street Journal,* February 28, 2002.

"Photographers Arrested in Aftermath of Attacks." Reporters Committee for Freedom of the Press, September 25, 2001, http://www.rcfp.org (accessed November 5, 2002).

"PM Compliments Putin on Courageous Handling of Hostage Crisis." *Asia Pulse,* October 27, 2002.

"Poll Shows Majority of Participants Oppose Closure of Al-Jazeera." BBC Monitoring Unit, June 5, 2002.

Postlewaite, Susan. "The Propaganda War—The View from the Middle East." *Advertising Age,* November 1, 2001, p. 4.

"POTO Threat to All Dissent." *Hindu* (India), November 4, 2001.

"Powell Lectures China on Human Rights Issues." Causes That Matter Clearinghouse, February 1, 2001, http://www.causesthatmatter.com (accessed July 1, 2002).

"President Salutes VOA's 60-Year Commitment to Freedom." PR Newswire, February 25, 2002.

"Press Freedom Being Tested by Bush Administration's Anti-Terrorism

Policy." Press release, Reporters Sans Frontières, http://www.ifex.org (accessed September 5, 2002).

"Press Freedom Organizations Concerned about Existing Criminal Defamation and Insult Laws in EU Member-States." Press release, International Press Institute, June 13, 2001, http://www.freemedia.at (accessed March 5, 2003).

"Prevent Abuse of POTO." *Hindu* (India), March 26, 2003.

"Proper Display of the Flag." Chicago Reader, October 12, 2001, http://www.chireader.com (accessed November 27, 2002).

"Public's Need to Know, The." Century Foundation, Homeland Security Project, http://www.homelandsec.org.

Puddington, Arch. *Broadcasting Freedom*. Lexington: University Press of Kentucky, 2000.

"Qatar Reports, 1997–2001." World Press Freedom Review, International Press Institute, http://www.freemedia.at (accessed January 7, 2004).

"Qatar's Al-Jazeera Television Forbidden to Report from Bahrain." *Gulf Daily News* (Bahrain), May 14, 2002.

Quenqua, Douglas. "Hughes to Launch New White House Crisis Communications Unit." *PR Week*, June 10, 2002, p. 3.

"Quirky Despot Key to Unlocking Oil Riches." *South China Morning Post* (China), November 17, 2002.

Ralston, Bill. "Truth—War's First Casualty." *Independent Business Weekly* (New Zealand), October 17, 2001.

Rashid, Ahmed. "Political Instability Will Leave Door Open to Extremists." *Daily Telegraph* (London), September 11, 2002.

Rayner, Jay. "Propaganda and Media—How Much Can We Believe It?" *Observer* (London), October 14, 2001.

"Read All about It." *Guardian* (London), October 16, 2001.

"Reorganization Plan and Report." Submitted by President Clinton to the Congress on December 30, 1998, Pursuant to Section 1601 of the Foreign Affairs Reform and Restructuring Act of 1998, as contained in Public Law 105-277, http://www.state.gov (accessed October 1, 2002).

"Repair U.S. Image with Truth, Not Lies" (editorial). *Greensboro News Record*, March 4, 2002.

Reporters Committee for Freedom of the Press. "Journalists Face Arrests, Obstacles after Terrorist Attacks." *News Media and the Law* 26, no. 1 (Winter 2002): 18.

Reporters, Writers, and Editors of *Der Spiegel* Magazine. *Inside 9-11: What Really Happened*. St. Martin's Press, 2002.

318   BIBLIOGRAPHY

"Resisting the Censor's Impulse" (editorial). *Washington Post*, September 26, 2001.

"Restrictions on Travel by Voice of America Correspondents." Memorandum for the Deputy Legal Advisor, Department of State, September 10, 1999, http://www.usdoj.gov (accessed August 27, 2002).

Reuters News Service. "Broadcasting Board Responds to Report on U.S. Public Diplomacy." August 5, 2002.

———. "Calling the Attacks on the World Trade Center and Pentagon 'a Wake-Up Call from Hell' Former Prime Minister Benjamin Netanyahu Said on Thursday the United States and Allies Must Be Relentless in Fighting Back." September 20, 2001.

———. "Key Events in Kidnapping of Daniel Pearl." February 22, 2002.

———. "Jazeera TV Says U.S. Bombed Its Kabul Office." November 13, 2001.

———. "Malaysia Detains Seven More Suspected Militants." January 19, 2002.

———. "Malaysian Rights Chief Criticized by Rights Groups." October 30, 2001.

———. "Malaysia Rights Group Says Studying Detention Law." May 24, 2002.

———. "Newsman Rather Tells Americans Ask More Questions." May 16, 2002.

———. "President Bush's Address to Congress and the Nation." September 20, 2001, transcript, September 23, 2001.

———. "Russian Duma Votes to Ban 'Terrorist Propaganda.'" December 20, 2001.

———. "State Department's Regret at VOA's Taleban Interview." Text of report by Voice of America *Communications World*, presenter Kim Andrew Elliott.

———. "U.S. Asks Media Not to Print Full bin Laden Comments." October 11, 2001.

———. "U.S. Envoy Hails Ties, Chides Russia on Chechnya." December 28, 2001.

———. "U.S. Says Russia Seige a Reminder of Terror Threat." October 26, 2002.

———. "U.S. Says Will Watch Gusinsky Case Closely." November 13, 2001.

Reuven, Frank. "TV in a Time of War." *New Leader*, November 2001.

Richardson, Ian. "Sand in Auntie's Face." *Independent* (London) April 28, 1997.

World Bank Institute. *The Right to Tell: The Role of the Mass Media in Economic Development*. World Bank Institute, 2002.

Rodriguez, Paul M. "Disinformation Dustup Shrouded in Secrecy." *Insight on the News*, May 6, 2002.

Rosen, Ruth. "The Day Ashcroft Foiled FOIA." *San Francisco Chronicle*, January 7, 2002.

Rosenthal, Phil. "Feelings Too Heavy to Hide—Late-Night Comedians, and One Usually Stoic Newsman, Bare Their Soul." *Chicago Sun-Times*, September 19, 2001.

Rosett, Claudia. "Spin Won't Win It." *Wall Street Journal Europe*, October 18, 2001.

Rowse, Arthur E. *Drive-By Journalism: The Assault on Your Need to Know.* Common Courage Press, 2000.

"RSF Criticizes U.S. 'Limitations' of Media Freedom Since 11 September." Reporters Sans Frontières, BBC Monitoring Unit, May 24, 2002.

"RSF Criticizes U.S. 'Limitations' of Media Freedom Since 11 September." Press release, Reporters Sans Frontières, May 23, 2002, BBC Monitoring Unit, May 24, 2002.

"RSF Protests Al-Jazeera Correspondent's Detention for Questioning." Reporters Sans Frontières, November 16, 2001, http://www.ifex.org (accessed August 28, 2002).

"RSF Says Censorship of Al-Jazeera TV 'Unacceptable.'" Reporters Sans Frontières, August 8, 2002, BBC Monitoring Unit, August 8, 2002.

"Rumsfeld Says Anti-Terrorism Efforts Are Broad-Based U.S. Military Build-up Dubbed 'Operation Enduring Freedom.'" Transcript, September 25, 2001, http://www.usembassy-israel.org.

Safire, William. "Giving 'Equal Time' to Adolf Hitler." *Seattle Post Intelligencer*, September 21, 2001.

———. "Our Voice Broadcasts Terror." *Times Union*, July 1, 2002.

———. "State Out of Step" (editorial). *New York Times*, July 1, 2002.

———. "You Are a Suspect" (editorial). *New York Times*, November 14, 2002.

Sage, Adam. "TV Channel Warned over al-Qaeda Videos." *Times* (London), November 9, 2001.

Salahuddin, Sayed. "Taliban Say Took 20 Days to Destroy Giant Buddhas." Reuters News Service, March 26, 2001.

Sandler, Robert. "MU 'Deeply Regrets' that Policy Banning KOMU Reporters from Wearing Patriotic Symbols May Have Caused Offense." Missouri Digital News, October 4, 2001, http://www.mdn.org (accessed November 27, 2002).

Sands, David R. "Karimov Bolsters His U.S. Standing—Rights Issues Not a Barrier to Pacts." *Washington Times*, March 13, 2002.

———. "VOA Director Was Undermined by Doubts—'Principled Conservative' Driven Out." *Washington Times*, September 5, 2002.

Sanford, Bruce W. *Don't Shoot the Messenger*. New York: Free Press, 1999.

Sarq News Agency (Azerbaijan). "Azeri Politician Urges Practical Help to USA in Fighting Terrorism." October 8, 2001.

"Saudi Papers Slam Qatari Foreign Minister, Al-Jazeera's 'Malicious Programmes.'" *Al-Watan*, July 31, 2002.

Scarborough, Rowan. "Rumsfeld Expresses Doubts on New Propaganda Office." *Washington Times*, February 25, 2002.

Schmidt, Sarah. "Experts Say Al-Jazeera's Translation of bin Laden Statement Was Inaccurate." *National Post*, October 9, 2001.

Schulz, William, and Robert L. Maginnis. "Symposium. (Human Rights Versus National Security." *Insight on the News* 18, no. 25: 40.

Schulz, William F., and Robert L. Maginnis. "Has the White House Ignored Human Rights in the Name of National Security?" *Insight on the News*, July 15, 2002.

"Seeking the New Patriotism." PR Newswire, June 26, 2002.

Seib, Gerald F. "U.S. Changes Attitude Toward Al Jazeera TV." *Wall Street Journal* (Europe), October 17, 2001.

Sen, Amartya. *Development as Freedom*. New York: Oxford University Press, 1999.

"September 11 Shook the World Profoundly But Above All It Shook the United States." *El Pais* (Spain), English edition, September 4, 2002.

Shapiro, Bruce. "Information Lockdown." *Nation*, November 12, 2001, http://www.thenation.com (accessed August 26, 2002).

Sherwin, Adam, and David Charter. "TV News Chiefs Resist Any Interference by No. 10." *Times* (London), October 16, 2001.

"Should bin Laden Be Abridged?" *Intelligencer Journal*, October 11, 2001.

Shulman, Holly Cowan. *The Voice of America: Propaganda and Democracy, 1941–1945*. Madison: University of Wisconsin Press, 1990.

Sierra, Javier. "Be Careful What You Say." Libertad de Prensa, October 9, 2001, http://www.libertad-prensa.org (accessed September 2, 2002).

———. "In the U.S., It's a Battle of Security vs. Freedom." Libertad de Prensa, November 21, 2001, http://www.libertad-prensa.org (accessed August 30, 2002).

Simon, Joel. "Look Who's Inspiring Global Censorship." *Columbia Journalism Review* (January 2002).

Singh, Tavleen. "Jurisprudence in the Flawed Indian Judicial System: POTO Will End Up as a Tool of Injustice." *India Today* (India), April 8, 2002.

Siskind, Lawrence J. "Who's Afraid of Osama bin Laden." October 18, 2001, http://www.law.com (accessed August 30, 2002).

Slevin, Peter. "At State—Giving Dissent Its Due—Department Honors Four Who Challenged System." *Washington Post*, June 22, 2002.

Smith, Christopher H. "Religious Freedom, A Casualty of War?" *Washington Times*, November 27, 2001.

Smyth, Frank. "The Price of Propaganda: Democracy Lessons from the Middle East." TomPaine.com, http://www.tompaine.com (accessed August 28, 2002).

Solomon, Norman. "The Discreet Charm of the Straight Spin." Fairness & Accuracy in Reporting, June 3, 2002, http://www.fair.org (accessed August 26, 2002).

———. "When Journalists Report for Duty." Fairness & Accuracy in Reporting, http://www.fair.org, October 3, 2003.

Sparrow, Andrew. "Blair Continues War of Words in Britain." *Daily Telegraph* (London), October 10, 2001.

"SPJ Appalled That Voice of America Pulls Reporter Off Air Amid Government Pressure." PR Newswire, February 8, 2002.

"Staff Have 'Misgivings' over New VOA Director." Text of Report by Voice of America *Communications World* on October 7, 2001, BBC Monitoring Unit, October 8, 2001.

Stancich, Rikki. "The Malaise of the Media." Worldreporter.com, August 19, 2002, http://www.epnworld-reporter.com (accessed September 2, 2002).

Starkweather, Gary. "They're Lying to Us Again—In the Name of War." http://www.deepcool.com (accessed December 5, 2002).

"Station Defends Decision Not to Air Bin Laden Tape—Questions Were Dictated, Reporter Was Intimidated, Statement Says." *St. Louis Post-Dispatch*, February 3, 2002.

"Stern Test for Media." *Business*, October 7, 2001.

Stifling America's Voice—Helm's Efforts Would Limit VOA's Effectiveness" (editorial). *Sarasota Herald Tribune*, October 26, 2001.

Ston, Damon. "Retreat of the Open Society." *Mercury* (Australia), October 10, 2001.

"Stop Trying to Censor News and Treating Us Like Idiots" (editorial). *Express* (London), October 15, 2001.

Straus, Tamara. "The CNN of the Arab World." October 26, 2001, http://www.globalissues.org.

"Supreme Court Throws Out 1876 Criminal Libel Statute." Reporters Committee for Freedom of the Press, November 19, 2002, http://www.rcfp.org (accessed March 5, 2003).

"Suter, Keith. "Fear and Loathing on the Campaign Trail." *Contemporary Review* (United Kingdom), January 2002.

Taheri, Amir. "Boob Tube—Unveiling Al-Jazeera." *Asian Wall Street Journal*, December 11, 2001.

"Tajikistan Hospitals to Receive New Bulk of Assistance Provided by U.S. State Department." *Asia Pulse* (Tajikistan), October 29, 2002.

Talbot, David. "Democracy Held Hostage." Salon.com, http://www.dir .salon.com (accessed September 10, 2002).

Tapper, Jack. "White House Whitewashers." Salon.com, September 27, 2001, http://www.dir.salon.com (accessed August 26, 2002).

"Target-Rich Environment." *Progressive*, September 5, 2002.

Taylor, Phillip. "Abduction, Death of Pearl Sparks Concern about CIA Agents Impersonating Journalists." Reporters Committee for Freedom of the Press, http://www.rcfp.org (accessed November 5, 2002).

———. "Journalists Confront Sporadic Restrictions in Aftermath of Sept. 11 Terrorist Attacks." Reporters Committee for Freedom of the Press, *News Media & the Law* 25, no. 4 (Fall 2001): 11, http://www.rcfp.org (accessed November 5, 2002).

Taylor, Stuart, Jr. "The Media, the Military, and Striking the Right Balance." *National Journal*, October 20, 2001.

Teinowitz, Ira. "Congress Will Support War of Ideas." *Advertising Age*, June 26, 2002, p. 4.

"10 IFEX Members Sign on to UNESCO Conference Resolution on Terrorism and Media" Press release, Article 19, May 3, 2002, http://www.ifex.org (accessed September 5, 2002).

"Ten Minutes of Freedom." *Economist* (London), November 14, 2002, http://www.economist.com (accessed January 13, 2003).

"Tension Between Protecting Security, Damage to Fundamental Freedoms Focus of World Press Freedom Day." M2 Press Wire, May 3, 2002.

Terashima, Jitsuro. "Washington Takes an Alarming Turn." *Japan Echo* (Japan), August 2002.

"Terrorism Has Unleashed War on the World." *Press Trust of India* (India), October 26, 2002.

"Terrorism, Refugee Link 'Disgusting.'" *Globe and Inner City News* (Australia), October 10, 2001.

"Terrorist Could Sneak into Australia Among Boat Loads of Asylum Seekers." *South China Morning Post* (China), November 8, 2001.

"Testimony of Marc B. Nathanson, Chairman, Broadcasting Board of Governors, House Committee on International Relations, October 10, 2001." http://www.house.gov. (accessed August 27, 2002).

"Text of Belarusian Law on Fighting Terrorism." January 15, 2002.

Thatcher, Jonathan. "Bloody Raid Ends Moscow Theatre Siege." Reuters News Service, October 26, 2002.

Tomlinson, Kenneth Y. "VOA Led Astray." *Washington Times*, October 14, 2001.

———. "VOA Needs Returning for War against Terror." October 8, 2001, http://www.humaneventsonline.com (accessed October 3, 2002).

"Total Information Awareness" (editorial). *Washington Post*, November 16, 2002.

Total Information Awareness (TIA) System, http://www.darpa.mil (accessed December 17, 2002).

Total Information Awareness Resources Center, http://www.geocities.com (accessed December 17, 2002).

"Trial of Wei Jingsheng, The." House Republican Policy Committee, Policy Perspective, December 12, 1995, http://www.fas.org (accessed March 21, 2003).

"Trofimov, Yaroslav. "Powell's PR Thrust Draws an Arab Parry." *Wall Street Journal*, October 5, 2001.

Turkmenistan Opposes Afghanistan's Division, Says President." Turkmen Radio 2, Asgabat (Turkmensitan), *BBC Monitoring International Reports*, August 27, 2002.

"2002 Pen/Newman's Own First Amendment Award Recipient, Vanessa Leggett."http://www.pen.org (accessed March 5, 2003).

"TV Cans al-Qaeda Broadcasts: 'Could Kill Americans.'" *Gold Coast Bulletin*, October 12, 2001, p. 9.

"TV Reporter Banned for 10 Days." IPR Strategic Business Information Database, August 5, 2002.

"TV Reporter Blown Off Chair by U.S. Missile." *Birmingham Post* (United Kingdom), November 14, 2001.

"TV Station Under Fire." *Gold Coast Bulletin*, October 12, 2001, p. 6.

"Tyrannical New Law POTA (sic) Being Abused." *Pakistan Press International*, May 10, 2002.

"Under Secretary Feith Breakfasts with Defense Writers Group." February 20, 2002, http://www.fas.org (accessed September 3, 2002).

"Uprooting Terrorism and Extremism—Common Task of Society." *Asia Pulse* (Tajikistan), November 7, 2002.

"U.S. International Broadcasting Chronology." http://www.ibb.gov (accessed October 1, 2002).

"U.S. Missile Destroyed Al-Jazeera Office in Kabul." *Hindu* (India), November 16, 2001.

"U.S. President for Further Expansion of Cooperation." *Asia Pulse* (Tajikistan), March 7, 2002.

"U.S. Presses for Censorship of Jazeera TV." Human Rights Watch, October 15, 2001, http://www.hrw.org (accessed August 28, 2002).

"U.S. Pussyfoots Around Egypt Military Courts." Middle East Times, http://www.metimes.com (accessed February 25, 2003).

"U.S. Ambassador Against Ocalan Interview on VOA." January 6, 1999, http://www.byegm.gov.tr (accessed October 17, 2002).

"U.S. Backs Putin on Chechnya Peace Bid." Courier Mail (Australia), September 28, 2001.

"U.S. Backs Turkmen-Pakistan Gas Pipeline project, Ambassador Says." Neytralnyy Turkmenistan (Turkmenistan), translation, BBC Monitoring International Reports, July 6, 2002.

"U.S. Confronts Image Problem." BBC News, July 30, 2002, http://www.news.bbc.co.uk (accessed September 3, 2002).

"U.S. Congressmen Rap Uzbekistan for Rights Failures." Birlik Web site, BBC Monitoring International Reports, March 16, 2002.

"U.S. Could Add Chechen Groups to 'Terrorist List.'" Johnson's Russia List, Center for Defense Information, November 1, 2002, http://www.cdi.org (accessed January 22, 2003).

U.S. Department of Defense. "Strategic Influence Office 'Closed Down,' Says Rumsfeld." FDCH Regulatory Intelligence Database, February 26, 2002.

U.S. Department of Justice. "New Attorney General FOIA Memorandum Issued." http://www.usdoj.gov (accessed December 12, 2002).

"U.S. Government to Continue Funding Radio-TV Marti." Text of a Report by Communications World by Voice of America, BBC Monitoring Unit, January 11, 1999.

"U.S. Launches Radio for North Caucasus Despite Protests." Editorial Analysis by Chris McWhinnie, BBC's Monitoring Foreign Media Unit, April 3, 2002.

U.S. State Department. "Closure of Independent Media in Russia Politically Motivated." Statement by Richard Boucher, spokesperson. April 18, 2001.

———. "Commission Endorses Freedom Protection Act of 2002." April 8, 2002, http://www.state.gov (accessed October 1, 2002).

———. Country Reports on Human Rights Practices. http://www.state.gov (accessed January 7, 2003).

———. "Craner Says Can't Ignore Human Rights in War on Terrorism." December 24, 2002, http://www.usinfo.state.gov (accessed January 7, 2003).

———. "U.S. Advisory Commission on Public Diplomacy to Release Global Communication Recommendations." *M2 Presswire*, August 8, 2002.

"U.S. Tramping on Principles It Holds Sacrosanct" (editorial). *Daily Star*, October 6, 2001.

"U.S. Turns to Propaganda in War Against Bin-Laden." BBC Monitoring Unit, October 18, 2001.

"U.S. TV Limits Bin Laden Coverage." October 11, 2001, http://www.news .bbc.co.uk (accessed August 30, 2002).

"USA Will Always Be with Uzbekistan." Uzbek Television (First Channel), *BBC Monitoring International Reports*, March 16, 2002.

"U.S.-Based Watchdog CPJ Concerned about Pressure on the Press." Press release, Committee to Protect Journalists, March 8, 2002, BBC Monitoring Media, March 11, 2002.

Uyttebrouck, Olivier. "Professor Speaks Out on 'Nightline.'" *Alburquerque Journal*, October 4, 2001.

"Uzbek Leader Gets Bouquets Not Brickbats During U.S. Visit." *BBC Monitoring International Reports*, March 14, 2002.

Vatikiotis, Michael, Ben Dolven, and David Murphy. "China-U.S. Relations: Terror Throws U.S./China Together, For Now." *Far Eastern Economic Review* (November 1, 2001).

Venkatesan, J. "National Security above Press Freedom." *Hindu* (India), November 7, 2001.

Vidaillet, Tamora. "U.S. to Reinforce Rights Concerns in Northwest China." Reuters News Service, December 18, 2002.

"VOA Airs Interview with Taliban." *Kyodo News* (Japan), September 27, 2001.

"VOA Airs Report over Objection of State Department—Segment Includes Interview with Head of the Taliban Militia" (editorial). *Washington Post*, September 27, 2001.

"VOA Defies State Department, Airs Interview with Taleban Leader." Text of Report by Radio Netherlands "Media Network" Web site on September 26, 2001, BBC Monitoring Unit, September 27, 2001.

"VOA Journalistic Code." http://www.voa.gov (accessed October 17, 2002).

"VOA Journalists Under Pressure." Committee to Protect Journalists, http://www.cpj.org (accessed August 27, 2002).

"VOA News Head Honored for Defying White House." Text of Report by Radio Netherlands "Media Network" Web site on June 26, 2002, BBC Monitoring Unit, July 2, 2002.

"Voice of America Will Retool for Arab World." *New York Times*, April 1, 2001, http://www.refuseandresist.org (accessed August 26, 2002).

Vuong, Andy. "Walter Cronkite Says Government, Media Should Provide More Information." *Denver Post-Colorado*, June 13, 2002.

Wain, Barry. "September 11, One Year On—Unfriendly Fire—The United States Is Newly Engaged with Southeast." *Far Eastern Economic Review* (September 12, 2002).

"War Propaganda Is Failing the West." *PR Week*, November 9, 2001, p. 12.

Ward, Stephen. "The Fog of Patriotism." *UBC Journalism Review*, Thunderbird Online Magazine, http://www.journalism.ubc.ca (accessed October 11, 2002).

Wastell, David. "The West at War—America's Latest Fear." *Daily Telegraph* (London), December 24, 2001.

Waugh, Paul. "Broadcasters Summoned for Propaganda Talks." *Independent* (London), October 15, 2001.

"We Just Reported the Insults." *Guardian* (London), October 9, 2001.

Weinstein, Henry, Daren Briscoe, and Mitchell Landsburg. "Civil Liberties Take Back Seat to Safety." *Los Angeles Times*, March 10, 2002.

Wells, Matt. "Al-Jazeera Accuses U.S. of Bombing Its Kabul Office." *Guardian* (London), November 17, 2001.

———. "CNN to Carry Reminders of U.S. Attacks." *Guardian* (London), November 1, 2001.

———. "How Smart Was This Bomb?—Did the U.S. Mean to Hit the Kabul Offices of Al-Jazeera TV?" *Guardian* (London), November 19, 2001.

"Western Democracies Undermining Freedom of Expression." Press release, World Association of Newspapers, May 27, 2002.

"What's Relevant, What's Not." *Investor's Business Daily*, September 25, 2001, p. 18.

White, Aidan. "Journalism and the War on Terrorism: Final Report on the Aftermath of September 11 and the Implications for Journalism and Civil Liberties." *International Federation of Journalists*, September 3, 2002.

"White House Warns Networks on Bin Laden Messages." NewsMax.com, October 11, 2001, http://www.newsmax.com (accessed August 30, 2002).

"White House Warns TV Networks about Bin Laden Tapes." *Dow Jones International News*, October 10, 2001.

White, Jerry. "White House Lied about Threat to Air Force One." World Socialist Web Site, September 28, 2001, http://www.wsws.org (accessed December 10, 2002).

White, Michael. "Campbell Takes a Spin to the White House." *Guardian* (London), October 29, 2001.

————. "Downing Street Gives Propaganda Warning—Media TV Urged to Be Wary on Bin Laden Tapes." *Guardian* (London), October 16, 2001.

Whittel, Giles. "Warning by U.S. on Chechnya Alarms Moscow." *Times* (London), January 26, 2001.

Wickham, DeWayne. Comment: "Strength through Freedom of Speech." *Times Union*, September 25, 2001.

Williams, Amy. "White House Tried to Stop VOA Broadcast of Dissident Wei Jingsheng into China." http://www.bulldognews.net (accessed August 27, 2002).

Windrem, Robert. "They Are Trying to Kill Us." *Columbia Journalism Review*, http://www.cjr.org (accessed September 3, 2002).

Wines, Michael. "As Russia Renews Crackdown, Chechen Fighters Down Copter." *New York Times*, November 4, 2002.

Wintour, Patrick. "Government to Raise Security Issue with Broadcasters— Blair Summons Media." *Guardian* (London), October 15, 2001.

Woodward, Bob. *Bush at War*. New York: Simon & Schuster, 2002.

Woolacott, Martin. "The World Six Months On." *Guardian* (London), March 11, 2002.

Wright, Jonathan. "Rogue Memo Tries to Block VOA Editorial on Cole." Reuters News Service, October 18, 2000.

Xinhua News Agency (China). "Britain Welcomes End of Russian Hostage Drama." October 26, 2002.

————. "Egypt Bans TV Program on Terrorism." October 10, 2001.

————. "Jordan Calls Back Ambassador over Closure of Qatari TV Office." August 10, 2002.

————. "Pakistan Condemns Attack on United States." September 11, 2001.

————. "Palestinians Call for Distinguishing Terrorism from Just Struggle."October 16, 2001.

————. "Russia Lashes Out at U.S. Criticism on Human Rights." March 7, 2002.

————. "U.S., Indonesia Agree to Strengthen Cooperation Against Terrorism." September 19, 2001.

————. "U.S. Praises Pakistan's Elections as 'Relatively Free.'" October 11, 2002.

Yarushin, Andrei. "Egypt Supports Fight against Terrorism on Global Scale." ITAR-TASS World Service, September 24, 2001.

Zahn, Paula. "America's New War—Patriotically Incorrect." Transcript, *Live at Daybreak*, CNN, October 1, 2001.

Zednik, Rick. "Inside Al Jazeera (Perspectives on War)." *Columbia Journalism Review* (March 2002): 44.

Zeidler, Sue. "U.S. Talk Radio Loud and Clear in Wake of Attacks." Reuters News Service, September 28, 2001.

Zelizer, Barbie, and Stuart Allen, eds. *Journalism after September 11*. Routledge, 2002.

Zelnick, Bob. "Bush Should Manage the War, Not the News." *Wall Street Journal*, October 17, 2001.

Zengerle, Patricia. "World Responds Quickly, Not Clearly, to Bush." Reuters News Service, September 21, 2001.

Ziauddin, Sardar. "Sultans of Spin or of Truth." *New Statesman* (London), October 22, 2001, http://www.newstatesman.co.uk.

Zimmerman, Sacha. "Right to Fire." New Republic Online, October 23, 2001, http://www.thenewrepublic.com (accessed September 10, 2002).

INDEX